ON THE CLOCK: DETROIT RED WINGS

ON THE CLOCK: DETROIT RED WINGS

Behind the Scenes with the Detroit Red Wings at the NHL Draft

HELENE ST. JAMES

Foreword by Jimmy Devellano

TRIUMPH
BOOKS

Library of Congress Cataloging-in-Publication Data available upon request.

This book is available in quantity at special discounts for your group or organization. For further information, contact:

Triumph Books LLC
814 North Franklin Street
Chicago, Illinois 60610
(312) 337-0747
www.triumphbooks.com

Printed in U.S.A.
ISBN: 978-1-62937-985-2
Design by Preston Pisellini
Page production by Alex Lubertozzi
All photos courtesy of *Detroit Free Press*

To Sophie, Peter, Annie, and Elsie

CONTENTS

FOREWORD

MY FIRST DRAFT with the Red Wings was in 1983. I joined the team in July 1982, right after the Ilitches had bought the team. We got the superstar in Steve Yzerman we needed to get started in '83. He gave the franchise hope. He gave the fans hope. The 1989 draft gave us 20 years with four Stanley Cups and a playoff run that may never be equaled. That was the year we drafted Nicklas Lidström and Sergei Fedorov in the third and fourth rounds, and Vladimir Konstantinov in the 11th. With those players plus Yzerman—boy, those drafts really defined us. We won four Stanley Cups with those people.

When I was named general manager of the Wings, I used to say I wouldn't trade a first-round pick, I wouldn't trade an eighth-round pick, and I wouldn't trade a 10th-round pick. I was trying to tell the public we were going to use the draft to get better. We weren't messing around. In later years we did trade draft picks—thank God people forgot what I had said—but we were really good by then.

So much has changed. When I first started drafting in 1967 for the St. Louis Blues, the National Hockey League was 12 teams. When I got to Detroit in 1982, there were 21 teams. Now what's hard for a guy like Steve Yzerman is there are 32 teams drafting, and we've had a draft lottery thrown into the mix. The draft lottery has been awful to us, just awful. Steve and I were driving to Grand Rapids to watch a Griffins game in October 2021, and I said to him, "Steve, you played here 22 years. You only missed the playoffs twice. Now you're back as manager." He said, "I know where you're going with this. I'm 0-for-2 already." Steve has got a bigger mountain to climb than I did. When I was a manager, 16 out of 21 teams made the playoffs. Five missed. Now 16 teams miss.

We had just done some analytics that showed that after the third round, there are so few players who make it. They mostly come out of the top three rounds. It's become a tougher proposition to build a team through the draft because of a 32-team NHL.

You need to use free agency and trades to build a team now, but the draft is still a very important tool. Steve already put his personal stamp on the entry draft, because of his first two first-round choices, Moritz Seider and Lucas Raymond. They came in as rookies and were impact players for the Red Wings. They were important picks.

What makes drafting hard is you're looking at a 17-year-old or 18-year-old kid and trying to figure out what he's going to be at 22. You're assuming he's going to be better, but some don't get better. We have all these things we measure now before the draft, but what you can't measure when you draft is the size of the heart. Steve Yzerman was quiet—he still is—but, boy, did he have a big heart. He was our best player when he was just 18 years old.

I've never patted myself on the back that I drafted Steve Yzerman—you haven't heard me say that because the truth is he fell to us. The franchise wanted Pat LaFontaine—he was a local boy. Now both are in the Hockey Hall of Fame. Steve had the better career. History will tell you he should have gone No. 1. But we got him at No. 4. Lucky us.

I think the world of Helene St. James. She has developed sources because she is trusted. She's been a respected reporter on the Red Wings and the NHL for a long time. I admire how she does her homework, and I know this will be a terrific book.

—Jimmy Devellano

Detroit, November 2021

Red Wings general manager, 1982–1990, 1995–1997

Red Wings senior vice president of hockey operations,

1990–present

ACKNOWLEDGMENTS

I **N THE COURSE** of writing my second book about the Detroit Red Wings, a scout I interviewed said in regard to one draft in particular, "We could have done better, we could have done worse."

The Wings are one of the most storied franchises in the National Hockey League, and the most successful team in the United States. The first group of players who made the Wings so successful predated the draft, but the second group shows just how often the Wings did very, very well at the draft.

Every draft concludes the same way: team executives and scouts are abuzz with enthusiasm over the players added to the organization. There is no more hopeful day in the NHL than the day after a draft: every first-round pick projects to be a winner; the later-round picks project to be sleepers. Players are so excited at being one step closer to realizing a boyhood dream. It is fascinating to evaluate how the choices turned out—and to look back at what might have been.

I very much enjoyed writing this book, and was delighted when Jimmy Devellano agreed to provide the foreword. He was the first big hire made by Mike and Marian Ilitch after they bought the Wings in June 1982 and set about restoring it to the glory befitting an Original Six team. Devellano is passionate about drafting, and he was in charge at the two drafts that dramatically impacted the franchise's fortunes.

So many people set aside time to talk to me for the book, and I am grateful for their generosity. Steve Yzerman had great insight into everything from his own experience being drafted (he knew the Wings coveted Pat LaFontaine) to running a draft table himself. Christer Rockström shared the story of how doing a favor for a colleague led him to join the Wings, and Håkan Andersson of how he gave up being a fishing guide in Argentina. Neil Smith, Ken Holland, and Jim Nill—all men who had significant impact on whom the Wings have drafted—likewise were full of good stories. Thank you, too, to Nicklas Lidström, Niklas Kronwall, Mark Osborne, Ryan Martin, Scotty Bowman, Mark Howe, and many others.

Gene Myers, my fellow outdoors enthusiast and my former editor at the *Detroit Free Press*, was a great help and wonderful sounding board. Jeff Fedotin, my editor at Triumph Books, was supportive at every stage. The most obscure statistic was checked by reaching out to Greg Innis, the longtime statistician for the Wings. Adam Engel compiled the list of draft picks from 1963 through 2021.

The *Detroit Free Press* archives were an invaluable resource thanks to the work put in by Keith Gave, Bill McGraw, Jason La Canfora, Nick Cotsonika, George Sipple, Joe Lapointe, and others.

Most of all, I am thankful for the support from my family, who have and continue to cheer my every endeavor and adventure.

ON THE CLOCK:
DETROIT
RED WINGS

1

CAPTAIN CONSOLATION

STEVE YZERMAN WAS 16 years old the first time Jimmy Devellano scouted him. It was clear Yzerman had a great deal of ability, that he was a very good skater and possessed tremendous hockey sense. But the coach he played for tended to divide playing time fairly equally, so Yzerman's statistics weren't as astronomical as some of his contemporaries. Years later, Devellano viewed that as a determining factor in what turned out to be the greatest consolation story in Detroit sports history.

In June 1983, Mike Ilitch had owned the Red Wings for one year. He was determined to distance them from the "Dead Wings" era of the 1970s, to restore the franchise to glory. He wanted the team to be the buzz of the city and he wanted fans crammed in the stands.

Salvation presented itself in the form of a winsome local hockey prodigy by the name of Pat LaFontaine. He was as good-looking as he was gifted, as grounded as he was genial. LaFontaine had gone to Canada to play junior hockey but had grown up in Waterford Township, just outside Detroit. Devellano, whom Ilitch had hired in July 1982 to be the general manager, and who had immediately bestowed upon himself the additional title of director of scouting, openly coveted LaFontaine. Devellano talked about LaFontaine to the Ilitches, talked about LaFontaine on the radio and on television, and talked about LaFontaine to the newspaper reporters who covered the team every day. By the time the draft neared, nobody in hockey was unaware how much the Wings wanted LaFontaine. He was a hometown hero whose impact on ticket sales projected to be meteoric.

"He would have been a superb marketing tool," Devellano said in 2021. "We had 2,100 season ticket holders in 1983, and had missed the playoffs for the [fifth] year in a row. We needed someone special."

The Wings were bad, but not bad enough to guarantee LaFontaine would be theirs. They finished 18th out of 21 teams, giving them the fourth pick. The order was: the Minnesota North Stars (with Pittsburgh's pick), the Hartford Whalers, the New York Islanders (with New Jersey's pick), and the Detroit Red Wings.

Knowing Devellano's situation, North Stars general manager Lou Nanne tried to take advantage. In May, the two were at the Marriott Hotel in Uniondale, New York. Nanne approached Devellano and suggested the two make a deal. By flipping picks and trading down, Nanne's plan was to draft goaltender Tom Barrasso. The Wings would get the first pick—and with it, LaFontaine—but Devellano was wary.

"I'm not trading with you; you've never made a bad deal," Devellano told Nanne.

Devellano went into the draft with the hand he was dealt—and with a good deal of anxiety.

"Of the players I had scouted, there were three I would have been satisfied with," he said in 2021. "That became problematic because we got the fourth pick, and I only liked three. The players I liked, in no order, were Sylvain Turgeon—he was a big, strong kid who could score, who was a good overall player—then there were two young men that were very, very, very similar in how they played, their hockey sense, and their size. One was Pat LaFontaine, the other was a young boy in Peterborough [Ontario] called Steve Yzerman. Of course, at that time, nobody knew who Steve Yzerman was in Detroit. They knew who Pat LaFontaine was, but not Steve Yzerman.

"I had to sweat it out because if the three people I liked went one, two, and three, I felt I would not get a difference-maker at four, which would have been a disaster in trying to turn the Red Wings around. A disaster."

Disaster was averted as soon as the North Stars selected Brian Lawton. The Whalers grabbed Turgeon, and the Islanders took LaFontaine. Out on the draft floor, Yzerman waited to hear his name.

"Detroit was the only team that I really had a feel for that I might be going to," Yzerman said in 2021. "Jimmy D was very honest and said they were going to take the highest rated player on their board. The picks were called out really quickly. There wasn't interviews in between picks like there is now.

"My name was called, and I quickly went down to the table and met Jimmy D., Mr. and Mrs. Ilitch, and some of the scouts. It was a very exciting day for me."

Choosing Yzerman turned out to be the best consolation in franchise history.

Yzerman became a beloved player in Detroit, a name as synonymous with the franchise as Gordie Howe's had been 30 years earlier. The Captain, as Yzerman became known, won three Stanley Cups as a player and a fourth as a member of the front office. His No. 19 was hoisted to the rafters six months after he retired. When he hung up his skates in July 2006, he paced his draft class with 1,755 points.

But on June 8, 1983, at the Forum in Montreal, Yzerman wasn't who Ilitch wanted. Yzerman was a reserved, shy teenager, presciently wearing a red tie, but he was not a name that resonated with the two people who had turned one pizza store into a multimillion-dollar business and who then had turned to reviving the Wings.

"I had invited Mike and Marian Ilitch to the first draft, to sit at the table and observe how we operate," Devellano said. "They came, a little bit due to my big mouth talking about LaFontaine all previous winter. They wanted him. They wanted Pat LaFontaine.

"Bill Torrey, the Islanders manager, took him at three. While I wasn't down and disappointed because I knew I was getting the equal or more in Steve Yzerman, it bothered me more for Mike and Marian Ilitch, because they didn't know Yzerman. Mike Ilitch came over to where I sat at the draft table and said, 'Jimmy, we need Pat LaFontaine. You go over to Bill Torrey and you give him Yzerman and $1 million for

Pat LaFontaine.' That's when Mrs. Ilitch tapped her husband on the shoulder and said, 'Mike, you hired Jimmy to run the draft, let the man do his work. Let the man do his work.'"

Devellano and Marian Ilitch convinced Mike Ilitch to let the matter drop.

"I said, 'Mike, I can't go over there and do that. Don't worry about it, please,'" Devellano said. "I told him, 'Mike, save your money. Yzerman will do just fine.' He returned to his seat. Marian helped me. Mike hadn't seen any of the players. She didn't like that. So she said, 'Mike, let the man do his work.' He slipped back to his seat, but he was very disappointed. And I understood."

Yzerman posted 91 points in 56 games with the Peterborough Petes in the Ontario Hockey League in his draft year. (LaFontaine, playing in the Quebec junior league, posted 234 points in 70 games with Verdun.) Two months after they drafted Yzerman, the Wings signed him to a contract. Yzerman, a native of Cranbrook, British Columbia, was living with his parents in Nepean, Ontario. The Wings hoped he'd soon be moving to Detroit.

"We are all very hopeful that Steve can step right in and help our club, and we believe he has a bright future in the NHL," Devellano said at the time.

The desire to imprint the Wings with players brought in under Ilitch's ownership, brief as it was at the time, prompted Devellano and coach Nick Polano to declare Yzerman had made the club even before training camp began. Yzerman was thrilled.

"This is great," he said on the first day of camp, as he gazed at a locker room that included Ron Duguay, Brad

Park, Eddie Mio, and Eddie Johnstone. "It's like Christmas." Yzerman didn't need until Christmas to show what a gift he was. By early November he was leading the rookie scoring race. He was quick, smart, and sometimes sensational, centering the team's top line.

"He came into camp low-key," teammate Danny Gare said. "He listens a lot. He takes a lot in. You see him watching things. He was very confident, but quiet."

Park described Yzerman as having "tremendous poise and tremendous natural ability."

Yzerman had grown up in Nepean, moving there when he was still in grade school. His father, Ron, a social worker who was director of welfare services for the Canadian government, said in a 1983 interview in the *Detroit Free Press* that Yzerman always seemed more mature than his age. When it became clear his hockey ability surpassed that of his older brother, Mike, Yzerman didn't flaunt it.

"He never said, 'I'm better, I deserve the better skates,' that sort of thing," Ron Yzerman said. "I think it was a conscious decision on his part."

Lottie Garvey, who housed Yzerman for two years while he played for the Peterborough Petes, described what a thoughtful, well-raised teenager Yzerman was: "He always took his plates to the sink."

In Detroit, Yzerman shared a two-bedroom apartment downtown with Lane Lambert, who had been drafted one round after Yzerman. Sometimes Devellano would drop in and take them out to dinner to make sure they were eating well.

Devellano had reason to be pleased: Yzerman's performance was drawing fans. In mid-November 1983, the Wings led the NHL with an average attendance of 17,752, a 5,904 increase at Joe Louis Arena from the previous autumn.

The NHL recognized Yzerman with its Rookie of the Month award for December, during which he had 10 goals and seven assists. The award came with a video cassette recorder. In January, Yzerman was the only rookie named to the NHL All-Star Game.

Yzerman had a sensational rookie season, leading his draft class with 87 points in 80 games. (Brian Lawton, the No. 1 pick, had 31 points in 58 games; No. 2 Sylvain Turgeon was right behind Yzerman with 72 points in 76 games; and Pat LaFontaine had 19 points in 15 games—LaFontaine had deferred joining the Islanders to play in the 1984 Winter Olympics.)

April heralded news that Yzerman was a finalist for the Calder Trophy, given to the NHL's rookie of the year. He lost out to Buffalo's Tom Barrasso, who became only the third goaltender in league history to win the Calder and the Vezina Trophy. But while Yzerman wasn't tops in the eyes of the voting members of the Professional Hockey Writers Association, who gave Barrasso the winning numbers, 242–203, Yzerman was No. 1 in Ilitch's eyes. Minutes before the awards ceremony got underway in Toronto, Ilitch gave Yzerman an envelope with a $25,000 check. Yzerman, Ilitch said, was his rookie of the year.

"I was shocked," Yzerman said in response to getting such a bonus.

The team was doing better, and ownership and management couldn't be happier with Yzerman. He was a quiet star, a teenager who scored big goals and still called his mom to ask advice about doing laundry. In October 1985—a little more than two years after drafting him—the Wings signed Yzerman to a seven-year contract, the longest in franchise history. It was estimated to be worth around $350,000 a year.

"Steve Yzerman is one of the cornerstones of our building process," Devellano said, "and we're very pleased that he's going to have a long career with the Red Wings."

What happened next was dreadful. The Wings endured their worst season in franchise history, finishing in last place with a 17–57–6 record. Yzerman struggled to produce. He had just 14 goals in 51 games when an injury put him on the sidelines. Looking back after the season ended, Yzerman said, "[I] had a lot of things going on. I bought a house, got a new contract, and I was starting to enjoy things a bit. Then, having a bad season made me more aware of what it's really all about.

"I've always had my confidence, even through last year. But I know I've got to prove a lot to a lot of people."

Yzerman was down on himself, but not so those around him. With Danny Gare having been released after the season, the Wings were without a captain. Jacques Demers, who had just been named coach, knew the man he wanted.

"I want to be sure whoever it is, is capable of wearing the C for many years to come," Demers said in September 1986. "Steve Yzerman seems to fit the bill."

Yzerman was only 21 years old and one of the most reserved players in the locker room, but Demers saw in him all the qualities needed in a leader.

Steve Yzerman, in his second year with the Wings, folds his laundry in his Riverfront apartment, November 30, 1984. *Photo by Mary Schroeder*

"The captain has to be a guy who can play, a guy who on and off the ice shows some class, a guy who wears the Detroit Red Wings sweater with some pride, and a guy whom the other players look up to and respect," Demers said. "He doesn't have to necessarily be a rah-rah guy, but someone who will stand up when times get tough and say, 'Let's go, guys, this is it.' And he has to be able to see the coach's side as well as the players' side. There's a lot of pressure."

Demers saw all those things in Yzerman.

"He's our franchise," Demers said. "He's got it all—looks, money, intelligence, modesty; he's a superb talent, super person, a kid you trust and respect."

The announcement took place at Oak Park Ice Arena after a practice on October 7. Yzerman reacted as expected: With quiet resolve. "I'm not a real vocal guy or anything," he said. "I'd try to do it by working hard, by being a good example."

Before making the announcement, Demers met with Yzerman. Giving him the C was a big deal: at 21, he'd be the youngest captain in franchise history. "I asked him about it," Demers said. "He hesitated. He wondered, 'Am I really ready for this challenge?' I said, 'I think you are.'"

Yzerman had been in the organization for a little more than three years. He was the face of the franchise and was beloved by ownership and fans. He had led the team into the playoffs his first two years and did so again his first year as captain. He was their most effective player and leading scorer, and he embraced being a leader. When a six-player trade in January 1987 rattled his teammates, Yzerman confronted Demers and told him as much.

"He's a concerned captain," Demers said. "He worries about the team. That's a good captain."

That dreadful 1985–86 season had worried Yzerman—both for the team and himself. He revealed just how much in an interview over lunch in February 1987. "People laughed at the Red Wings," Yzerman said over a meal of clam chowder, a grilled cheese sandwich, french fries, and several glasses of orange juice. "We lost a lot of pride and respect. We had some tough years before that in Detroit, but even though we did bad, we still had some respect. We lost that last year."

Yzerman himself had played poorly and suffered a broken collarbone in his 51st game. "All summer I worried about it," he said. "I was on the edge of becoming a run-of-the-mill player. Never a day went by when I didn't think, *Geez, if I'm not careful, in a couple of years I could be out of hockey.* It worried me every day."

The C on his sweater changed Yzerman. Harold Snepsts, who already had played in the NHL for a decade when he joined the Wings in 1985, said naming Yzerman captain improved the team. "Jacques put some responsibility on him. He was so quiet and reserved last season—it's almost like he wasn't even part of the team."

Yzerman had been lonely after Lane Lambert and Claude Loiselle, his close friends and teammates, were sent to the minors. He was alone in the condo he had bought in West Bloomfield, alone when he drove the Porsche 944 he had bought after signing that seven-year deal. "I like to deal with things alone, but I didn't know what do," Yzerman said. "Last year we had a lot of unhappy people. There was a lot of complaining. It was always somebody else to blame.

"I didn't fit in anywhere. I didn't feel comfortable. It was a tough position to be in. But I couldn't say anything, because I was one of the major reasons we didn't do well."

Yzerman could speak freely in 1986–87—he led the Wings with 90 points in 80 games. The Wings advanced to the playoffs, dispatching Original Six foes Chicago and Toronto in the first two rounds.

"I don't know if it's being captain or just growing up," Yzerman said, shortly before his 22nd birthday. "I'm taking things a lot more seriously. I'm saving more money, watching what I spend. I've cut out a lot of distractions.

"I know we're paid money to do this, but the Stanley Cup, that's what it's really all about. That's really why you play the game. If it wasn't, why bother?"

That was in 1987. Yzerman was the most famous and most beloved hockey player in Detroit since Gordie Howe. Devellano, the man who had drafted Yzerman, referred to him as "a pure Red Wing," someone Devellano envisioned playing his whole NHL career in Detroit.

It would take 10 more years before Yzerman would realize his dream of winning the Stanley Cup. There were personal joys (marriage, fatherhood), accomplishments (scoring 50 goals in 1987–88, then 65 the next season), and professional trials. During a game in March 1988, Yzerman crashed into a goal post and tore ligaments in his right knee. Yzerman avoided reconstructive surgery, but the knee would trouble him the rest of his career. In the fall of 1993, Yzerman suffered a spinal injury and underwent a procedure to have two cervical disks fused together, requiring him to spend six weeks in a halo-shaped device to immobilize his spine.

It was a trying time. The Wings were an immensely talented team—the 1989 draft had brought in Nicklas Lidström, Sergei Fedorov, and Vladimir Konstantinov—but they kept coming up short in the playoffs. In 1993, the Wings were expected to compete for the Cup but lost to the Toronto Maple Leafs in the first round. That summer, the legendary Scotty Bowman was brought in to coach. Still the playoffs brought pain: in 1994, the Wings were upset in the first round by the upstart San Jose Sharks. The dream of hoisting the Stanley Cup kept eluding Yzerman.

The following June marked a dozen years since he had been drafted. The Wings advanced to the Stanley Cup Final. Four victories stood between Yzerman and his dream. He was 30 years old and had thought about the Cup for so long it was almost unbearable. "I don't remember if I've ever really actually touched it or gotten close to it," Yzerman said. "The last few years, I've made a point of not really going near it. I really have no desire to get near it until I get the opportunity to win it.

"When you build on things, each year you're expected to do a little more, little more. We had such good teams the last two years and were expected to do well. It was really, really disappointing, particularly two years ago and last year the same thing happened. It really sets you back and makes you wonder at times what's going on, wondering about yourself."

When the Final ended on June 24, it was the New Jersey Devils who were partying with the Cup. Yzerman knew then that losing in the Final hurt even more than losing in the first round.

It was a trying time for Yzerman in 1995. For the second time in his career he endured rumors that he might be traded.

The first time was in 1992, when there was talk between the Wings and the Buffalo Sabres about swapping Yzerman and LaFontaine. (The Sabres had acquired him from the Islanders in 1991.) Ilitch nixed the trade.

Two years later, Bowman played mind games with Yzerman, letting it be known publicly that there was talk of trading Yzerman to the Ottawa Senators. As the Wings had wanted with LaFontaine in 1982, Yzerman was a chance for the Senators to market a hometown hockey hero. That was in October 1995.

Ultimately, Bowman guided Yzerman to become a complete player, to the point he was recognized as the NHL's top defensive forward in 2000. But the prize Yzerman really wanted finally arrived on June 7, 1997, when The Captain carried the Cup for a lap around the Joe.

"I was glad when the game was over, but then I didn't want the game to end," Yzerman said. "I've been watching hockey since I was five years old. I always dreamed of the day I would get the Stanley Cup. Sometimes I wondered if I would ever get there. It was the one thing in my career I didn't have. I wanted dearly to have my name on the Stanley Cup before I retired."

Yzerman was 32 years old when he won the Cup. He first got on the ice with a stick in his hand when he was five years old. His father, Ron, had been persuaded to coach his six-year-old son Michael's team with the understanding that Steve could come along. The kids looked like water bugs on ice, skittering along after a puck. Steve was the one who got to the puck first, and Michael would lie down in front of the net and play goalie.

When Steve was 10 years old, his family moved from Cranbrook, British Columbia, to Nepean, just outside Ottawa. It was there that Yzerman grew into a teenager who would catch the Wings' attention. When he was 15—a year before Devellano first scouted him—Yzerman was busted by his parents for forging his father's signature on a note that allowed him to miss school every Tuesday morning so that he could play hockey. Yzerman's parents were with him three years, later, on that June day in 1983 when Devellano selected Yzerman, and Ilitch relinquished his dream of Pat LaFontaine. In a quiet moment, off to the side, Ilitch and Ron Yzerman chatted about being hockey parents. Ron joked about the money it cost. Ilitch turned to Ron and said, "I guess I'll be taking care of that from now on."

Yzerman won the Stanley Cup as a player in 1997, 1998, and 2002. He retired in 2006. In January 2007, his No. 19 was hung in the rafters at Joe Louis Arena. In 2008, Yzerman won a fourth Cup, as a member of the hockey operations personnel. He had transitioned from the ice to the front office, seeing his future in hockey management. In 2009, he was inducted into the Hockey Hall of Fame.

On April 19, 2019, the man who had worn No. 19 returned to the franchise after leaving in 2010 to manage the Tampa Bay Lightning. When Yzerman left Detroit, Marian Ilitch had refused to say good-bye to Yzerman for fear she would cry uncontrollably. In 1983 she had convinced Mike, who passed away in 2017, that drafting Yzerman would work out, to let go of LaFontaine. When Yzerman returned, Marian Ilitch, then 86, was at the news conference at Little Caesars Arena.

"I'm very, very happy," she said.

Yzerman brought life back to the Red Wings, brought pride back to the franchise. He turned out to be the most successful player from the 1983 draft by a landslide, leading the class in goals (692), assists (1,063), and points (1,755 points). Nearly 40 years later, the man who headed up the Wings' table in 1983 thought about what might have been.

"Sometimes you wonder about the course of history," Devellano said in 2021. "What if Yzerman had gone to the Islanders? LaFontaine would have come to us. Would we have won three Cups with him? Would Steve have won in New York? We'll never know."

THE WONDER OF DETROIT

Pat LaFontaine grew up in a nine-room home on the shores of Williams Lake in Waterford Township, about 30 miles north of Detroit. His dad, John LaFontaine Sr., would set up a makeshift rink on the lake every winter, piling up snow to simulate boards. He installed eight spotlights so Pat and his older brother, John Jr., could play in the evenings.

In 1983, LaFontaine was beloved in Montreal and coveted in Detroit. The fantastically talented center was a superstar in the Quebec Major Junior Hockey League (QMJHL) and seemingly the perfect player to revive interest in the Red Wings.

His hockey credentials were sublime. In 1981–82, LaFontaine had recorded 175 goals and 324 points in 79 games with Detroit Compuware. On January 5, 1983, the 17-year-old LaFontaine broke Guy Lafleur's 12-year-old record for consecutive-game scoring in the QMJHL. Prime Minister Pierre Trudeau was among the many well-wishers who sent congratulations via telegrams.

Jimmy Devellano, the general manager at the time, described LaFontaine as "a franchise-type player. He's a Marcel Dionne–Wayne Gretzky-type player. He has fantastic vision and makes fantastic plays. The puck just seems to follow him around, as it does for all the great players."

LaFontaine finished the 1982–83 season with 104 goals and 234 points for the Verdun Juniors, surpassing Mike Bossy's 70 goals as a rookie, out-performing future NHL superstar Mario Lemieux, and winning the Jean Béliveau Trophy as the top scorer. LaFontaine's face was on buttons and posters; he appeared daily in newspapers and as the subject of discussion on talk shows. He would spend 45 minutes after games signing autographs. Admirers wrote messages in the dust on his car.

"I've never seen a kid loved like him," Verdun general manager Eric Taylor said. One Montreal newspaper referred to LaFontaine as "La Merveille de Detroit"—The Wonder of Detroit.

LaFontaine had it all: elite skills, good looks, a grounded personality. He graduated from Waterford Kettering High School the same month he was drafted. "I started to dream about the NHL as a little kid," LaFontaine said. "Then I set goals for myself and followed them."

At the Montreal Forum on June 8, 1983, New York Islanders general manager Bill Torrey announced LaFontaine's name with the third pick. LaFontaine, seated in the second row, hugged his parents.

That September, he decided to postpone his NHL dreams until after the 1984 Winter Olympic Games in Sarajevo, Yugoslavia. The U.S. failed to advance to medal contention, and LaFontaine returned to the Islanders. He had just turned 19.

LaFontaine made his NHL debut on February 29, 1984, in Winnipeg, Manitoba. He didn't get a point because the goal he set up was disallowed, but on March 3, in his second game, LaFontaine looked every bit the teenage sensation, recording three goals and two assists. He played only 15 games that season, but tallied 13 goals and six assists.

LaFontaine was a star for the Islanders, but he arrived as the team entered a decline following four consecutive Stanley Cup championships. The playoff runs grew shorter, but LaFontaine thrived. In 1989–90, he scored 54 goals and put up 105 points in 74 games. The Islanders made the playoffs, but LaFontaine was knocked unconscious after being crushed between the New York Rangers' James Patrick and Chris Nilan in Game 1 of the division semi-finals on April 5. La Fontaine suffered a concussion and was hospitalized overnight, though he was able to return for Game 5 eight days later.

As the Islanders continued to sputter, LaFontaine grew frustrated. He staged a contract holdout at the start of the 1991–92 season, and on October 25, the Islanders traded their cornerstone center to the Buffalo Sabres. LaFontaine responded with 93 points in 57 games.

He enjoyed his best season in 1992–93, recording 95 assists and 148 points in 84 games. LaFontaine finished second in the scoring race behind Mario Lemieux's 160 points, was a finalist for the Hart Memorial Trophy (most valuable player), and a finalist for the Lady Byng Trophy (most sportsmanlike player). He was awarded the Bill Masterton Trophy (perseverance and dedication to hockey).

LaFontaine's career was defined by talent and derailed by concussions. In November 1996, news emerged that LaFontaine suffered from severe post-concussion effects and would miss three months. The previous month, he had suffered the fifth concussion in his 14-season career. There was talk he would be forced to retire, but LaFontaine was traded to the New York Rangers in September 1997. During a game on March 16, he collided with teammate Mike Keane and was again sidelined. On August 11, 1998, LaFontaine announced his retirement. He was 33 years old.

LaFontaine recorded 468 goals and 545 assists in 1,013 games. He played in five NHL All-Star Games and for two U.S. Olympic teams, and was inducted into the Hockey Hall of Fame in 2003. The Wonder of Detroit played his entire NHL career for New York teams, marking his career with grace and excellence.

2

THE PERFECT
PICK

THE STORY OF how the Red Wings came to draft Nicklas
Lidström involves deceit, disappointment, and a dish of
pizza that left one scout reeling.

The credit for drafting him is shared by Christer Rockström, Neil Smith, and Jimmy Devellano, but it all began with
Jörgen Holmberg. In 1988–89, he was playing for Västerås
IK in Sweden's top hockey league when he noticed a young
defenseman who was called up from Västerås's lower-level
team. Holmberg was eight years older than Lidström and was
in his sixth season in the top-level Elitserien, but he couldn't
beat Lidström in practice. Lidström didn't get into many
games, but still, Holmberg thought it was worth alerting his
friend, Rockström, who scouted for the Wings.

"I went to see him practice, first of all," Rockström said in a 2021 interview. "And then my friend called and said there were some defensemen who were injured, so Nick was going to play the next game. That's how I saw him play. Then I got Neil to see him play, and he said he was really good and put Nick on their list to draft him."

There were other NHL scouts at Västerås games, but they came to see Patrik Juhlin, a forward who would end up being drafted 34th by the Philadelphia Flyers in 1989. Lidström had played just 20 games, notching two assists. He didn't put up eye-catching numbers in the lower league, either, recording a goal and four assists in 15 games in Allsvenskan. He wasn't physically imposing—at the time of the draft, Lidström was listed as 6'1", 178 pounds. But there was something about the way he played that stood out: Lidström never made a mistake. He never was out of position, he never got beat, he never threw away the puck.

"When I saw him play, he was a natural," Smith said in 2021. "He was a fantastic skater. I mean, never did you ever in your wildest dreams think he would win seven Norris Trophies. But you did know he was better than anything we had back in North America.

"I remember taking him to a Pizza Hut in Västerås to talk with him. I don't remember anything startling said. The most startling thing was how much the pizza cost. I was blown away by how much it was. Back then, I didn't have much money myself."

The price of the pizza was lost to time, but not so the period leading up to June 17, the day the 1989 draft was held at the MetCenter in Bloomington, Minnesota. (Mats Sundin was the first overall pick; he leads the draft class with 1,349 points. Lidström ranks first with 1,564 games. Appropriately, the ground where the MetCenter stood is now home to an IKEA, the Swedish superstore.) Smith returned to Detroit, determined to keep Lidström's name quiet.

"I was so scared somebody was going to find out about him," Smith said. "I told our staff, 'You're not allowed to talk about him with each other.' I was so excited, but I was scared to death somebody was going to find out about him. There was some cloak and dagger there."

While Smith tried to keep Lidström a secret in North America, Rockström tried to do the same in Sweden. One night he was at a Västerås game with Don Meehan, an NHL agent who was looking for potential clients.

"He and Christer were friends," Lidström said in 2021. "Donny would ask Christer, 'Who's that No. 9 guy, who's he?' Christer would be like, 'I'm not sure who he is. But look at the other guys you are here to see.' After the end of the game, Donny asked again, 'What's the deal? I know that No. 9 guy is pretty good. How come you're not telling me about him?' So Christer told Donny, 'Okay, but you have to be quiet. You can't tell anyone about that No. 9 guy, that Lidström player.'"

The draft drew closer. Eventually, Meehan called Smith.

"Donny was a good friend," Smith said. "He asked, 'Neil, do you know about this kid in Sweden, named Lidster?' I swear he said 'Lidster.' I went, 'Lidster, Lidster—no, I don't know any Lidster.' Then he said, 'Oh, Lidström.' And I said, 'No, I don't know who you're talking about.'"

The politesse stopped, and an expletive-laden, truth-baring exchange ensued.

"Donny goes, 'Fuck off, Neil, you know about this guy, Lidström,'" Smith said. "And I said, 'Donny, I do know about him, but you better not fucking tell anybody about him. Do not fucking tell anybody about him, and do not bring him to the draft. Because I have to get this guy.' That shows how paranoid I was. Donny was a really good friend of mine, and I wouldn't even admit to knowing who he was. That was hilarious."

It wasn't as funny for Lidström, not at the time, anyway. Meehan had invited him to the draft. A week before he was to leave, Lidström was told to stay home.

"Christer called and said not to come," Lidström said. "He had gotten a call from Neil telling him to tell me, 'We can't have him there. Someone might see him and someone else might pick him ahead of us.' I was so fired up that I was going to be able to go. It would have been my first trip to the United States, and then it never happened. And this was the year Mats Sundin was drafted first overall, so the draft was a huge deal for European players. It was hyped up in the papers in Sweden because of Mats."

At the time, there was a rule that teenagers had to be drafted in the first three rounds. Sundin aside, there was also a bias against European players—they weren't considered as "tough" as North American players. The Wings played it safe in the first two rounds, drafting forward Mike Sillinger at No. 11 and defenseman Bob Boughner at No. 32.

The Wings' next time on the draft board was at No. 53.

"We get to the third round, and I was begging Jimmy D. to let me take Lidström," Smith said. "Because if we didn't take him in the third round, you couldn't take him after that because of the way the rules were back then. I said, 'Next year he'll go in the first round, and we won't get him.' I said, 'Please, please, let's take him.'"

All that time keeping quiet about Lidström for fear of tipping off rival scouts was over. Smith implored. Rockström expounded.

"In the third round, oh my goodness," Devellano said in 2021. "I'm sitting there and on one side, I had my head scout, Neil Smith, with his right-hand guy, the young Ken Holland. He had just become a scout for us. On my other side was our head of European Scouting, Christer Rockström. Neil said to me, 'We want to take a Swede. We want to take a Swede.' I said, 'All right, describe him to me.' Neil asked Christer to tell me what he liked about this kid. 'Well, he's a really smooth hockey player.' I asked what position does he play? 'Defense. He's really smooth, he can skate, he's got good hockey sense.' I asked whether he's big and strong enough to play in the NHL, because when I heard smooth, I'm thinking, 'Will that translate to the NHL?' Neil said yes, but that if we draft this player, he needs to stay in Sweden an extra year or two. We can't bring him over right now. He needs to get a little more beef on his body. I was a little bit concerned, because I would have liked to bring him over and put him in Adirondack. But Christer and Neil felt that this kid had enough sense and savvy that they wanted to draft him. They were the ones who saw him. So I said, 'Okay, he's your pick.' So we drafted Nick Lidström."

Banished from attending the event, Lidström waited with his parents at their house in Avesta, Sweden, seven hours ahead of Bloomington, Minnesota. "It was late in the evening,"

Lidström recalled. "My parents said, 'If the phone rings, you have to answer it.' Because they were afraid to answer it and hear someone speaking English. So I answered the phone every time it rang that night. When the Wings finally rang, I was very happy to be drafted, to know I was one step closer to the NHL.

"It's funny how things turn out. From when I was drafted to when I came over, those two years, my career really took off. I made the national team, I played on TreKroner, I made the world championship team that won gold in Finland. Everything went really fast for me after I was drafted."

In May 1991, Lidström signed a three-year contract with the Wings. When the Wings began the 1991–92 season, they had two rookies on the back end in 21-year-old Lidström and 24-year-old Vladimir Konstantinov, an 11th-round pick from the same draft as Lidström.

Every time Lidström played he looked like he should have been a first-round pick. He was the NHL's rookie of the month for November, and then won the award again for December. He led the rookie scoring race with six goals and 35 points in early January, and was third in the NHL with a plus-23 rating. In February, during a trip to play the Quebec Nordiques, the French-Canadian press speculated the Wings could be a landing point for Eric Lindros, the phenomenally hyped prospect who had been drafted No. 1 in 1991 by the Nordiques but refused to report. The Quebec press suggested it would take a package involving both Lidström and Fedorov—to which Wings general manager Bryan Murray responded, "Eric Lindros must be one hell of a hockey player."

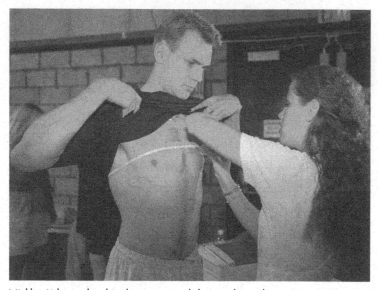

Nicklas Lidström has his chest measured during physical exams at training camp on September 9, 1997. *Photo by Mary Schroeder*

Lidström tied Pavel Bure for third in the rookie scoring race with 60 points, and led rookies with a plus-36. Bure won the Calder Trophy as the NHL's top rookie, and Lidström finished second. (The year before, Fedorov was runner-up for the Calder behind goaltender Ed Belfour.)

Lidström had a subpar second year with the NHL, recording just 41 points, a 19-point drop from his sensational rookie year. The 1992–93 season ended with a numbing Game 7 overtime loss to the underdog Toronto Maple Leafs in the first round. When Lidström's third season began, Scotty Bowman had been installed behind the bench.

Lidström rebounded, recording 56 points. He nearly missed a stretch early on in 1993–94 when he jammed his left thumb, causing swelling, but a cast made it possible for

9 TO 5

Before there was a No. 9 guy with Västerås IK, there was, of course, a No. 9 guy with the Red Wings.

Gordie Howe's number was retired by the Wings on March 12, 1972, in a ceremony at Olympia Stadium in Detroit attended by Vice President Spiro Agnew. Nicklas Lidström was a month shy of turning two years old and living in Sweden.

Nearly two decades later, in fall of 1991, Lidström showed up at Joe Louis Arena hoping to make the Wings. In the two years since he had been drafted, Lidström had kept up with the Wings as much as possible. This was before the Internet made everything hyper accessible, so Lidström's options were limited.

"The year before I came over, I was watching the Wings play in a playoff game and saw that there was no No. 9 on the ice," Lidström said. "So I was hoping that if I can make it, maybe I can have No. 9. So when I came over, I asked one of the trainers if I could have the number, and he said, 'Come with me, I'll show you something. And I looked up at the rafters at the Joe, and it showed No. 9 was hanging there. I knew to keep my mouth shut after that."

Retiring numbers wasn't common in Swedish hockey leagues, and there were none retired in Västerås when Lidström played there. When he learned who had worn No. 9 with the Wings, Lidström didn't make another request.

"No. 5 was handed to me," he said. "That was the number I got when I first came. I was just happy to get a number."

On March 6, 2014—almost 42 years to the day the Wings retired Howe's No. 9—Lidström's No. 5 went to the rafters.

him to play. When the season finished, Lidström had a flawless attendance record, having played all 248 games possible since entering the league.

"I take pride in this," Lidström said. "If possible, I play."

The more he played, the more he was recognized for how superbly he played. That special something Rockström and Smith had seen in Lidström—that ability to define perfection on ice—helped carry the Wings to the Stanley Cup Final in 1995. In 1996, Lidström was named to the first of 12 All-Star Games. In 1996–97, he finished third in scoring among NHL defensemen with 57 points. On June 7, 1997, Lidström scored late in the first period of Game 4 against the Philadelphia Flyers, helping secure a 2–1 victory and his first Stanley Cup championship. His first call was to his parents, who, much like that June day in 1989, were waiting by their phone. It was about 5:30 in the morning when Jan Erik Lidström answered—no wariness this time of hearing anyone speak English. On each side of the Atlantic Ocean, father and son Lidström swigged champagne.

Lidström won a second Cup in 1998. In 1999, Yzerman described Lidström as "our best player. He plays in a lot of situations; he plays against the opposition's top players. He's expected to be great defensively and great offensively. He does everything."

Lidstrom's excellence both on and off the ice prompted teammates to nickname him "The Perfect Human."

In 2001, Lidström won the first of seven James Norris Memorial Trophies as the NHL's top defenseman. After the 2002 Cup, Lidström was recognized with the Conn Smythe Trophy as the most valuable player of the playoffs, becoming

FROM CHAUFFEUR TO SCOUT

It began with a favor to a friend.

Christer Rockström was at home one day when Verner Persson called. Persson worked for Central Scouting in Stockholm, and he wanted to know if Rockström could pick up two NHL scouts at the airport. Persson was supposed to meet them, but he couldn't make it. Sure, Rockström told Persson. No problem. He drove to Arlanda Airport and collected Neil Smith and Gary Darling.

That meeting led to one of the most famous draft picks in Wings history. Like many stories with a great ending, it had an inauspicious beginning. "I wasn't really interested in being a scout at that time," Rockström said in a 2021 interview. "I just took them around as a favor for my friend.

"I knew that age group of players, so when we got to the game, I helped Neil and Gary get lineups and circled the names of some of the better players. I wasn't even with them during the game. After the game I took them to their hotel. That's how it all started."

Smith worked for the Wings, and Darling scouted for the Philadelphia Flyers. Both were in Sweden for about a week, and Rockström drove them to a couple games.

"They were nice guys," Rockström said. "They took my phone number, and a few days later Neil called me and asked if I wanted to help them. At first I said no, I don't have time. I wasn't really sure what it would be—there weren't a lot of scouts in Europe at that time. So I said no, I'm going to do what I've been doing, which was being a skills coach.

"He called me a week or two later and said, you need to think about it. Why don't you help us a little bit? So I started doing some work part-time. There was basically no money involved. It was more helping first Verner, and then Neil, whom I liked. That's where it started."

Rockström worked for the Wings from 1984 to 1989. In 1988–89 he was one of the few scouts to see Nicklas Lidström and convinced Smith he should see the young defenseman, too. In those days it wasn't unusual for European players to go unnoticed, but the Wings had shown their savvy—and their situation—in hiring Rockström.

"Detroit at that time wasn't very good, so they started to go into Europe to look for talent," Rockström said. "Neil was very proactive in that way. He was the guy pushing to go in another direction than everyone else. There were a few teams that were going into Europe—Philadelphia was one of them, New Jersey was one of them, Detroit was one of them. The Rangers were one of them. But some teams didn't go at all."

Rockström left the Wings shortly after the 1989 draft, opting to go to the New York Rangers with Smith. "It was hard to leave, but my contract was up, and I decided to go to the Rangers with Neil," Rockström said. "I can only say good things about Detroit. It was great to work for them."

the first European-born and -trained winner. Lidström won the Norris again in 2002, 2003, 2006, 2007, 2008, and 2011. When Yzerman retired in 2006, Lidström succeeded him as captain—and in 2008, he became the first European-born and -trained captain of a Stanley Cup–winning team.

Lidström announced his retirement on May 31, 2012, at age 42. In 1,564 games, Lidström recorded 264 goals and 878 points—and set numerous franchise records for defensemen, including for points (80) and assists (64) in one season; and career playoff goals (54) and points (183). He ranks first in team playoff games with 263.

Lidström spent 20 seasons with the Wings, during which they never missed the playoffs. He was recognized as one of the best to ever play the game, and in 2015 he was a first-ballot inductee into the Hockey Hall of Fame. Those who saw Lidström in 1989 with Västerås knew there was something about him, that he was worth taking out for ridiculously priced pizza and worth all the precautions so that no rival would discover him.

"Nick Lidström was one of the only times in all my career that people think you find these diamonds-in-the-roughs—which you don't—but he was one," Smith said. "Everybody knows about everybody. It's just about who happens to take them at the right time. But Lidström truly was a diamond in the rough. All of a sudden, he's this superstar, and you got [him] when nobody else really had him rated. He really was amazing."

3

THE BEST YOUNG PLAYER IN THE WORLD

SHORTLY AFTER THE Red Wings chose Sergei Fedorov in the fourth round of the 1989 draft, Jimmy Devellano gleefully told reporters the Wings had drafted, "the best young player in the world."

They had also drafted a Russian, and at that time, NHL teams were wary of drafting Soviet players because they might never emerge from behind the Iron Curtain. Slava Fetisov—who would go on to have a history-making career with the Wings—had been drafted by the Montreal Canadiens in 1978 with the last pick in the 12th round, at No. 201, but Fetisov was unable to leave the Soviet Union and reentered the draft in 1983, when he was selected by the New Jersey Devils in the eighth round, at No. 145. Fetisov finally debuted with the Devils in the fall of 1989, when he was 31 years old.

Drafting a Russian was risky, but after making their first three selections on June 17, 1989, Devellano and his top scout, Neil Smith, weighed the risk against the potential reward. No one doubted Fedorov would succeed in the NHL. Christer Rockström, the chief European scout, was dazzled by him. "He was so quick, and he played such a good two-way style," Rockström said in 2021. "You could tell he would be a fantastic player in the NHL."

Smith and Nick Polano, the assistant general manager, had traveled to watch Fedorov play in the World Championships in Sweden in 1989. They returned to Detroit and told others in the organization that Fedorov was head and shoulders above everybody else.

"The thing about Fedorov was, you knew if you got him over here, he would be a superstar player," Smith said in a 2021 interview. "I had seen him enough the year before and I wanted to take him then. He was so gifted, you could see that even as a teenager. The only doubt was, would you ever get him over here?"

Fedorov's obvious talent was one factor guiding the Wings' decision. Another was time: it had been seven years since Mike and Marian Ilitch bought the franchise and brought in Devellano to run it. Devellano had promised his bosses a Stanley Cup championship within eight years, and by the summer of 1989, it was clear that would not happen. Devellano decided the draft was the place to gamble and turned to his top scouts—Smith, Rockström, and Ken Holland.

"I quizzed them and asked, 'Okay, who is the best young player in the world?' Now, we weren't dead last, so we wouldn't get him if he were North American," Devellano said in 2021. "But I wanted to know. I said, 'Forget about the Iron Curtain. Who's the best 18-year-old in the world?' They told me, 'Well, that's Sergei Fedorov. He's a Russian.'

"I said, 'Okay, so are you telling me if we had the first pick in the draft and there was no Iron Curtain, and you knew you could get him, he would go No. 1?' They all agreed—'Oh, yeah, yeah, he would. But he's behind the Iron Curtain, and you're never going to get him.'"

Back then there were rules about where players could be drafted, based on nationality, age, and experience—for example, the Wings had had to draft Lidström in the third round, or else he would not be available again until the 1990 draft.

When the fourth round began, Devellano decided to stick his neck out.

"I said to myself, *Jimmy, you've been drafting fourth-round picks forever. It's rare one of them makes the NHL.* A fourth-round player is usually a player that goes to the American Hockey League and plays there, and is okay. That would be nine times out of 10. And so I'm saying to myself, *I know nobody's ever taken a guy from behind the Iron Curtain this high, but you know what, I'm going to tell Neil and Kenny we're taking him.*

"My thought process was, I might get fired in the meantime because we haven't advanced. But I'm going to be able to go to the Ilitches and say, I may not be here, you may not keep me around, but if you get him even 10 years from now, when Sergei Fedorov is 28 or 29 years old, you'll have a great player."

Four years earlier, the Ilitches had used their business contacts and wealth to help facilitate Petr Klima's escape from what was then Czechoslovakia. He was a star player, and in Fedorov, the Wings saw a superstar.

"People thought we were wasting a pick, because there was an Iron Curtain," Devellano said. "But Neil and Kenny told me Sergei was the best young player in the world. I had great confidence in the Ilitches, that they might find a way to get Sergei out. They might pay off the Russian government, they might open pizza stores in Moscow. They can do some things that ordinary people can't do. So we drafted him.

"There were snickers all over the draft floor—'There's Devellano, drafting a Russian.' Well, look how that turned out. Look at the impact he had. We had Steve Yzerman, now we had a second superstar center. Between Mike and Marian and Jim Lites, they found a way to get him to Detroit."

When the Wings' turn came in the fourth round, Smith made the announcement. "The Detroit Red Wings are happy to select, from the Central Red Army in the Soviet Union, Sergei Fedorov."

It was the highest a Russian played ever had been drafted.

Fedorov was 6'2" and 195 pounds, and blended explosive power with elite skill. In April 1990, Yzerman played against Fedorov in the World Championships in Switzerland, and returned to Detroit raving about him. "I was at the World Championships in 1990, the year after we drafted him," Yzerman said in 2021. "Sergei and I were on the ice at the same time, and he was just flying. He took a slap shot inside our blue line—this was on international ice—and ripped the puck right over our goalie's shoulder. His speed and strength were awesome."

The Wings had been in contact with Fedorov since August 1989. In July 1990—three months after the glowing report from Yzerman—Fedorov was in Portland, Oregon, for an exhibition game in the lead-up to the Goodwill Games. His military service had ended, and it seemed an opportune moment to stage his defection. Wings executive vice president Jim Lites and scout Nick Polano checked into the same hotel where Fedorov was staying. While Fedorov was playing in the game, Lites used the key Fedorov had slipped beneath his door to access Fedorov's room and collect his belongings. Lites waited in the hotel lobby for the Russian team to return. When Fedorov saw him, he followed Lites to a waiting taxi. Lites tipped the driver $100 to stop asking questions and take them to the airport, where Mike Ilitch's private airplane was ready.

"I was excited to see nice plane," Fedorov said. "I was looking forward to landing in Detroit and getting on with a new life."

In Detroit, Fedorov made an immediate impression. Bryan Murray, the coach, joked that Fedorov's English was limited to "give me the puck." A dictionary helped solve the conundrum elicited in the training staff when Fedorov told them, "I need love." The word Fedorov wanted was *glove*.

Nothing was lost in translation on the ice. His style was a combination of finesse and fierceness, of physicality and

Sergei Fedorov in August 1990. *Photo by Steven R. Nickerson*

grace. "He's willing to go into traffic, go to the corner, go to the front of net," Murray said. "Anything to make the plays."

The last obstacle to getting Fedorov into an NHL game was cleared October 1, when he received his work visa. The risk the Wings had taken at the draft started to pay off in the first game. Fedorov scored in his debut on October 4. It was the first of 31 goals in his rookie season, in which Fedorov recorded 79 points in 77 games. But it wasn't just his offense that dazzled, it was how good he was defensively. This was at a time when it was okay for star scorers to be one-dimensional—Petr Klima used to brag, "I never play defense. I score goals."

Not so for Fedorov. He had grown up skating on frozen soccer fields in his hometown of Pskov, 10 miles east of the Estonian border. As a teenager, he'd lie on the ice, jump up, race to the other end, kneel, jump up, and race back. He hated getting beat, with or without the puck.

"Fedorov is probably the best defensive player to come out of Europe," Polano said. "I don't think there's ever been a European player who understands his defensive responsibilities like he does."

Fedorov's 79 points were 20 more than first-overall pick Mats Sundin, who played three more games. As Yzerman had done in 1984, Fedorov lost out on the Calder Trophy as rookie of the year to a goaltender: in Yzerman's case it was Tom Barrasso; Fedorov was runner-up to Ed Belfour.

Fedorov was 21 years old. Everything that made the Wings decide to draft him was reinforced—he was a fantastic player, a combination of strength and skill. In 1993–94 he recorded 120 points, 10 behind league-leader Wayne Gretzky. A herniated disk limited Yzerman to 58 games, and in his absence, Fedorov thrived as the top go-to guy. During the 26 games Yzerman was sidelined, Fedorov scored 17 goals while racking up 45 points, leading the Wings to a 16–8–2 record en route to the best record in the Western Conference.

"With Stevie out, I feel like I've got to do something extra," Fedorov said. "It's part of the job. Bigger responsibility—and pressure."

(That season was also a harbinger of the trouble the Wings would have with Fedorov. He was, by league standards, underpaid at $295,000 per season, but Fedorov switched agents while the Wings were trying to rework his contract in December 1993, stalling the process.)

There were nights Fedorov played close to 30 minutes, nearly half the game. In March 1994, he celebrated his first hat trick, fueling a 5–2 victory over the Calgary Flames, in what was Fedorov's 293rd game. It was the first time he had scored three goals in a game since he was 15. His second goal gave him 100 points.

That June, Fedorov became the first-ever Russian to win the Hart Trophy as the league's most valuable player. Members of the Professional Hockey Writers Association also awarded Fedorov the Frank J. Selke Trophy as the league's best defensive forward. Fedorov received 194 Hart votes to 86 for Buffalo Sabres goalie (and future Wing) Dominik Hasek's 86, and topped Toronto Maple Leafs forward Doug Gilmour 175–107 in Selke voting.

Fedorov was ecstatic.

"The greatest time I have ever had," he said. "I am so excited to win these awards. It's a great honor." He thanked Mike and Marian Ilitch for getting him to Detroit.

All the subterfuge in Portland had been well worth it. Five years after he had been drafted in the fourth round, Fedorov lead his draft class with 372 points in 312 games. Sundin, the No. 1 pick, had 334 points in 324 games.

Fedorov was the second franchise center, behind Yzerman, that the Wings had drafted since the Ilitches bought the team. But the playoffs continued to be a disappointment. Scotty Bowman had been brought in to coach after the Wings lost in the first round to the Toronto Maple Leafs in 1993, but the 1994 playoffs weren't any more fun. In Game 7 at Joe Louis Arena, goaltender Chris Osgood gave away the puck and with it, the first-round series.

It would be another three years before the Stanley Cup finally came to Detroit. During that time Bowman assembled the Russian Five, putting Fedorov on a line with countrymen Igor Larionov and Slava Kozlov, and with Vladimir Konstantinov (another product of the 1989 draft) and Slava Fetisov on defense. It was like nothing ever seen in the NHL, the way the five comrades played as one, commandeering the puck to the despair of opponents. *Sport Express*, a daily newspaper in Russia, sent a reporter to Detroit to document the group in 1996. Ever since Fedorov had defected in 1990, interest in the Red Wings in Russia had surged.

On December 26, 1996, Fedorov recorded his best individual game, scoring all five of the Wings' goals, the last one in overtime, in a 5–4 victory over the Washington Capitals at Joe Louis Arena. Fedorov described the night: "Like rolling stones from the mountain coming at me." Only one player in franchise history had ever done better: Syd Howe, who on February 3, 1944, scored six goals against the New York Rangers.

"It was like a dream game," Bowman said.

It would turn into a dream season. Fedorov scored in the clinching game of the Western Conference Finals against the Colorado Avalanche, sending the Wings onto the Stanley Cup Final. He scored the game-winning goal in the Game 1 against the Philadelphia Flyers, putting the Wings up 1–0. Fedorov set up a goal by Brendan Shanahan as the Wings cruised to another 4–2 victory in Game 2. In Game 3, Fedorov scored twice, including the winning goal, and also recorded two assists. When the playoffs ended in jubilation on June 6, Fedorov had delivered a team-leading 20 points in 20 games.

Eight years had passed since the Wings had drafted "the best young player in the world." Fedorov had amassed 592 points in that time, beating Sundin by 34 points, in 23 fewer games. He had made Wings brass look like geniuses. Then he broke their hearts.

Fedorov became a restricted free agent in the summer of 1997. He didn't report to training camp that fall. The months dragged on, and still talks stalled. When his teammates received their Stanley Cup rings at a gala ceremony in November, Fedorov wasn't there. He got his ring in January, when he was at Joe Louis Arena to meet with general manager Ken Holland. The Wings had offered long-term deals averaging $5.5 million annually. Fedorov wanted $7 million.

Fedorov forced the Wings' hand in a manner that was especially painful to Ilitch, signing an offer sheet with rival Detroit businessman Peter Karmanos, owner of the Carolina Hurricanes. The offer sheet, signed while Fedorov was at the 1998 Nagano Olympics, was for six years, $38 million, and prohibitive in how it was designed. Beyond an immediate $14 million signing bonus, Fedorov stood to make another $16 million if the Hurricanes made the Conference Finals. There was little risk of the Hurricanes doing so, but the Wings were favored to repeat, putting Ilitch on the hook to, potentially, owe Fedorov $28 million if the Wings won three playoff rounds.

Ilitch gave permission to match, and once again a decision involving Fedorov paid dividends, as the Wings celebrated another Stanley Cup championship that June. But while the two shook hands when Fedorov returned from the Olympics, there was lingering damage. Fedorov helped the Wings win the Stanley Cup again in 2002, when he was part of a star-studded lineup, and he posted 83 points in 2002–03, the last year of the Carolina-authored contract. He had demanded a trade in 1997, and in 2003, he mastered his own departure. Fedorov deliberately chose to become a free agent, rejecting a personal offer from Ilitch for five years and $50 million. It was a bold and unprecedented offer, and the $10 million a year still stood in April, though reduced to four years and $40 million. The Wings lost in the first round of the 2003 playoffs to Anaheim, and Fedorov consoled himself by buying a $650,000 Ferrari Enzo. Publicly, he said he wanted to stay "because I live here for 13 years and I play my best hockey and I love it here," but that wasn't what he said in private.

The Wings were full of glee in 1989 when they drafted Fedorov and engineered his escape. In 2003 they were full of gloom. Fedorov may have craved the southern California lifestyle afforded when he signed with the Ducks, and he may have craved being out from the shadow of Steve Yzerman, but the Wings weren't the same without him, and his NHL career never reached anywhere near the glory he enjoyed in Detroit. The Ducks jettisoned him on November 15, 2005, trading him to the Columbus Blue Jackets, a franchise that was in its fifth season and had never qualified for the playoffs. Fedorov wore a Ducks uniform when he became the first Russian to reach 1,000 points and a Blue Jackets uniform when he became the first Russian to reach 1,000 games.

At the 2008 trade deadline, Fedorov was traded to the Washington Capitals, where he played through 2008–09. Fedorov ended his NHL career with 1,179 points, second only to Sundin's 1,349 points for his 1989 draft class.

Fans in Detroit booed Fedorov when he returned to the Joe. It wasn't until he was inducted into the Hockey Hall of Fame in 2015 that fans relented, giving him a standing ovation when he appeared for a ceremonial puck drop. Fedorov, who had maintained a residence in the Detroit area after he left, blamed his departure on misunderstandings.

"I had the best years of my life here," Fedorov said.

The Wings believed they got the best young player in the world when they used a fourth-round pick to draft Fedorov. They took advantage of a bias against Russian players and gambled on getting around the Iron Curtain, and for 13 years, Fedorov proved a great reward.

4

BEFORE THE DRAFT

BEFORE THE RED Wings built Stanley Cup championship teams through the draft, they built them with leather jackets.

Gordie Howe is synonymous with the franchise, but he almost ended up with another Original Six team. When Howe was 15 years old, in 1943, he attended the New York Rangers' training camp in Winnipeg, Manitoba. The Rangers told Howe they wanted him to play junior hockey at Notre Dame Cathedral in Wilcox, Saskatchewan, but Howe wasn't Catholic and didn't think it was a good fit.

The next year Howe traveled to Windsor, Ontario, to attend Wings camp, invited by a scout named Fred Pinkney. Jack Adams, the team's coach and general manager, liked what he saw and signed Howe to a contract that stipulated he receive a leather team jacket.

Howe was assigned to the Galt Red Wings in the Ontario Hockey League. He ended up not playing because the team already had three players from Western Canada, which was the limit allowed in the lineup.

In 1945, Howe was assigned to the Omaha Knights in the United States Hockey League, where Tommy Ivan coached. That was a great fit for Howe, because Ivan guided his development on the ice and was kind to him off the ice, inviting Howe over for dinners and to celebrate Christmas. After Howe recorded 22 goals and 26 assists in 51 games in 1945–46, Ivan told Adams that Howe was ready for the NHL.

Howe would go on to play 25 seasons for the Wings, from 1946 to 1971. He led the NHL in points from 1950–51 to 1953–54, and again in 1956–57 and 1962–63. He ranked among the top 10 in scoring for 21 consecutive seasons. He was hurt for all but the first game of the playoffs when the Wings won the Stanley Cup in 1950, but contributed significantly when the Wings won the Cup again in 1952, 1954, and 1955. In 1972, he was inducted into the Hockey Hall of Fame.

WHERE HOWE WAS enticed by a jacket, Ted Lindsay wanted cash.

His path to the Wings began in the fall of 1944, when he was invited to try out for a spot on the team. The season before, in 1943–44, Lindsay put up 29 points in 22 games playing junior hockey in Toronto for St. Michael's College.

The Wings' camp was in Windsor, Ontario, across the river from Detroit. There was no air conditioning at Windsor Arena, and practicing there often was uncomfortable.

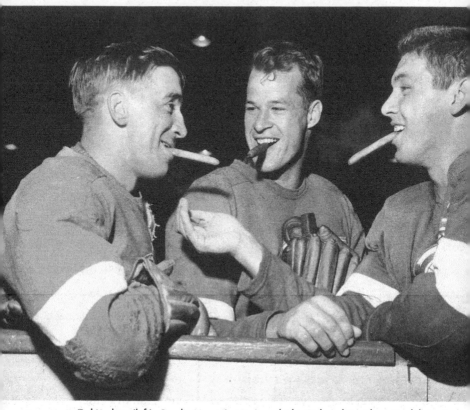

Ted Lindsay (left), Gordie Howe (center), and Alex Delvecchio, who joined the Wings long before the NHL Draft.

Sometimes Lindsay would be told to take part in evening practices, which were held for the guys who had day jobs. When that happened, Lindsay had to put on equipment that was still wet and smelly from being used by other players during the day.

Even as a 19-year-old, Lindsay showed the mettle that one day would lead him to form the Players Association. He figured he would have much more of an opportunity to be an impact player if he returned to his junior team, St. Mike's, and that's what he said when Adams offered Lindsay a contract to sign with the Wings.

Lindsay discussed the situation with Paul McNamara, his junior coach. McNamara told Lindsay to grab the opportunity. Lindsay did so—but with conditions. He asked Adams to include a clause that Lindsay wouldn't be sent to the minors, and that he would appear in at least 40 games. Adams conceded on all counts. On top of that, Lindsay received a $2,000 signing bonus, an astronomical sum in those days. (By comparison, Howe's salary in 1946–47 was around $5,000.)

Lindsay was 19 when he debuted with the Wings in 1944. He played for them until 1956–57, and again in 1964–65. He won the Cup four times and served as captain from 1952 to 1956. In July 1957 Adams traded Lindsay to Chicago, five months after the formation of the NHLPA. Lindsay served as general manager from 1977 to 1980 and as head coach in 1979–80.

FOR THE MOST part, there was little discussion about paperwork. Alex Delvecchio met Adams at a hotel, signed a contract, and suited up.

The 1950s were a glorious time for the Wings. Howe, Lindsay, Delvecchio, Sid Abel, Terry Sawchuk, Red Kelly—these were the players who made the franchise a byword for glory. Long before the NHL Draft took shape, before it became the fountain from which teams were built and nourished, they were the ones to sign tryouts and take what was offered.

Howe's jacket became part of Red Wings lore. No one is exactly sure when, his son Mark said in 2021, but at some point down the road, Howe still hadn't gotten it. Howe went to Adams, who asked what was wrong. Howe told him he hadn't gotten the jacket. "Just go grab one," is what Adams replied according to the story Howe told his children. Howe did.

The jacket—a varsity-style with tan sleeves and a red bodice, with a *D* on the left chest embroidered with "Red Wings"—was worn by Howe for a number of years, and after that, his son Marty wore it. Eventually, the Howes added it to the family's memorabilia collection, recognizing the jacket's place in history. Once worn by the face of the franchise, it's a relic of how the Wings built a dynasty before the draft.

5

HOW IT BEGAN

THE DRAFT HAS become a major building tool for teams, but when it began, it was a task that begat little thought.

The first draft was held in 1963, in the days of the Original Six. The Red Wings, Black Hawks, Bruins, Canadiens, Rangers, and Maple Leafs agreed to institute what was then called an "amateur draft" to create a more egalitarian method for teams to acquire promising young players. Previously, teams sponsored players, essentially buying their rights.

On June 5, 1963, executives for the six teams met at the Queen Elizabeth Hotel in Montreal. Sid Abel, a member of the Wings' famed Production Line, was the general manager, having succeeded the legendary Jack Adams the previous year.

The draft was limited to players who would reach 17 years of age between August 1, 1963, and July 31, 1964.

Players already under sponsorship were not eligible. The NHL allowed team executives to essentially decide in which order they would make selections, rather than go by where teams finished in the standings. The order for the first round was Montreal, Detroit, Boston, New York, Chicago, and Toronto. The Canadiens had first pick in all four rounds. The Red Wings, however, had only two selections in the entire draft, the second pick of both the first and second rounds.

The draft was a noble idea, but in its first iteration had almost no impact. All the best young players already had sponsorships with teams. The 1963 draft was such a sparse event that there were only four rounds, and teams could pass on making a selection.

The Wings made one of the few good picks when they selected Pete Mahovlich at No. 2. Mahovlich, the younger brother of Frank Mahovlich, who would be inducted into the Hockey Hall of Fame in 1981, debuted with the Wings on December 28, 1965. Mahovlich earned an assist in his first game, but he struggled to make an impact and spent time in the minor leagues. Frank Mahovlich joined the Wings in 1967–68 and was a great fit on a line with Gordie Howe and Alex Delvecchio, scoring 49 goals in 1968–69. That same season, Pete Mahovlich had four points with the Wings.

It wasn't until his 1969–70 move to the powerhouse Canadiens that Pete Mahovlich's career took flight. He regularly topped 30 goals a season and topped 100 points in 1974–75 and 1975–76. "Little M," as the 6'5", 220-pound Pete was nicknamed because his brother was "Big M," recorded 82 assists in 1974–75 on a line with Guy Lafleur and Steve Shutt. Known for his deceptively quick stride and deft puckhandling,

Pete Mahovlich won the Stanley Cup four times with Montreal between 1971 and 1977, the only player from the 1963 draft class to do so.

Mahovlich also played for the Pittsburgh Penguins before finishing his playing career where he started it, back in the Wings organization. The team was in terrible shape—it was during the "Dead Wings" era, but Mahovlich once again was relegated to the minors.

The Wings selected Bill Cosburn, a forward for the Hamilton Red Wings, in the second round. He never made it to the NHL, spending parts of three seasons in Sweden's lower levels until 1970–71. The Wings passed on making a selection in the third round, and again in the fourth round.

By the fourth round, only the Canadiens, Bruins, Rangers, and Maple Leafs made picks. Of the 21 players drafted in 1963, only five ever played in the NHL: Garry Monahan (No. 1, Montreal, 748 games), Mahovlich (884 games), Walt McKechnie (No. 6, Toronto, 955 games), Jim McKenny (No. 17, Toronto, 604 games), and Gerry Meehan (No. 21, Toronto, 670 games).

The second draft wasn't much more effective in yielding talent. The Wings had the No. 1 pick in 1964, but Claude Gauthier, a forward in the Quebec leagues, never made it to the NHL. Their second choice, Brian Watts, a forward playing in Toronto, appeared in four games. Ralph Buchanan, a defenseman out of Montreal, likewise never played in the NHL; it was Rene LeClerc, a forward from Quebec, who turned out to be the best selection. He played 87 games for the Wings, and then found success in the World Hockey Association, where he played from 1972–73 to 1978–79.

It wasn't until 1969 that the Wings drafted a player who had a long career in Detroit. Jim Rutherford, a goaltender from Ontario, was selected at No. 10. He began his NHL career with the Wings in 1970–71, playing 29 games. He spent three seasons with the Pittsburgh Penguins, then returned to Detroit in 1973. He was with them during the Dead Wings era, playing 305 of his 457 NHL games in a Wings uniform.

The draft had grown to 10 rounds in 1969. It ballooned all the way to 21 rounds in 1978, when, basically, the draft kept going until every team passed. It was at 12 rounds from 1983 (the year the Wings drafted Steve Yzerman) to 1991, and has been at seven since 2005.

6

THE MEN
WHO BURIED THE
DEAD WINGS

THE 1983 DRAFT brought life back to the Red Wings. It marked a turning point after a decade of poor talent development and poorer finishes in the standings, distancing the club from the dismal days of the 1970s, when the team was so awful it spurred the sobriquet the "Dead Wings." It yielded The Captain and the Bruise Brothers and an enigma from the Czech Republic.

It was the first draft for the group of men who had breathed hope into the franchise the previous summer. Mike Ilitch bought the Wings in early June 1982, too late to install his own people before the draft, which was held June 9.

The 1983 draft, especially the club's first pick, carried all the more importance in light of what had happened the previous draft. Despite finishing with the second-worst record in 1981–82, the Wings didn't pick until near the end of the first round because of a trade with Minnesota in the summer of 1981. North Stars general manager Lou Nanne swindled Wings counterpart Jimmy Skinner, convincing him to swap first-round picks in exchange for two players—Greg Smith and Don Murdoch—who made little to no impact on the Wings. The North Stars finished sixth and picked second; the Wings finished 20th and picked 17th.

The 1983 draft was, in fact, the first time since 1979 the Wings retained their own first-round pick, having traded away their first-round picks in 1980, 1981, and 1982. (All the trades were disastrous for the Wings, while their trade partners benefited from being able to draft Larry Murphy in 1980 and Brian Bellows in 1982.)

As Devellano and his top aide, Neil Smith, proceeded through their first season, they zeroed in on three players who they thought could be game-changers: Pat LaFontaine, Sylvain Turgeon, and Steve Yzerman. When the buzzer sounded on the regular season in May, the Wings sat in the 18th spot, giving them their first pick at No. 4. As soon as the Minnesota North Stars took Brian Lawton with the first overall pick, Devellano and Smith knew they'd get one of their guys. LaFontaine was the top choice because he was a prodigy from the Detroit area, but when the New York Islanders grabbed him at No. 3, after the Hartford Whalers had taken Turgeon, the Wings took Yzerman.

"I saw Steve quite a few times, particularly in the second half of the season," Smith said in 2021. "As the season went on, we were getting closer and closer to figuring out where we would land in the draft. It was always Sylvain Turgeon, LaFontaine, and Stevie. We saw each of them quite a number of times. We had them rated pretty equally, but LaFontaine was the local guy."

When he arrived in Detroit that summer, local papers included explanations on how to pronounce Yzerman: *I-zer-man*. But soon he was known simply as Stevie, and then "The Captain"—he was honored with the *C* on his sweater in 1986 when he was 21 years old, making him the youngest in franchise history. Yzerman was quiet but played a thunderous game. He was stoic through playoff heartbreaks, and when he finally won the Stanley Cup on June 7, 1997, at age 32, he embodied a city's return to glory as he skated a lap with the Cup, his gap-toothed smile an instant, iconic image. Yzerman had won three Stanley Cups by the time he retired in 2006. He had his No. 19 retired in 2007, won another Cup as a front-office member in 2008, and was inducted into the Hockey Hall of Fame in 2009. Yzerman's 692 goals, 1,063 assists, 1,755 points, plus-184 rating, and 1,514 games all are best in his draft class.

Yzerman alone would have changed the Wings, but as the rounds wore on, the Wings continued to find players who would revive the franchise: Lane Lambert at No. 25, Bob Probert at No. 46, Petr Klima at No. 86, and Joey Kocur at No. 88.

"We had really done some good work, myself and the scouts," Devellano said in 2021. "We had done a lot of good scouting, because in the second round we got Lane Lambert, who played two or three years for us. Unfortunately, he sustained an eye injury and he never really advanced into the player we thought he could become. But he was an NHL player.

"Further on, we got two 18-year-olds that would a few years later become the two toughest players in the NHL—third round, Bob Probert; fifth round, Joey Kocur. They became known as the 'Bruise Brothers.' And, boy, were they tough. And did they ever sell a lot of jerseys. In a later round, we got another tough guy in Stu Grimson [No. 186]. He didn't play much for us, but he played in the NHL for a long time, and we drafted him—we get credit for him."

The other picks were defenseman David Korol at No. 68, goaltender Chris Pusey at No. 106, forward Bob Pierson at No. 126, defenseman Craig Butz at No. 146, defenseman Dave Sikorski at No. 166, forward Jeff Frank at No. 206, and forward Charles Chiatto at No. 226.

While Yzerman and Klima in particular had been drafted for their skill, Devellano was excited by how big some of the picks were that year. "You can see by the size of some of these guys that the Red Wings aren't going to be pushed around much longer," he said at the time. In addition to Probert, Kocur, and Grimson, Devellano liked Pierson, who stood 6'3" and weighed 213 pounds. "Hopefully, he'll be one of our goons in the future."

Lambert had been expected to go in the first round, and even after the eye injury he was billed as a tough, aggressive forward who was good at creating scoring opportunities around the net. He appeared in 176 games for the Wings, and

Steve Yzerman (left) and Lane Lambert, both drafted in 1983, stand in front of Joe Louis Arena in 1984. *Photo by Mary Schroeder*

in July 1986 was part of the trade that brought over goalie Glen Hanlon from the New York Rangers.

When the Wings drafted Probert, he was a 6′3″, 206-pound 18-year-old whose hard punches belied the soft hands he showed around the net. He started playing for the team in 1985 and was named to the All-Star Game in 1988. His popularity was enormous—fans cherished Yzerman but adored

THE GRIM REAPER

The month after he made 6'5", 208-pound forward Stu Grimson the 186th pick in the 1983 draft, Jimmy Devellano laid out how he envisioned Grimson contributing to the Red Wings.

"Hopefully," Devellano said, "he'll be grinding bodies and banging them in the corner."

Grimson had one point, an assist, and 105 penalty minutes in 48 games with the Regina Pats in the Western Hockey League in 1982–83. He showed significant growth over the next two years in juniors, posting 56 points and 248 penalty minutes in 71 games in 1984–85. But Devellano did not sign Grimson, and so in 1985 he reentered the draft and became property of the Calgary Flames when they selected him at No. 143. It wasn't until a decade later that Grimson appeared in a Wings sweater, when he was acquired from the Mighty Ducks of Anaheim in a package deal that cost the Wings Mike Sillinger (a first-round pick from 1989) and Jason York. "A lot of people felt we needed to be a little stronger, bigger, tougher up front," Devellano said April 4, 1995, the day the trade was finalized. On April 9, Grimson won his first fight in a Wings uniform, against Chicago's Jim Cummins. A year later, Grimson battled Bob Probert, the first time the two heavyweights met with Grimson fighting for the Wings and Probert for the Blackhawks. The much-anticipated renewal of their rivalry was something of a dud: neither landed any good punches, and it was more of a wrestling match.

"We stared each other down, and it appeared the appropriate time, so we just fought," Grimson said. "I thought it was important if I stepped up, for whatever good it did, to try and send a little message."

Grimson was with the Wings during their run to the 1995 Stanley Cup Final and their 62 victories in 1995–96. But as Scotty Bowman continued to fine-tune the roster toward a championship, Grimson became expendable. The day after the Wings acquired Brendan Shanahan in October 1996, Grimson was placed on waivers. "We like him as a person," Bowman said. "We like a lot of things about him. But we have other players we're using." The Hartford Whalers—who had just traded Shanahan to the Wings—plucked Grimson off the waiver wire.

Grimson enjoyed a long career in the NHL, playing 729 games, but only 68 of those appearances were with the Wings.

Probert. He fought opponents and fought the law—he scored big goals and got busted for cocaine—and he sold jerseys. He was a combination of big, skilled, and tough not seen in a Wings uniform since Gordie Howe retired. The Wings held onto Probert through multiple arrests, kept him even when he broke curfew and went out drinking the night before Game 5 of the 1988 Conference Finals. It wasn't until Probert's play declined—and he was arrested for drunk driving again—that the Wings finally cut ties with him in 1994. But fans still loved him, and cheered, "Pro-bie! Pro-bie!" when he appeared at Yzerman's number retirement ceremony in 2007. Probert's 259 points in a Wings uniform ranks second in his draft class; his 2,090 penalty minutes leads the class.

"He was such a good player," Devellano said in 2021. "He could score 20 goals, he was tough as nails. He could play with Steve Yzerman, could protect him. He gave you that in flashes. You just don't dump a guy of that caliber—they're too hard to get. So we tried to deal with it. We put him in rehab. We invited psychologists to work with him. We tried everything. But Bob's addiction was so strong. If I had to do it over again, I might not be tolerant.

"Every time he got caught, he would come back and play, and guess what would happen at Joe Louis Arena? He would get a standing ovation. It would go on and on. And I would sit in the stands, and the names on the backs of the jerseys were Yzerman—he was No. 1—and Probert was No. 2."

Probert played with Yzerman, fought with Kocur, and drank with Klima. Klima was a daring pick: he was a gifted player, but he was stuck behind the Iron Curtain, and in 1983 that made it uncertain the Wings would ever get him. It took Klima ditching the Czechoslovakian national team during a training exercise in West Germany in 1985 and defecting to Detroit. His immigration status was aided by Ed Meese, the U.S. Attorney General. On opening night at Joe Louis Arena in October 1985, fans greeted Klima with a five-minute standing ovation. Klima was a riveting player, scoring 32 goals in his rookie year, 30 in his second year, and 37 in 1987–88. But with him there were also numerous off-ice problems: he was arrested three times for drunk driving, and Klima was drinking with Probert at the nightclub Goose Loonies in 1988, during the playoff series against the Edmonton Oilers. In November 1989, Klima was part of the trade that brought Jimmy Carson to Detroit. Klima's 223 points with the Wings ranks third in the draft class.

"We stepped outside the box and we took a skilled, skilled player, a player that our scouts assured me would be an NHL player, in Petr Klima," Devellano said. "And he did become a very skilled player."

Kocur's contributions in the 1980s were pugilistic—he and Probert gave the Wings a potent tandem of enforcers. When Kocur was traded to the Rangers in March 1991 (where Neil Smith was then the general manager), Kocur had 111 points in 399 games—and 1,714 penalty minutes.

(In January 1997, the Wings brought Kocur back, signing him after he'd been playing for their alumni team and in an over-40 league. The Wings needed someone to keep opponents from taking cheap shots at their stars, and Kocur was a terrific fit. He helped them win the Stanley Cup and played until 1999.)

The 1983 draft transformed the Wings. Yzerman led the team into the playoffs in his first year, and soon he, Probert, Klima, and Kocur restored the franchise's good name. They made the Wings a better team in the 1980s—not a Stanley Cup team, but for the most part, a playoff team. That draft class enabled the Wings to win a few playoff rounds, to sell tickets, to fill Joe Louis Arena. It took them from really bad to really competitive, from unwatchable to entertaining. The change began when Ilitch bought the team and when he hired Devellano. But it was Yzerman, Probert, Klima, and Kocur who buried the Dead Wings.

7

THE MASTER
DRAFTER

THE DRAFT WAS the first thing Jimmy Devellano talked about when Mike Ilitch interviewed him to run the Red Wings after buying the team in June 1982. Devellano had a reputation as a master drafter, having helped build what was then the best team in the National Hockey League.

When the New York Islanders became an NHL team in 1972, Devellano became their scout in Eastern Canada. In 1974 he was promoted to head scout, a position he held, along with other titles, until he left for Detroit. During Devellano's decade with the Islanders, they became a remarkable story, advancing from winning 12 games their first season to being Stanley Cup champions in 1980, 1981, and 1982. Devellano's list of draft picks included Bryan Trottier, Mike Bossy, Denis Potvin, and

Clark Gillies. When the Islanders won a fourth Cup in 1983, only five players on the team were not drafted by the team.

In contrast, the Wings were in dismal shape in 1982.

"When I arrived, the team had missed the playoffs 14 of the previous 16 seasons, and I guess that is why I was hired," Devellano said in 2021. "The reason Mike and Marian Ilitch chose me, basically, was the drafting I had done with the New York Islanders. That's why I got the job.

"I wasn't a former player. I was short and didn't look like a hockey guy. I wore glasses and was heavyset. It was a 21-team league, and 16 teams made the playoffs—and yet somehow the Red Wings, an Original Six team, had missed the playoffs 14 of the last 16 years. They were in the Detroit River. Now along come the Ilitches and purchase the franchise from Bruce Norris, and they bring me in from the New York Islanders to get the show on the road."

After his introductory press conference, Devellano and Mike and Marian Ilitch lunched together. Devellano asked how many season tickets holders there were at Joe Louis Arena, which seated a little over 19,000. Marian said that Norris had told her there were 5,000. After their meal, the three returned to the Joe, and Marian suggested a trip to the box office.

"Marian wanted to get an exact count," Devellano said. "She asked a gentleman at the box office, 'How many season ticket holders do we have?' He said, 'Marian, can I give you that answer in about 10–15 minutes?' She said, 'We'll be in Jimmy's office.'

"Of course, when I heard '10–15 minutes,' I thought, *It can't been too many if you can figure it out that quickly.* And, sure enough, he comes down and he gives us the bad news: 2,100. So there we sit on July 12, 1982. The Ilitches had just purchased the team, and I look up at the arena and I see 20,000 seats. And we have 2,100 tickets sold."

Devellano believed drafting well was the only way to make the team competitive and, in turn, make fans want to pay to see them. Devellano was the team's fourth general manager in 10 years, and there would be no more mortgaging of the future. (The Wings didn't have a first-round pick in 1981 and didn't select until 17th in 1982 despite finishing 20th because of a bad trade made by Jimmy Skinner, Devellano's predecessor.)

"I will make a commitment right now," Devellano said at his introductory news conference. "As long as Jimmy Devellano is the general manager of the Detroit Red Wings, we will not trade a draft choice. We won't trade a first pick, a third pick, a sixth pick, a 10th pick. We will keep our draft picks. Hopefully, we will be able to get some good players in here. You don't build a Stanley Cup contender through trades. You do it through the draft."

Devellano estimated that out of a 12-round draft, a team should be able to find three or four players who would make it to the NHL within five years. "If you keep your draft choices," he said, "you'll get 120 players over 10 years. Out of that, you should get 40 to 50 players.

"I've got a plan. I'm going to stick to it. The only question is whether my heart will last that long."

Devellano, known in hockey circles as "Jimmy D.," was 39 when he joined the Wings. He grew up in the Toronto area, where he became coach of a youth team in Scarborough, Ontario, when he was 19. He rose through the ranks of hockey as a scout, always signing his reports, "Hockey Is Happiness." (During a scouting trip to Detroit in the early 1980s, Devellano's rental car was burglarized outside Joe Louis Arena, and all of his scouting reports were stolen. When Wayne Maxner, then the Wings coach, heard about it, he said, "I hope it was one of our scouts who did it.")

Devellano was at the Islanders' table when they drafted Potvin with the first overall selection in 1973. In 1974, the year Devellano was promoted to chief scout, he selected Gillies, who would become one of the most feared players in the league, in the first round. In the second round, Devellano chose Trottier, a future Hockey Hall of Fame inductee.

It was an impressive track record to try to match in Detroit. Devellano tried to balance building fan excitement with realistic expectations. He suggested new slogans for the Wings—"We're Not Easy Anymore" and "We'll Earn Our Wings"—and preached patience to fans.

"I think what you have to tell the fans is you have a man who is committed to building this, not just into a good hockey club, but into a great hockey club," Devellano said. "I know they've suffered a long time, but I hate to say they may have to suffer some more. I'm sorry, but I think that's the best way to do it, to build a successful hockey club."

Ilitch did what Devellano refrained from doing, putting a time frame on the situation. "I'm hoping we can do it somewhere in the area of three years," Ilitch said. "I think the fans will hold out that long because they'll see the players we're putting on [the ice] and what we're bringing in."

There wasn't anything for Ilitch or the fans to like in the first year, as the Wings won just 21 games and failed to

Jimmy Devellano working his formula in mid 1980s to make the Red Wings a Stanley Cup champion. *Photo by Mary Schroeder*

qualify for the playoffs. Devellano spent much of his time on the road, preparing for the 1983 draft.

"I said to Mike and Marian, 'Look, the team is what it is,'" Devellano said in 2021. "'I'll do my best to improve it with unrestricted free agents, but basically it's not going to be a great team. I'll attend most of the home games, but when the team goes on the road, I won't be going with the team, I'll be going to Ontario. I'll be going out west, I'll be going out looking at the draft picks that our scouts are looking at.'"

Devellano and his top aide, Neil Smith, zeroed in on three players they judged could be game changers: Pat LaFontaine and Sylvain Turgeon, two forwards out of the Quebec junior league; and Steve Yzerman, a forward in the Ontario Hockey League. Devellano had them rated pretty equally, but LaFontaine had a tremendous advantage for a team trying to restore pride—he was from the metro Detroit area.

"The thing that was appealing to us was simply that LaFontaine…was Yzerman's equal as an 18-year-old, but he was a local," Devellano said. "We had 2,100 season tickets. That was the reason we wanted Pat LaFontaine."

Yzerman became the face of the franchise, spending 22 seasons as a player before retiring in 2006, moving to the Wings' front office until 2010, and returning in 2019 to be the general manager. As he had done with the Islanders in 1974, Devellano made his mark on the Wings with the 1983 draft—in addition to Yzerman, Devellano drafted Bob Probert (who Devellano framed as a Clark Gillies–type player), Petr Klima, and Joe Kocur, all of whom would play key roles in reviving the Wings that decade.

"That first draft of mine set the franchise up for the '80s and allowed us to go to the Conference Finals on two occasions," Devellano said in 2010. "Yzerman was a big part of it. The Bruise Brothers—Probert and Kocur—were a big part of it. Petr Klima was a big part of it. That draft in '83 set us up to be at least a somewhat respectable team by the mid- to late '80s."

But the Wings endured their worst season in franchise history in 1985–86, winning just 17 games. There was chatter in hockey circles when Harry Neale was fired from his coaching job midway through the season that it might cost Devellano his job, too. Devellano was in the last year of his contract. But he survived because five players from the '83 draft were playing for the Wings: Yzerman, Lane Lambert, Kocur, Probert, and Klima. They were the ones fans came to see.

"We had 10,000–11,000 season tickets by our fourth year," Devellano said in 2021. "It was a big improvement, but I was getting frustrated because we continued to draft NHL players—Shawn Burr, Brent Fedyk, Yves Racine, Steve Chiasson, and several others—who improved our record, but they weren't difference-makers. I had Steve Yzerman, a young superstar, but ordinary NHL players around him. We had to take the team to the next level."

That happened in 1989, with a draft class that would play 5,955 games: Mike Sillinger in the first round, Bob Boughner in the second, Nicklas Lidström in the third, Sergei Fedorov in the fourth, Dallas Drake in the sixth, and Vladimir Konstantinov in the 11th. It was the draft the Wings rode to Stanley Cup championships in 1997, 1998, and 2002.

"I always said, and history proves it, while the Yzerman-Probert-Klima-Kocur draft set us up for a respectable decade through the '80s, the '89 draft with Lidström, Fedorov, and Konstantinov, set us up for two decades worth of success," Devellano said in 2021. "Over the years I've been a great

THANK GOODNESS FOR GORDON GUND

Mike Ilitch bought the Red Wings from Bruce Norris on June 2, 1982. Even before the NHL Board of Governors officially approved the purchase, Ilitch started interviewing people. Jimmy Devellano was named general manager in July, but Ilitch first tried to hire Minnesota North Stars general manager Lou Nanne.

"I called Gordon Gund, who is the owner, for permission to talk to Nanne, because he was first choice," Ilitch said at the time. "And he said, 'I appreciate your interest, but we feel the same way you do. We've got him on a six-year contract.'"

Had Nanne been in charge at the 1983 draft, the Wings might not have drafted Steve Yzerman. The North Stars had the first pick, and Nanne chose Brian Lawton. (The Hartford Whalers drafted Sylvain Turgeon at No. 2 and the New York Islanders took Pat LaFontaine at No. 3.)

Within a few seasons, Nanne knew if he had a redo, he would have taken Yzerman. "I guess I would," he said in January 1988. "I can't think of anybody ahead of him."

studier of the entry draft. I have yet to see a better draft in the NHL. Lidström, 20 years; Fedorov's great career; and what might have been with Konstantinov. It's the best draft in the history of hockey."

Under Devellano, the Wings were frontrunners in drafting from Europe and behind the Iron Curtain, and their decision to chance a pick on the latter, especially, drew doubters. "We were able to get Klima to defect, and later we would be able to get Fedorov to defect, and Konstantinov to defect, and that took a lot of behind-the-scenes skullduggery," Devellano said. "It took a lot of work. I was laughed at a little bit about that—'Look at Devellano drafting all those Europeans. He probably won't get most of them. Imagine a franchise like that, and here he is running around drafting these guys and they need help now.' And they might have been right if the players didn't turn out."

The 1989 draft gave the Wings the players they needed to win championships, but Devellano still needed to find the right coach. In the 1993 playoffs, the Wings suffered a first-round upset at the hands of the Toronto Maple Leafs—despite a roster than included Yzerman, Fedorov, Lidström, Konstantinov, Probert, Keith Primeau, Paul Coffey, Vyacheslav Kozlov, and Mark Howe. The Wings were ousted May 1; later that month, Bryan Murray stepped down as coach, and Devellano set to work finessing who should be the successor.

"Mike Ilitch felt Mike Keenan would be that man," Devellano said. "I wanted Al Arbour or Scotty Bowman. To Mike's credit, he said, 'If you can deliver one of them, I won't go after Mike Keenan.' We delivered Scotty Bowman. So now we had a coach in place that wasn't going to be intimidated by ownership, management, the media, or fans. Scotty was 60 years old and had a ring on every finger. He was quirky, he was nutty, but a genius."

When Devellano was hired in 1982, he told Mike and Marian Ilitch he'd win them a championship in eight years. (It took 15.) A year later he wondered how long his heart would hold out in such a stressful job. Five years after that, Devellano pondered how long he would remain with the Red Wings. "Jack Adams had his job for 35 years, but he couldn't have done that if he had to deal with agents and 20 other clubs. I'll know when I'm burned out here and step aside."

When Steve Yzerman was named general manager in April 2019—36 years after being the best consolation pick in franchise history—one of his first calls was to Devellano, to discuss the state of the Wings. By then Devellano was a senior vice president, nearing his fourth decade with the organization. He had come to Detroit with a reputation for drafting, and cemented that prestige with draft picks that led to Stanley Cup championships in 1997, 1998, 2002, and 2008.

A BOUQUET OF PANSIES

Willie Huber was the Wings' prize pick from the 1978 draft, chosen with the No. 9 selection. He was a promising prospect: a towering defenseman coming off a stellar junior career. He won the Memorial Cup with the Hamilton Fincups in 1976 and represented Canada at the 1977 and 1978 World Junior Championships.

He stepped into the Wings' lineup right away and looked at home, recording 31 points in 65 games in 1978–79. The offense came easily, with Huber notching a career-high 49 points in 1980–81. But as everything with the Wings changed in the early 1980s—ownership, management, coaching—Huber's star faded. At 6'5", 230 pounds, he was one of the biggest players in the NHL, but to the Wings' chagrin, he played like someone half his size. Fans at Joe Louis Arena derisively called him "Baby Huey."

In 1982, the Wings hired an aerobics instructor named Marilyn Smith. New coach Nick Polano thought the Wings, especially Huber, were too slow. "She will help with flexibility and speed," Polano said.

Three weeks into the 1982–83 season, Huber's performance came under fire. It was deemed so far below expectations, "It's not even funny," Polano said.

Jimmy Devellano, barely four months into his job as general manager, was aghast. "You think of what maybe he could be, and you hope and pray he'll get that spark in his own system to allow him to become the player he's capable of becoming," Devellano said. "It's there. It's up to Willie. You've got to go at 100 percent. The feeling sometimes is that Willie goes at 80 percent."

It wasn't pretty on the ice and borderline ugly off. Huber wanted to renegotiate his contract. Devellano refused. He was willing to talk extension, but he wasn't about to give Huber a raise on his $130,000 annual salary.

Huber's offensive numbers—43 points in 74 games in 1982–83 were good enough to land him an All-Star invitation, but as the season neared the finish line, it was clear Huber's time in Detroit wouldn't last much longer. "He didn't play like an All-Star," Devellano said in April. "We didn't get the type of season we need from a Willie Huber. The biggest problem that I found with Willie is the lack of emotion. I don't know if those things will ever change."

Two months later, Devellano pulled the trigger on his biggest trade since taking control of the Wings. He traded Huber, Mike Blaisdell, and Mark Osborne to the New York Rangers for forwards Ron Duguay and Eddie Johnstone and goaltender Ed Mio. The Wings had drafted Blaisdell at No. 11 and Osborne at No. 88 in 1980, but it was worth giving them up to rid the team of Huber.

"Willie was an enigma," Devellano said. "More frustrating than disappointing."

When he found out about the trade, Huber was delighted. "I'm in a great mood," he said. "I'm just so happy to go to a good team, a team with a chance to win the Stanley Cup."

It took trading Huber for him to show the mean streak the Wings had craved to see in the big guy. In September, just before the start of training camp for the 1983–84 season, Huber let loose. "Devellano and Polano better watch out for their jobs," he said. "Jimmy D. knows so much about the game—he's never played it in his life. He has a lot of people buffaloed."

Devellano responded by writing Huber a letter. A hate letter.

"He called me a liar," Huber said.

"I called him a liar and I signed it," Devellano said.

That was in November. In January, after the Rangers improved to 3–0 against the Wings since the trade, there was scuttlebutt that Devellano had sent Huber a bouquet of pansies.

"I never got them," Huber said. "I expect that of Jimmy D. That's why I wanted out of Detroit."

When he heard Huber's claim, Devellano was contrite. Sort of.

"That's a shame he didn't get the pansies," Devellano said. "I'll have to send him some more."

8

FOUR CUPS AND A SNOWMOBILE

HÅKAN ANDERSSON WAS watching the Swedish national camp in 1991 when he noticed a forward who buzzed around the net like a maniac. The player wasn't a good skater and he wasn't very big, but his competitiveness stood out, and this was on a squad that included future NHL stars in Peter Forsberg and Markus Naslund.

Andersson jotted down the name—Tomas Holmström— and noted his attitude.

"The first time I saw Tomas, he was 18 and he was very small, probably about 5′10″, 165 pounds," Andersson said in 2021. "But he showed some ability around the net. He got into fights with the defensemen because he wouldn't give up even though the whistle had blown. So that makes you remember a player.

"A year or so later, I was talking to a friend of mine who was coaching in northern Sweden, in the second-highest league. Back then, the divisions were more regional—the northern teams stayed up there, and the southern teams stayed in the south. I was talking to my friend and asked, 'Who are some of the best players in your league?' And he said, 'The best one is probably on my team. His name is Holmström.' And I said, 'Yeah, I know that little guy.' And he said, 'No, no, no, he's probably about 6', 190 now.'"

Andersson liked the sound of that, so he made arrangements to see Holmström. He was playing in the northeast corner of Sweden, for Boden IK, in what was considered third-division hockey. "He was bigger than when I first saw him, and so competitive around the net," Andersson said. "I liked what I saw."

Holmström tallied 23 goals and 16 assists in 34 games in 1993–94. At the draft, held June 28–29 at the Hartford Civic Center in Hartford, Connecticut, Andersson knew he had to find the right time to push for Holmström. The Wings took a Russian defenseman, Yan Golubosky, with their first pick, at No. 23. In the second round, at No. 49, they took Mathieu Dandenault. Although Golubovsky only played 56 games in the NHL, Dandenault was part of three Stanley Cup championships with the Wings and went on to play for the Montreal Canadiens, retiring after having played 868 games.

The rounds dragged on—third, fourth, fifth, sixth, seventh. Eighth. Ninth.

This was his fourth draft with the Wings, and Andersson had observed that the later-round picks tended to be dismissed as soon as training camp three months later, when their deficiencies against proven NHL players came to the forefront. So Andersson figured, why not pitch Holmström?

The Wings took him in the 10th round, at No. 257. Nobody else they drafted after the second round in 1994 played in the NHL. When Holmström retired following the 2011–12 season, he was fifth in his draft class with 1,026 games, trailing only Ryan Smyth (1,270), Daniel Alfredsson (1,246), Patrik Elias (1,240), and Ed Jovanovski (1,128).

Holmström stayed in Sweden for two seasons after being drafted. In spring 1996, he helped his club, Lulea, win the Swedish league championship. In summer, the Wings signed him to a two-year contract. In fall, he represented Sweden at the World Cup along with future Wings teammate—and future best friend—Nicklas Lidström.

There was turmoil at training camp, with Keith Primeau holding out and asking for a trade. Holmström, by then 6' and 200 pounds, was a bright spot. Wings personnel were curious about this hard-charging forward who was known in Sweden as "Demolition Man."

"Homer came in and right in training camp was very combative," Steve Yzerman recalled in a 2021 interview. "That's the way he played, and he was unapologetic for it. You're kind of cruising through practices a little bit in training camp, and you've got this guy who is all elbows and stick and whatnot, and you just think, *Oh, God*. And he didn't apologize for anything—he just scowled and looked at you and away he went. The more he played, the more you really appreciated him."

Holmström quickly learned what happens to forwards who go to the net in the NHL. In October he got into a fight with Los Angeles Kings defenseman Rob Blake, resulting in a punch to the nose that sent Holmström to the ice. "I'll stand up, anyways," Holmström said. "I try, anyways, to learn from a lot of the guys who can fight."

Holmström's perseverance won him admiration from the coach, Scotty Bowman. "He causes the other team to lose their focus," Bowman said. "I think in time he'll be an effective player for us."

Holmström played in 17 of the first 32 games in 1996–97 and was sent to the minors in December. He ended up playing 47 games his rookie season—one of them was March 26, 1997, when he fought Mike Keane as the Wings and Colorado Avalanche brawled. Overall, the season was a learning experience—specifically, how to do his job without getting his skates in the crease, because that led to goals being called back.

"I play more controlled around the goal area now," Holmström said in April. "I had a problem with that in the beginning. When I first played, I was maybe two or three feet from the goalie. Now I try four feet. It gives me a little more room to be pushed."

Holmström only played once in the 1997 playoffs. He was in and out of the lineup when the next season began. He finished 1997–98 with five goals and 17 assists in 57 games. He capped his season with four points in two games, and starred as the playoffs got underway on a line with Sergei Fedorov and Vyacheslav Kozlov. He scored his first playoff goal on April 30 when he deflected Kozlov's shot. The goalie was helpless. "That's how I know I'm in the perfect place," Holmström said. "When they are hitting me with the sticks, it's perfect. Because then I know they can't see the puck."

On June 16, Holmström won his second Cup. His 19 points were tied with Lidström for third in team playoff scoring behind Steve Yzerman's 24 points and Fedorov's 20. But Yzerman, Fedorov, and Lidström all averaged more than 20 minutes per game. Holmström averaged 11.

Four years later, Holmström won a third Cup. His eight goals were tied with Brendan Shanahan for second on the team, behind Brett Hull's 10. Two of them came in Game 7 of the Western Conference Finals against the Colorado Avalanche. On the first, Holmström was battling for position in the slot with Avs defenseman Greg de Vries when Steve Duchesne fired a shot from the blue line. Holmström was off-balance and still deflected the puck with his stick, right between de Vries's legs and past Patrick Roy. On the second goal, Roy stopped Robitaille's shot, but Holmström swiped the rebound into an open net. "On the first goal, I fake falling down so he doesn't know where I'm going to go," Holmström said. "It seems to fit me being around the net."

Holmström won the Stanley Cup for the fourth time in 2008. On February 10, 2012, he became the sixth player in franchise history to reach 1,000 games in a Wings uniform, joining Gordie Howe, Lidström, Alex Delvecchio, Yzerman, and Kris Draper.

The next day the Wings had an afternoon practice at Joe Louis Arena. When it ended, the doors to the Zamboni entrance opened, and Henrik Zetterberg (who would go on to play 1,000 games in a Wings uniform himself) rode in on a brand new snowmobile, emblazoned with Holmström's No. 96 on the side.

Mike Ilitch recalled a conversation he had had with Holmström during his rookie season, when Holmström was struggling to understand what Bowman wanted from him. "He was telling me, 'I don't understand this coach. I can play. I don't understand why I'm not in there.' And he wanted us to go talk to Scotty," Ilitch said. "I told him, 'Look, I'm not talking to Scotty.' I told him owners don't talk to Scotty or tell him what to do.

"I was impressed with the fact he told me, 'I can play.'"

Holmström retired January 22, 2013, the day before his 40th birthday. Over 15 seasons he proved what perseverance can accomplish. The knock on Holmström early in his career was that he was the rare player to come out of Sweden who wasn't a good skater. He amended for that by being relentless around the net. He was disciplined on the ice, refusing to retaliate when opponents whacked away at him, and good-natured off the ice, gamely playing along when teammates teased him about being from so far north in Sweden he must be neighbors with Santa Claus. He recorded 243 goals and 530 points, both of which rank seventh in his draft class. During the 2002 championship run, Holmström was part of one of the best fourth lines ever, next to Igor Larionov and Luc Robitaille. Later, Holmström played on the top line with Zetterberg and Pavel Datsyuk. The Wings have found several players in later rounds who impacted the team, but none rival Holmström, who emerged from the 10th round in 1994 to become one of the most successful players of his draft class.

9

THE GREATEST
DRAFT CLASS

THE YEAR BEFORE the Wings would come away with the most amazing draft class in NHL history, only one of their 11 players selected made it to the NHL. Drafting is a gamble, and sometimes the winnings are slim.

In 1989, the Wings hit the jackpot.

They drafted two players, Nicklas Lidström and Sergei Fedorov, who were inducted into the Hockey Hall of Fame the first year they were eligible, and a third who probably would have made it, too, had his career not been cut tragically short. Four players each celebrated 1,000-game milestones, and four won the Stanley Cup with the Wings.

When general manager Jimmy Devellano, assistant general manager Neil Smith, and a cadre of scouts arrived at the

1989 draft on June 17, the Wings were coming off a first-round playoff exit. They had advanced to the Western Conference Finals in 1987 and 1988 on the strength of the 1983 draft class that was headlined by Steve Yzerman, but all the pieces for a Cup run were not there.

"I was getting frustrated with the process," Devellano said in 2021. "And then in 1989, we went to Minneapolis for the draft. It turned out to be my last draft in my first run as general manager of the Detroit Red Wings, because we would bring Bryan Murray in to replace me, and I would be booted upstairs.

"Boy, did that draft make a difference. I would be telling a lie if I knew what would eventually take place. But all of a sudden, we had Lidström, we had Fedorov, and then further down, a kid by the name of Dallas Drake—didn't play a long time for us, but he played a long time in the NHL. And then we got Vladimir Konstantinov. He would have been a huge part of all of those Cups if not for what happened."

Konstantinov played 446 games for the Wings from 1991 to 1997, when a limousine accident six days after the Wings' Stanley Cup championship ended his career. He was renowned for his fierceness, beloved by teammates, and despised by foes. Konstantinov, born March 19, 1967, was not physically imposing—he stood 5'11", 176 pounds—but he was a scrapper who leveled opponents with bone-rattling hits and an imperturbable disposition.

Konstantinov was the second Russian the Wings drafted in 1989. They took him at No. 221, after taking Sergei Fedorov in the fourth round, at No. 74.

"It was different then because of the climate at the time," Smith said in 2021. "There was a prejudice at the time. You had to take the major junior guys out of Canada first, because that's who everybody wanted. The Europeans, and especially the Russians and the Czechs, who were still behind the Iron Curtain, there was a lot of doubt about how long it would take you to get them."

Teams were gradually embracing looking beyond North America. Mats Sundin, a Swede, was so good the Quebec Nordiques grabbed him right away, the first time a European was drafted first overall. Bobby Holik, from Czechoslovakia, was drafted at No. 10 by the Hartford Whalers, and Olaf Kolzig, from West Germany, at No. 19, by the Washington Capitals. Drafting a Russian, though, meant dealing with the Red Army. The Wings drafted Mike Sillinger, a Canadian, with their first-round pick at No. 11, and another Canadian, Bob Boughner, in the second round, at No. 32.

Then they looked overseas, taking Lidström in the third round, at No. 53, and Fedorov in the fourth round. "Even though you knew in your heart that Lidström was better than Sillinger or Boughner, you couldn't convince the other guys who had never seen him of that, because they wanted Canadian guys," Smith said. "The NHL was all studs from the junior leagues. So you sort of said, 'Well, it's time to take these guys.' Even though it was out of order based on talent. By jumping in, in the third round, we're still jumping in ahead of everybody else. By picking Fedorov in the fourth round, that was the highest a Russian had ever been picked in the draft."

Lidström and Fedorov were cornerstones of the team that won Cups in 1997, 1998, and 2002. The organization wanted Fedorov to spend his entire career with the Wings, but he left as a free agent in 2003. Lidström did stay, captaining the 2008 team and celebrating the retirement of his No. 5 in 2014.

"You added three players—Nick, Sergei, and Vladdie—who had incredible impact," Yzerman said in 2021. "But for the car accident, Vladdie would be a Hall of Famer. So you would have gotten three Hall of Famers out of one draft class. Sergei came over in '90, Nick and Vladdie in '91. Out of one draft class, Sergei comes in, and our team significantly improves. We got a top centerman to put right into our lineup. A year later, you get two top-four D. Both of them were top-four D the day they stepped into the NHL. Those three had the biggest impact of any incoming group of our era. They turned the franchise around. From the day all three got here, we made the playoffs every single year. And they were the reason why."

Lidström played 1,564 games. Fedorov played 1,248 (908 with the Wings). Sillinger played 1,049 (129 with the Wings). Drake played 1,009—only 184 were in a Wings uniform, but he began his career in Detroit and ended it there, helping them win the Cup in 2008. Overall, half of the 14 players the Wings drafted in 1989 appeared in the NHL, logging a combined 5,955 games.

The remarkable coda to the Wings' draft class in 1989 is that they almost added another superstar in Pavel Bure to their haul. The impression was that Bure had to be drafted within the first three rounds because, at 18, he had not played enough games in his native Russia to be taken in later rounds.

But as the draft wore on, Christer Rockström, the Wings' chief European scout, kept pushing for Bure.

"Christer is telling us that we should draft Bure," Ken Holland, then a scout, said in 2021. "Christer was convinced that he could prove Pavel Bure had played enough games so that he was eligible to be picked after the first three rounds."

Devellano and Smith had a good deal of faith in Rockström, because he really knew the European and Russian players. Smith brought up the Bure issue with Gil Stein, the NHL vice president and counsel at the league's draft table. "Gil told Smith that Bure wasn't eligible, and that if we picked him, we'd lose the player," Holland said. "So Neil comes back, scared off. But Christer kept pushing, round after round."

The Wings already had gambled in picking Fedorov, hoping they would be able to get him out of Russia. In the sixth round, they decided to do the same with Bure, even if it meant wasting a pick.

The Wings picked at No. 116. Three spots before they were ready to call his name, however, the Vancouver Canucks drafted Bure. There had been a great deal of buzz around Bure because he was such a talented player, but between the Red Army and red tape, teams hadn't dared to pick him in the first three rounds. When the Canucks made their bid for him, teams protested. Jack Button, the chief scout of the Washington Capitals, protested to the NHL that Bure was ineligible. It took a year before the NHL finalized an investigation that proved the Canucks—and Rockström—right: Bure was eligible. The Wings could have taken Bure in the fifth round, instead of Shawn McCosh, who played nine NHL games. Injuries limited Bure to 702 games, but he leads the 1989 draft class with a 1.11 points-per-game average.

The 1989 draft was a defining one for the Wings. Lidström and Fedorov, and for too short a time, Konstantinov, were those missing pieces the franchise needed to be the last team standing when the playoffs ended, to finally end a 42-year drought and bring the Stanley Cup home to Detroit.

10

THE 1,000 CLUB

WHEN STEVE YZERMAN dressed in his Red Wings uniform to play on February 19, 1997, he became the first player drafted by the club to reach 1,000 games. It was a fitting accolade for a player who had become as synonymous with the franchise as the first man in NHL history to surpass 1,000 games: Gordie Howe.

Howe was a headliner during the Wings' first Stanley Cup dynasty, Yzerman during their second. Howe combined sheer strength and scoring prowess; Yzerman blended immense talent with sheer durability.

The draft was still two years away when Howe reached his milestone on November 26, 1961, against the Chicago Black Hawks, in what was Howe's 16th season. Howe had five shots on goal in the game, but the Wings lost 4–1. The second player in franchise history to reach that plateau was

Alex Delvecchio, who played in his 1,000th game on February 13, 1966, against the Canadiens, recording a goal and an assist in a 4–3 loss in Detroit.

Yzerman is one of 14 players drafted by the Wings to surpass 1,000 games. He was selected at No. 4 in 1983 and retired in 2006 having appeared in 1,514 games. He recorded three assists in the Wings' 4–0 victory over the Calgary Flames in his 1,000th game, and in typical Yzerman fashion down-played the accomplishment. "It's a neat thing to do," he said. "It gives you a chance to reflect on different situations that you've been in."

Yzerman was in his 14th season when his odometer rolled past 1,000 games. Nicklas Lidström was in his 13th; the durable defenseman the Wings had nabbed at No. 53 in 1989 had missed just 17 games (playing in 999 out of a possible 1,016) when he celebrated the milestone on February 29, 2004.

Howe, Delvecchio, Yzerman, and Lidström were such incredibly skilled players that only injuries could have prevented them from reaching 1,000 games. Tomas Holmström, on the other hand, was a 10th-round draft pick from 1994 who was known as the rare player to come out of Sweden who was not a good skater. Holmström grew so frustrated his first year in Detroit when he wasn't getting into the lineup that he appealed to owner Mike Ilitch to intervene with coach Scotty Bowman, to no avail.

Holmström may not have been the best skater, but he could play. On February 10, 2012, he appeared in his 1,000th game, a home game against Anaheim. Teammates presented Holmström with a snowmobile, which he gleefully took for a spin around the ice at Joe Louis Arena.

The game against the Ducks featured a double milestone (or so the Wings believed at the time). In addition to being Holmström's 1,000th game, the Wings recognized Lidström for tying Delvecchio for the second-most games in a Wings uniform at 1,549, behind Howe's 1,687. It later emerged that Delvecchio had not been credited by the league for a game, and that he actually played 1,550 games.

Henrik Zetterberg could not have timed his admission to the Wings' 1,000-game club any better. It happened April 9, 2017, in what was the last game at Joe Louis Arena. Zetterberg was honored before the game against the New Jersey Devils, which featured a ceremonial puck drop by Yzerman. Lidström was also in attendance as Zetterberg contributed a goal and an assist in the 4–1 victory. "It was a good night for everyone," Zetterberg said. "To see all the legends here, it was something special." Teammates gifted him a Rolex timepiece.

Zetterberg, Holmström, Lidström, and Yzerman were drafted by the Wings and spent their entire careers with the franchise. To those who drafted him, Sergei Fedorov should have been on that list, too.

Fedorov had played 908 games when he left the Wings after the 2002–03 season and signed with the Mighty Ducks of Anaheim. The Ducks traded Fedorov to the Columbus Blue Jackets on November 15, 2005, and on November 30, Fedorov became the first Russian-born player to reach the milestone.

Two other players whom the Wings drafted in 1989 surpassed 1,000 games: their first-round pick, Mike Sillinger, and their sixth-round pick, Dallas Drake. Sillinger played just 129 games for the Wings before they traded him in April 1995 to the Ducks as part of a package deal to acquire tough guy Stu

Grimson. Jimmy Devellano, the senior vice president, predicted that Sillinger would "play in the NHL a long time." Make that a long and winding time: in addition to the Wings and the Ducks, Sillinger played for the Vancouver Canucks, Philadelphia Flyers, Tampa Bay Lightning, Florida Panthers, Ottawa Senators, Blue Jackets, Phoenix Coyotes, St. Louis Blues, Nashville Predators, and New York Islanders. It was during his last NHL stop that Sillinger played in his 1,000[th] game on November 1, 2007.

Drake began and ended his career with the Wings. He had appeared in 119 games when he was part of the package sent to the Winnipeg Jets for goaltender Bob Essensa in March 1994. Drake also played for the Coyotes and Blues before returning to Detroit in 2007. The following year was a banner one for Drake: he celebrated his 1,000[th] game on March 11, 2008, and celebrated his only Stanley Cup championship on June 4.

One of the players the Wings drafted in 1990 is also on the list: Vyacheslav Kozlov. He was the quiet member of the Russian Five, and was the price the Wings paid in the summer of 2002 to acquire Dominik Hasek from the Buffalo Sabres. He played 607 games for the Wings and was with the Atlanta Thrashers when he appeared in his 1,000[th] game on December 26, 2007. Appropriately enough, it was against the Blue Jackets, then home to former Russian Five linemate Fedorov.

The 1991 draft also yielded a player drafted by the Wings who would surpass 1,000 games—Mike Knuble, taken in the fourth round, at No. 76. Knuble did not play in enough games to get his name on the 1997 Stanley Cup, but he met the requirements in 1998. He was traded to the New York Rangers in October 1998 because the Wings had more players than roster spots, and went on to also play for the Boston Bruins, Flyers, and Capitals. Knuble appeared in his 1,000th game on December 20, 2011.

Two players who spent their entire NHL careers with the Wings came close to the milestone: Pavel Datsyuk, a sixth-round pick in 1998, and Niklas Kronwall, a first-round pick in 2000, each played 953 games.

It speaks to what a good year 2002 was for the Wings that they not only won the Stanley Cup that year but then went to the draft and chose a player in the third round who surpassed 1,000 games. Valtteri Filppula left as a free agent in 2013 having played 483 games, spent time with the Lightning, Flyers, and Islanders, and returned to Detroit in 2019. On February 1, 2020, he appeared in his 1,000th game.

Filppula was the 14th player drafted by the Wings to reach the milestone. Marcel Dionne was the first. Selected by Ned Harkness at No. 2 in 1971, Dionne recorded 139 goals and 366 points in 309 games his first four years. But Dionne was a star player at a time when the franchise was at its worst, and he was vocal about all the losing the Wings did during the "Darkness with Harkness" days. Harkness's successor, Alex Delvecchio, traded Dionne for Terry Harper and Dan Maloney, sending Dionne to the Los Angeles Kings. Dionne found fame there as a part of the Triple Crown line. Dionne was a prolific scorer, recording yearly goal-scoring totals of 40, 53, 36, 59, 53, 58, 50, and 56 through 1982–83. Appropriately enough, Marcel's 1,000th game came March 24, 1984, against the Wings. Dionne had a goal and two assists as the Kings topped the Wings 9–7.

THE 1-GAME CLUB

At the other end of the spectrum from the 1,000-game club—players drafted by the Wings who reached that milestone entirely in a Wings uniform—is a small group of one-timers.

In 1978, the Red Wings selected Bjørn Skaare in the fourth round, at No. 62. Skaare had been a standout player in Sweden and recorded 42 points in 38 games in his draft year for the Ottawa 67s in the Ontario Major Junior Hockey League. When Skaare suited up on November 29, 1978, he became the first Norwegian to play in the NHL. "Playing in the National Hockey League was always very big dream of mine," Skaare said in 1984.

Skaare spent the rest of the season in the Central Hockey League. He moved back to Norway, where he won the Norwegian Championship in 1981 and '82. Skaare also played in Austria, and had a brief reappearance in the CHL in 1983–84. Skaare was only 30 years old when he died in an auto accident in 1989.

Chris Pusey made his only appearance with the Wings on October 19, 1985. The Wings had drafted him in the sixth round, at No. 106, in 1983 (the Steve Yzerman draft). In 1985, Pusey was considered one of the top goalie prospects in the organization. He got his chance that fall, when Eddio Mio aggravated a knee injury, but didn't last long. Corrado Micalef got the start in the game against the Chicago Black Hawks, but was pulled in favor of Pusey to start the second period. Pusey surrendered three goals on 12 shots in 40 minutes of play and never saw another minute in the NHL. He was sent back to the minors on October 22 and played out his career in lower leagues.

Pusey had a small part in what turned out to be the Wings' worst season in franchise history. Their 1986 draft was notable because they had the first overall pick, which they used on Joe Murphy. But in the eighth round, at No. 148, the Wings selected Dean Morton, who would have a long career in the NHL—just not as a defenseman, and not for them.

Morton had such a good camp in the fall of 1989 that he was in the lineup when the Wings opened the season October 5. Morton scored a goal, but the Wings lost 10–7 to the defending Stanley Cup–champion Flames at Calgary. Three days later, Morton was sent to the minors. Management said Morton would figure heavily in the team's future, but that never came to pass. Two years later, Morton attempted to rekindle his professional playing career with the Michigan Falcons in the Colonial Hockey League. "Even if I never make it back, I've already achieved what a lot of guys can only dream of," Morton said. He was 23 years old.

Morton found his way back to the NHL, but as an official.

The fourth player to have the distinction of being drafted by the Wings and only appearing in one game is B.J. Young, a forward selected in 1997 in the sixth round, at No. 157. He joined the organization in the late 1990s, at a time it was deep with stars. Young's appearance was notably brief. He was called up from the minors and played 64 seconds on November 28, 1999. Young was 28 years old when he died in a car accident in 2005.

Mike Foligno came in at the tail end of the "Dead Wings" era, a breath of fresh air with his jubilance and confidence. Selected at No. 3 in the 1979 draft, Foligno was runner-up to Ray Bourque for rookie of the year in 1980 after scoring 36 goals. Fans delighted in Foligno's celebrations, cheering him on when he leapt into the air, knees tucked to the chest. He played only 186 games with the Wings, before being traded to the Buffalo Sabres along with Dale McCourt and Brent Peterson for Danny Gare, Jim Schoenfeld, and Derek Smith.

"Detroit treated me like gold, and I thank Ted Lindsay for drafting me," Foligno said in 2005. "I was in disbelief when I was traded and just wish I could have played with them longer as the team got better."

Foligno was a star with the Sabres before finishing his 15-season career with the Toronto Maple Leafs and Florida Panthers. He played his 1,000th game January 7, 1994. Foligno inflicted a lingering memory on Wings fans in the 1993 playoffs when he scored in overtime in Game 5 at Joe Louis Arena, helping the Leafs to go on to take the first-round series in seven games.

Murray Craven, selected at No. 17 in 1982, played just 46 games for the Wings before being traded to the Flyers as part of the deal that brought Darryl Sittler to Detroit ahead of the 1983–84 season. Sittler took several days to report to the Wings, deeply unhappy with the trade. He struggled to contribute, and was bought out at the end of the season. Craven went on to play 1,071 games, also playing for the Hartford Whalers, Canucks, Chicago Blackhawks, and San Jose Sharks, and celebrating his 1,000th appearance on March 30, 1998.

The Wings drafted Adam Graves at No. 22 in 1986, the year they had the No. 1 overall pick, which was used on Joe Murphy. Graves played just 78 of his 1,152 games with Detroit, because on November 2, 1989, he was part of a blockbuster trade between the Wings and Oilers. In return for Graves, Murphy, Petr Klima, and Jeff Sharples, the Wings received Jimmy Carson, Kevin McClelland, and a fifth-round pick in the 1991 draft. Graves spent two seasons with the Oilers before going to the Rangers. He finished his career with the Sharks, where on October 27, 2001, he appeared in his 1,000[th] game.

11

THE SWEDISH
CONNECTION

IT WAS A generally unhappy group of scouts and management personnel that sat around the Wings' draft table on June 26, 1999, in Boston. The buzz of the event centered on the Sedin twins, Henrik and Daniel, and how the Vancouver Canucks were going to draft both forwards, at Nos. 2 and 3. The Atlanta Thrashers took center Patrik Stefan No. 1 overall.

There was no buzz around the Wings. Hoping to make it three straight Stanley Cup championships, general manager Ken Holland did what was anathema to his mentor, Jimmy Devellano, and traded multiple picks. The first-rounder was part of the package that went to the Chicago Blackhawks for defenseman Chris Chelios. One second-round pick was used to acquire forward Wendel Clark, and another to acquire defenseman Ulf Samuelsson. By the time the dealing was done, the Wings didn't have a pick until the fourth round—120 spots into the draft. It was a meager outlook for amateur scouting director Jim Nill and his staff.

"That's the year we traded all the picks away and we lost in the second round," Nill said in 2021. "So we were really down. I remember we went to the draft, and Jimmy D. said, 'Let's just trade all the picks and get out of here.'"

One of names the Wings had on their list was that of forward Mattias Weinhandl, a Swedish forward that Nill and chief European scout Håkan Andersson had scouted together. It was while assessing Weinhandl that their attention was diverted by a small forward who would go on to become a career Wing.

"Håkan and I had gone to Finland to see a game to watch a guy who ended up getting picked by the Islanders," Nill said. "He was a really good player. But we kept seeing this one player out there who stood out, this Zetterberg. We said to each other, 'He's small but he always has the puck.' He was always on the puck. So we kept an eye on him. But he wasn't a great skater and he was small—like 5'9", 150–60 pounds."

Andersson used his connections to get a better feel for what kind of player Zetterberg was. One of the players in Timra was Jörgen Ericsson, the older brother of Anders Ericsson, who the Wings had drafted in the first round in 1993. "I called Anders's brother and said I've seen this Zetterberg kid," Andersson said in 2021. "The 1980-born Swedish team was very good—the Sedins and Weinhandl were on the first line. There were a lot of good forwards. Zetterberg was not one of the stars. He was a bottom-six forward. But I kind of

Henrik Zetterberg, in his rookie season, December 8, 2002. *Photo by Eric Seals*

liked some things about him. Anders's brother said the kid is smart. He's not strong and he's not fast. Anders Eriksson's brother was a great skater. He said, 'I can catch him with my speed, but he's smart. His head is always moving.' He really liked him."

The Wings liked Zetterberg, but there were others they liked more, like Weinhandl. But he went in the second round, long before the Wings got on the board. When they finally got to make a pick, in the fourth round, they drafted Jari Tolsa, another forward out of Sweden. At No. 149, they drafted Andrei Maximenko, a Russian forward. Neither would make it to the NHL. Their pick in the sixth round, forward Kent McDonnell, played 32 games with the Columbus Blue Jackets.

The draft had advanced to the seventh round when the Wings took Zetterberg at No. 210. "We liked a lot of guys ahead of him," Nill said. "Finally we decided, this is the time to take him. May as well take him."

Zetterberg was vacationing in Cyprus with friends when his parents called and told him he had been drafted. His buddies made him pay for dinner at that night's celebration.

"Thank goodness we got Z, because I don't think any of the other ones that year turned out," Andersson said. "But after we drafted him, things happened really fast with Z. The year after that, the coach told me he was better than the Sedins on Sweden's world junior team.

"We took him in June. The next season he was the leading player that brought Timra up to the highest league in Sweden. So a little over a year after we drafted him, he was the second player ever to play on the national team before he played a game in highest league. They had already put him on the national team before Timra advanced."

Zetterberg played for Timra for three seasons after being drafted. At the 2000 World Junior Championships, he posted five points in seven games (and was teammates with future Wings draft pick Niklas Kronwall).

Zetterberg's stature continued to rise. He made the Swedish national team that would compete at the 2002 Salt Lake City Games, a roster that included Red Wings Nicklas Lidström, Tomas Holmström, and Fredrik Olausson. When Sweden played Canada in an early marquee matchup, Zetterberg's first faceoff was against NHL star Eric Lindros. Zetterberg won it cleanly. Then he set up a goal in the 5–2 victory.

"He didn't look shy at all," Lidström said. After the game, Wings forward Brendan Shanahan, who was on Canada's roster, playfully tipped up the back of Zetterberg's helmet. Zetterberg smiled.

It wasn't the tournament the Swedes wanted, as they lost in the quarterfinals to upstart Belarus. But Zetterberg made a good impression over four games, holding his own against far more experienced players.

"He definitely has a lot of upside in terms of talent and skill," Toronto Maple Leafs captain and fellow Swede Mats Sundin said. "He needs to put on a few pounds, but he's definitely going to be a great player, I think."

A few months after the Olympics, the Wings invited Zetterberg and Kronwall (whom they drafted in 2000) to Detroit to watch them in the playoffs. The pace and physicality awed Zetterberg, who returned to Sweden and spent his free time in the gym.

In September, he debuted at Wings camp wearing a No. 15 sweater. Expectations were high, but cautious: he had performed well at the Olympics and had won the Golden Puck as the Swedish Elite League's top player the previous season, one year after being named rookie of the year. He had matured physically—at camp he measured 6′, 180 pounds. (Zetterberg said he spent his summer lifting weights and eating: "I ate a lot. All of the time, I think, I ate.")

Nill said the Wings hoped Zetterberg "can come and contribute, be a regular full-time player for us."

Zetterberg made his NHL debut October 10, 2002, the day after his 22nd birthday. On October 13, he recorded his first goal, tapping a rebound into an open net during a power play. Dave Lewis, the coach, put Zetterberg on a line with Shanahan and Sergei Fedorov.

Zetterberg finished with 22 goals and 22 assists; his 44 points led all rookies. He was a finalist for the Calder Memorial Trophy as rookie of the year, but lost to St. Louis Blues defenseman Barret Jackman.

While it was Lidström and other Swedes on the Wings who facilitated Zetterberg's transition to the NHL, it was a late-round pick from 1998 who became a bosom buddy. By 2003–04, Zetterberg and Pavel Datsyuk were so close that teammate Kris Draper dubbed them the Euro Twins.

In 2008, Zetterberg and Datsyuk both were finalists for the Frank J. Selke Trophy for best defensive forward. (It was won by Datsyuk, the first of three consecutive times.) Though Zetterberg didn't win that award, on June 4, he became a Stanley Cup champion and was awarded the Conn Smythe Trophy as the most valuable player of the playoffs. Zetterberg set up the first goal in Game 6, and scored the third goal in the clinching victory over the Pittsburgh Penguins, finishing with 27 points. His defense was as much a part of the recognition as his offense, as he had played a major role killing penalties.

Winning the Stanley Cup completed Zetterberg's membership in the Triple Gold Club, as he had won gold medals at the 2006 Olympics and 2006 World Championships.

When Lidström retired at the end of the 2011–12 season, Zetterberg was the natural choice to succeed him as captain.

He had been an alternate since 2006–07 and had all the traits the Wings wanted in a leader: superior play and superior character.

On April 9, 2017, in what coincided with the final game at Joe Louis Arena, Zetterberg played in his 1,000[th] game. Scotty Bowman proclaimed Zetterberg "a Hall of Fame player."

A bad back forced Zetterberg's retirement after the 2017–18 season. He made the announcement during training camp in Traverse City in September 2018, 16 years after his arrival there as a hot-shot prospect. Zetterberg finished third in his draft class with 960 points and 1,082 games, behind Henrik and Daniel Sedin—the second and third overall picks in 1999.

The Wings came into the 1999 draft with a dour disposition and left with a seventh-round pick who would evolve into one of the best picks in franchise history.

"That's why you go to games," Nill said. "We went to see a certain guy. We traveled way north in Finland. It was an U19 tournament. We just happened to be at the right tournament at the right time."

12

SOMETHING SPECIAL IN THE SIXTH ROUND

THE RED WINGS drafted Pavel Datsyuk for his head, which is what they kept telling themselves when he first came to North America.

Few in the organization had seen Datsyuk, who played in Russia's lower levels in Yekaterinburg, a city roughly 900 miles east of Moscow and famous for being the place where, in July 1918, Tsar Nicholas II and his family were executed by Bolsheviks. Håkan Andersson, the Wings' chief European scout, was one of the few who had laid eyes on Datsyuk, and he told Jim Nill, the team's director of amateur scouting, that Datsyuk had a head for hockey.

"After the first time he saw Pavel, Håkan called me and said, 'You know what, this guy reminds me so much of Igor Larionov,'" Nill said in 2021. That was high praise. Larionov was among the most cerebral and celebrated players in the game, and he had added to the glory of his career with the Red Army when he joined the Red Wings and won three Stanley Cups.

"We went through our scouting meetings," Nill said. "Håkan mentioned, 'Here is this kid, I've seen him once or twice.' Back then, Pavel was about 5′9″ and 140 pounds soaking wet, and he wasn't a great skater. But Håkan kept telling us, he's got the same head as Igor. So we kept an eye on him."

Andersson had gone to Russia to scout Dmitri Kalinin. Andersson traveled with Christer Rockström, the former Wings scout who at that time was scouting for the New York Rangers. "We knew Kalinin was a good player," Andersson said in 2021. "Me and Christer said, 'Let's travel into Russia early and see him.' So we picked a couple places, and one of them was near Datsyuk's team. Datsyuk was a small player, but he looked good. He was skilled. He worked hard."

Andersson liked Datsyuk enough to want another look. On his second attempt, he was on a plane at Moscow's airport, scheduled to fly to Yekaterinburg. So was a scout from another NHL team. It was snowing heavily. Suddenly Andersson heard a loud, whirring noise, and looked out the window. He saw what looked like an oversize flame thrower, a relic of a de-icing machine from the Soviet era. The snow intensified, and finally, around 5:00 in the afternoon, the flight was canceled. Andersson didn't get to see Datsyuk—but neither did the rival scout.

Andersson did eventually manage to get a second look at Datsyuk. Hoping to talk with him, Andersson had brought along a translator to the game. "We tried to talk with the kid, but he wouldn't even talk to us," Andersson said in 2021. "He looked at us from a distance, and the interpreter said, 'Hey, can you come over here? We want to talk to you.' And he just shook his head and left."

At the 1998 draft, Datsyuk was approaching his 20th birthday. The Wings were fresh off repeating as Stanley Cup champions. They selected a big Czech defenseman, Jiri Fischer, in the first round. The next six picks turned out to be utterly forgettable. Andersson kept bringing up Datsyuk. He hadn't done anything remarkable that season, posting seven points in 24 games, but Andersson was certain there was something special about the undersized Russian. Finally, when the Wings went to make their second pick in the sixth round, at No. 171, they selected Datsyuk.

Three years later, he arrived in Detroit.

"I still remember going to the airport to pick him up for camp," Nill said. "Here this little guy comes off the plane. Pavel doesn't look you in the eye. His head is down, he's hunched over. We brought him to camp. He couldn't do a bench press. We're sitting there thinking, *Boy, how is this guy going to be a pro hockey player?* Then he didn't like his sticks, so we had to get him the right sticks. All of a sudden on day two of the camp, he got on the ice and he started to get comfortable. And we were all, *Oh, my gosh. He's something special.*"

After a few exhibition games, "We saw he was something special," Scotty Bowman said. "Then we decided to keep him and just hope we'd have enough work for him."

It was Bowman's job as coach to distribute minutes, but Datsyuk's play demanded he get a role. It wasn't long before his teammates joined the fan club. "I didn't know anything about him before he came in, but right from the second day of camp, he really stood out," Steve Yzerman said in November 2001. "He's a tremendous talent—just a guy who is really, really good. He's been a real boost for the team."

That Datsyuk stood out reinforced all the praise bestowed upon him by Andersson. In 2001–02, the Wings were a roster of hockey gods: Yzerman, Larionov, Sergei Fedorov, Nicklas Lidström, Brendan Shanahan, Luc Robitaille, Brett Hull, Chris Chelios. For a rookie to gain such praise was remarkable.

"At the beginning of the year, he used to lose faceoffs," Robitaille said in November. "Now he's figured out how to beat bigger guys. He just figured it out. This guy is going to be a superstar in this league."

The biggest compliment of all came from Hull. He was 37 and one of the most prolific scorers in the NHL. And he was not one to keep his mouth shut if he didn't like how things were going. Hull was more than a decade removed from 1990–91, when he netted 86 goals, but he was still scoring regularly in the 30-goal range. He was also picky about his linemates. But Hull adored playing with Datsyuk, finding in the young Russian a center whose wizardry meant Hull had the puck on his stick. "He looks like an orangutan," Hull said in February 2002. "He goes this way, and all of a sudden he's over there. He's very talented."

Datsyuk played on a line with left wing Boyd Devereaux most of the season, with a rotation of right wings. When Hull joined the group, magic ensued. In one 16-game span that began in late December, the line accounted for 22 goals and 39 points.

"It almost seems perfect," Hull said. Fourteen years older than his linemates, Hull nicknamed the trio "Two Kids and a Goat."

That February, the NHL paused for the Salt Lake Olympics. Datsyuk was one of 11 Wings spread across five national teams. It was more hockey than Datsyuk had ever played in Russia, and as the regular season wound down, Bowman opted to sit Datsyuk a few games so he could rest for the playoffs. When he appeared overwhelmed in the playoffs, Bowman pulled Datsyuk the last two games of the first-round series against the Vancouver Canucks. But as he adapted to the hectic style of the playoffs, Datsyuk once again displayed that brainy style that made the Wings fall for him in the first place.

"He's so gifted, so smart," Hull said June 7, the day after Game 2 of the Stanley Cup Final. "He's got a great temperament for the game. When we get out there, we kind of work together, and it makes it easier for everybody."

Six days later, the Wings were Stanley Cup champions. Having teammate Maxim Kuznetsov do his translating, Datsyuk described the feeling "like seeing the sun coming up in the morning."

As the older players retired, Datsyuk's role on the Wings increased. The season after he won the Cup, he was joined by Henrik Zetterberg, a late-round pick from the 1999 draft. The Two Kids and a Goat line disappeared, to be replaced by the Euro-Twins. Datsyuk spent 14 seasons with the Wings, and when Datsyuk retired in 2016, he had won two Stanley Cups and appeared in 953 games. His 918 points ranks third in his draft class, behind Vincent Lecavalier's 949 points and Brad Richards' 932. Lecavalier went at No. 1. Richards went at No. 64. Datsyuk went at No. 171.

Soon after they drafted Datsyuk, while he was still playing in Russia, an NHL team wanted to know if he was available. "Anaheim had called and wanted to do a trade, and they wanted Datsyuk to get thrown in," Nill said. "We said no. It wasn't like you'd go to the games, and he was the best player. He was as weak as could be. But he showed flashes. You'd see him passing the puck and somehow finding guys who were open. There was something special there. That's part of drafting—will they get faster, will they get stronger? Some guys do, some guys don't. Pavel did. He always had the skill and the head."

13

SCOUTING SALMON

BEFORE HE SCOUTED hockey players, Håkan Andersson scouted salmon. Working as a fishing guide, he would meet clients in his native Sweden, in neighboring Norway—and in Argentina.

Fishing was a favorite pastime growing up, and so was hockey. In his mid-teens, Andersson bought a boat with a buddy. In his early twenties, Andersson found work with Frontiers, a company based outside Pittsburgh that specialized in sporting travel.

"They had fishing and hunting trips all over the world," Andersson said in a 2021 interview. "I was working mostly on rivers, for salmon fishing. I was one of the guides taking care of the guests, mostly in Norway and Sweden. Then they found a place in Argentina that they wanted to explore. The fishing was good, but they had no orientation. So they sent a couple of us down there to make maps of the river and mark where there were fishing places."

That assignment took Andersson to Rio Grande in Tierra del Fuego. From there, he would take clients to Ushuaia, which at the time still claimed the title of the southernmost city in the world.

Being a fishing guide was seasonal work—January, February, and March in Argentina, April and May in Sweden, June, July, and August in Norway. To make money the other months, Andersson drove a taxicab in Stockholm, his hometown.

In 1990, a conversation with a friend changed Andersson's life. "When I was 15, I bought a fishing boat in Sweden with Christer Rockström," Andersson said. "He was scouting for the Detroit Red Wings. When he left with Neil Smith to go to the Rangers, Christer asked if I wanted him to recommend me for the job. I asked, 'What is it?' 'Well, you have to look for players, do this and that.' And I said, 'Okay, may as well try it.'"

Thus began a career that led to more adventurous travel, locally and globally. The first years, though, were spent learning. "I remember my first draft was the '72-born players," Andersson said. "I had just started. I don't think I did anything in that draft. We drafted Slava Kozlov. I had watched him and liked him, but the Wings had already made up their mind they were taking him. Without or without me, they didn't care what I said."

In 1993, the Wings drafted Swedish defenseman Anders Eriksson at No. 22. Andersson had watched him, too, but had a limited voice in the selection because of where Eriksson was chosen. "I can't tell you one occasion when the local or regional scout makes the decision on the first-round pick," Andersson said. "That's all general managers and chief scouts. If I would have said, 'Stay away from him,' they may not have taken him. But I liked him, too. He was big and skilled. Now, it turned out he was a little bit soft, but he played 500–600 games. We probably could have done better, but we also could have done worse."

Andersson's first big catch for the Wings came in 1994, when he recommended a very atypical Swedish player named Tomas Holmström. Holmström wasn't a fluid skater like so many of his countrymen, but he was fierce and physical around the net.

At the same time, Andersson had noticed a trend he decided he could use to suggest players such as Holmström. When Andersson started scouting for the Wings, there were 12 rounds in the draft. The general manager's involvement in making decisions lessened as the rounds increased.

"I would be at the draft in June, and then you come to training camp in September, and some of those late picks from June were laughed at in September," Andersson said. "It was like, 'Oh, he's never going to play for us.'

"I see these guys, and they're not very good, they're probably not going to play in the NHL, or even the AHL. There are a lot of guys in Europe, so I said, 'Why not take a flyer on one of those in late rounds, if these guys are not turning out that good?' That's how we got Tomas."

Andersson influenced many great picks for the Wings, including Pavel Datsyuk, Henrik Zetterberg, Niklas Kronwall, Valtteri Filppula, Jiri Hudler, and Johan Franzén, but has a soft spot for Holmström. He was picked in the 10th round, at No. 257, and went on to rank fifth in his draft class with 1,026 games played. Holmström was a spectator when the Wings won the Stanley Cup in 1997 but was a key component in the 1998, 2002, and 2008 championships.

"Homer was a special guy," Andersson said. "His skating was pretty ugly. But what he did was tremendous."

Andersson endured winter storms to travel far north in Sweden to scout Holmström. That was nothing compared to trying to get eyes on Datsyuk. Andersson's most memorable—and most frightening—journey on behalf of the Wings came when he was trying to scout Datsyuk around Christmastime in 1997. "I had seen him one time," Andersson said. "And a month later, I was still thinking about him. So then I decided to go to Russia. I flew into Moscow and had a guy there who helped me. He said, 'We've got to be at the airport really early because the flight leaves at 10:00 and they like you to be there at least three hours before. So we left the hotel at 6:00, got to the airport at 7:00, checked in. It was snowing. They let us know the flight was going to be delayed because of the snow.

"At noon, we boarded the plane. On the flight there was another NHL scout who was going to the same game. We sat there, and it was still snowing. They said, 'We're waiting to be de-iced, then we're going to leave.' Then all of a sudden there was this big roar, like a huge hair dryer. I looked out the window and see this big machine. The diameter was probably 12 feet. It was lit up with gas. Behind they had a big fan blowing through the flames, so the air would be hot. They pulled it up and just started blowing on the plane to make the ice melt. Knowing the wings were full of gasoline, it made me really nervous."

Håkan Andersson, the Swedish scout who found numerous Wings, June 10, 1998. *Photo by Nico Toutenhoofd*

The wings were de-iced, but still the plane did not move. Finally, a little after 4:00 PM, six hours after scheduled departure, passengers were told to deplane because the flight had been canceled. "I remember leaving the hotel at 6:00 and getting back at 6:00," Andersson said. "Twelve hours later, without getting anywhere."

It was a frustrating and futile day spent for Andersson, but it turned out to be beneficial, too. Because as far as the Wings knew, that canceled flight meant no other NHL scout saw Datsyuk.

Andersson did get to lay eyes on Datsyuk one more time. "I still wanted to see him, and a month or two later, he was playing closer to Moscow, and I managed to get in to see him," Andersson said. "I liked what I saw."

WHAT A CATCH

For a while in the mid- to late 2000s, the Red Wings had a line with one of the best returns on draft investments.

That was when Henrik Zetterberg, Pavel Datsyuk, and Tomas Holmström played so well together that teammate Kris Draper described them in 2007 as "being on another planet. The way they're seeing each other, the way they see the ice, it's unbelievable." A month into the 2007–08 season, the trio had accounted for 45 percent of the team's goals and 71 percent of those scored on power plays.

Zetterberg and Datsyuk both were world-class puck movers, able to maneuver their way through opponents. When opponents zeroed in on those two, Holmström would go to the net and be open to tip a shot, something he had mastered since entering the NHL a decade earlier.

"A team cannot take a shift off against them because they can win the game for you in one or two shifts," veteran forward Kirk Maltby said.

It was all the more remarkable given where the three, all found by scout Håkan Andersson, had been drafted. The Wings found Holmström in 1994 in the 10th round, at No. 257. In 1998, they drafted Datsyuk in the sixth round, at No. 171, and followed up a year later by selecting Zetterberg in the seventh round, at No. 210. The three players' draft position averages out to No. 213.

Dealing with competition from fellow scouts is part of the job. But in the early 2000s, Andersson learned a hard lesson about revealing what he did for a living. A friend of his called from the western part of northern Sweden, where there's not a lot of hockey teams compared to the rest of the country. The friend recommended Andersson make a trip to see this young defenseman who was big and strong and a good skater.

"I flew up there, watched him play, liked what I saw," Andersson said. "But the team wasn't very good, and it was going to be done soon. So I wanted to see him again. My mistake was that I called the coach and said, 'My name is Håkan Andersson, I'm a scout, and I'm thinking of doing this seven-hour drive, one way, to where you are playing because I want to see one of your players. I just want to check that he's healthy and will play.' And the coach said, 'Yeah, he's playing.'

"Then the coach hung up and called a friend who was an agent."

The agent alerted other NHL teams to the defenseman, but there were so few games left in the season that the Vancouver Canucks were the only other club to have a scout see the player. At the draft, the agent called Andersson to see if they wanted to meet with the player. "I said, 'No, we have no interest,'" Andersson said. "I was trying to downplay it."

The Wings didn't have a pick until the third round, at No. 97. The Canucks didn't have a pick in the second or third rounds because of trades. Andersson knew they weren't going to use their first-round pick on the Swedish defenseman, so there was hope he would be there for the Wings in Round 3.

"We have Johan Franzén on the list, but above Johan Franzén is this defenseman I had seen, Alexander Edler. We're at the table at the draft, and we're saying to each other, 'We've got to draft the Edler kid in the third round, and then we have Johan Franzén in a later round.'

"All of a sudden with about five picks to go, Vancouver traded for a pick. I said to Jim Nill, 'If they don't pick Alexander Edler, I will eat all the paper on this table.' Sure as hell they picked him. If I wasn't so stupid to call the coach, we would have had them both. I messed up."

As with fishing, luck plays a role in scouting. It wasn't on Andersson's side that time, but it was when that snowstorm prevented his plane from leaving Moscow. What began as a part-time job with the organization, as he tested the waters as a scout, became a full-time passion that grew from decade to decade.

In the mid-2000s, Holland offered Andersson a promotion that would have meant working out of the front office in Detroit. Andersson declined, preferring to stay in Sweden and operate out of Stockholm.

"I'm 56 and hoping for another 10 years," Andersson said in 2021. "It's been a fantastic job. But someday I want to go back to Rio Grande and go fishing again."

14

A GOOD BALL HOCKEY PLAYER

CHRIS OSGOOD STARTED more than 500 games for the Red Wings and won more than 300. He is the most successful goaltender who was drafted by the franchise, and what sealed his selection was not ice hockey, but ball hockey.

Ken Holland was the chief amateur scout in 1991 when the Wings drafted Osgood in the third round, at No. 54. Holland, who got his start scouting Western Canada for the organization, had seen Osgood dozens of times and gotten to know him personally. Osgood was quiet, but there was something there that appealed.

"Chris was playing for Medicine Hat in the Western Hockey League," Holland said in 2021. "He was a bit slight, not a big guy for a goaltender. Now you're looking for goalies who are 6'5", 6'6", but back then you were happy if they were 6'1", 6'2".

"Chris wasn't big, but he was competitive. I watched him in the playoffs. They went to the division finals, lost a seven-game series to Lethbridge, one of the best teams in the league. It was Ozzy and Jamie McLennan, and they were both outstanding."

Osgood posted a 23–18–3 record in 1990–91 with a .901 save percentage. Holland saw a goalie who played better than his numbers reflected, but it was when the two ended up on the same ball hockey team that Holland really got to know Osgood.

"Twice a week we'd see each other," Holland said. "I was impressed with his competitiveness. About two weeks before the draft, I told him, 'If you're on the board, we might take you in the second round. If you're there in the third, we'll definitely take you.'"

The Wings didn't have any goaltending depth in their system at the time. They had not drafted a goalie in 1990 and had waited until their last pick, at No. 246, in the 1989 draft to take one (Jason Glickman, who never appeared in the NHL). They had not used one of their 11 picks in the 1988 draft on a goalie, either.

The hope at the time was that Osgood would develop into an NHL-caliber player within a few years. That's what had happened with Tim Cheveldae, who the Wings took at No. 64 in 1986. By 1990, he was the team's starting goalie.

Osgood stayed in the WHL through 1991–92. He began his professional career with the Adirondack Red Wings in 1992–93 and made his NHL debut October 15, 1993, when he was called up to play against the Maple Leafs in Toronto. Cheveldae was sidelined by a sprained right knee, Vincent Riendeau had been benched, and Peter Ing was on a conditioning stint in the minors. Osgood, 20 years old, was the team's best goaltending prospect and excited for the opportunity.

"It's a big opportunity for me because if I play well, I might have a chance to stay here," he said.

Osgood lasted less than 33 minutes, allowing four goals on 12 shots. Afterward he said he wasn't going to let it get him down. It was that mindset that had appealed to Holland, that had played into the decision to draft Osgood. It was a trademark of Osgood's throughout his career that he did not let a bad outing fester. He won his first game in his third start, making 23 saves October 27 against the Kings. Osgood brought a packed house at Joe Louis Arena to its feet with a diving glove save on Alexei Zhitnik, delighting fans desperate for competent goaltending. "I'll remember it the rest of my life," Osgood said.

Osgood won his next two starts, reassuring higher-ups in the organization that their depth at the position was in good shape. Osgood was 4–3–1 with a 2.96 goals-against average and .893 save percentage by mid-November. In mid-January, there were signs Cheveldae was nearing a return to action. The organization was not eager to have him stay and serve as a backup to Cheveldae, because young players are better off playing than watching games, but Osgood's performances made it difficult to demote him.

It was Scotty Bowman's first season behind the bench, and he had been brought in to lead the Wings to success in the playoffs. While Osgood played well, Cheveldae was not viewed as a playoff-caliber goalie. In March, he was traded to the Winnipeg Jets for Bob Essensa. But Essensa was benched after losing the playoff opener in the first round against the San Jose Sharks, and Osgood was back in the spotlight. He delivered a 22-save performance in Game 2, evening the series. When he gave up two goals on two shots in a 6–4 loss that left the Wings on the edge of elimination, that trademark *sangfroid* was in evidence when Osgood said the next day, "[I] already am over it."

Osgood's philosophy was to focus on the next game, but that only works when there is one. There was no getting over how Game 7's overtime period ended: Osgood mishandled an attempted clearing pass, instead giving the puck to Jamie Baker, who flung the puck into the open net. Osgood wept at his stall for an hour afterward.

"I just hope that people stick with me," he said. "I'll try my best again next year."

Over the summer, the Wings brought in goaltender Mike Vernon, a Stanley Cup winner with the Calgary Flames in 1989. Osgood outplayed Vernon during the 1994–95 season, starting 19 games and posting a 2.26 goals-against average and a .917 save percentage. But Bowman gave the nod to Vernon in the playoffs because of his experience.

When the 1995 playoffs ended with the disappointment of being swept by the New Jersey Devils in the Final, attention returned to Osgood. He was only 22 years old, but Holland had great belief in the guy he had drafted.

"I don't see why Chris Osgood can't do what Martin Brodeur did," Holland said, referring to the Devils' Stanley Cup–winning goalie."

After a breakout season in 1995–96, Osgood was again the backup when the Wings won the Cup in 1997. But he was their go-to guy for the repeat in 1998. It was a banner spring for him: he fought Colorado nemesis Patrick Roy on April 1, earning the adoration of the crowd that a year earlier had cheered Vernon's bout with Roy. When he let in a 90-foot shot by Dallas's Jamie Langenbrunner in overtime of Game 5 of the Western Conference Finals, Osgood delivered a shutout in the next game. On June 16th, he danced with the Cup.

Osgood had made it, going from third-round pick to starting goaltender on a Stanley Cup–championship team. He was in a great situation, playing for an Original Six team and, with Holland's promotion in July 1997, under a general manager who had drafted him.

Then the Buffalo Sabres called.

Holland could not resist the offer to acquire six-time Vezina winner Dominik Hasek, even though it meant Osgood would be out of a job as a starting goaltender. The deal stung Osgood, and he asked to be traded. Holland called and talked to Osgood, talked to his mom.

"I've known him since he was 17, so there's a personal relations as well as the business side," Holland said. "That was one of the things we talked about, was separating the personal from the business."

Three years after the Wings won the Stanley Cup with Osgood in goal, and one year after signing him to a contract extension, the Wings lost Osgood on waivers. He spent time with the New York Islanders and the St. Louis Blues, while maintaining the strong friendships he had grown in Detroit. Holland, too, kept up a relationship with Osgood. In

A FIERY TYPE OF COMPETITOR

In 1991, Bryan Murray was in the charge of the Red Wings draft and wanted to use their first pick on somebody he deemed would fit the identity he was trying to establish in what was Murray's second year with the franchise.

The pick at No. 10 must be "someone who's hard-working, with character and discipline, a guy who really loves to play and will do whatever it takes to be a winner."

Murray had instructed his scouts to look into the background of potential candidates, to interview junior coaches and teammates, family members, and billet families to complete the picture. "We have to get to know the person as well as the player," Murray said.

Three players in particular stood out as possibilities: Alex Stojanov, a 6'4" forward who scouts compared to Bob Probert; Phillipe Boucher, a 6'3" defenseman with a booming slap shot; and Martin Lapointe, a 17-year-old, 5'11" forward known as a scorer who liked to play in front of the net.

Stojanov was taken at No. 7 by the Vancouver Canucks. The Wings went with Lapointe.

"My sense is that Martin is a guy with a real level of maturity for a young guy," Murray said. "He relates very strongly. He knows what he wants to be, and I think he knows where he's going. He's a fiery type of competitor. It was an easy selection to make."

An easy one, and a good one. The Wings signed Lapointe to a four-year contract three months after drafting him. He reinforced what a good choice he was during exhibition season, scoring goals and finishing checks and fighting. For the sake of his long-term development, it was deemed best to send him back to juniors, but by 1993–94 he was making a name for himself with the Wings. The Winnipeg Jets asked for Lapointe when the Wings inquired about trading for goaltender Bob Essensa in February 1994, but that was a no-go. Lapointe was looking like a good piece for the Stanley Cup–chasing Wings, a thick-bodied right winger who played with emotion and provided toughness.

"He's as close to untouchable on our team as anybody," Scotty Bowman said in 1995, when his roles covered coaching and serving as director of player personnel. "He's a strong skater, good hands. He's just going to get better."

That's just what Lapointe did. In the 1997 playoffs, he displayed the blend of skill and brawn that appealed to the Wings when they drafted him. He tallied 16 goals and 33 points in 1996–97, and followed up with four goals, one of them in overtime, in the playoffs. Lapointe surpassed that the following spring, when he had nine goals and 15 points as the Wings won a second straight Cup.

Lapointe continued to raise his profile, scoring 27 goals in 2000–01. He chose to see what he could get on the free-agent market rather than stay with the team that drafted him, and struck it rich with a four-year, $20 million offer from the Boston Bruins. Lapointe played 991 games in the NHL, but he never repeated the success he had during his 552 games with the Wings.

the summer of 2005, Holland brought Osgood back. While Osgood had been gone, Hasek had left—but he returned, too, in 2006. The two shared the net for two seasons, sharing the 2008 William M. Jennings Trophy for fewest goals allowed in a season. When Hasek struggled in the first-round series against the Nashville Predators, he was pulled midway through Game 4 and replaced by Osgood. Osgood took command of the starting position. He finished the 2008 playoffs 14–4 with a 1.55 GAA and another Cup party.

Osgood retired in 2011. He led his draft class with 401 victories in 713 appearances. Jamie McLennan, the first goaltender drafted (at No. 48, by the Islanders) won 80 games in 254 appearances.

Osgood won 317 games in a Wings uniform.

"I thought he might be good," Holland said in 2021. "I had seen him play, had developed a personal relationship with him. What a champion he turned out to be."

15

PICKING FOR
THE PIPES

CHRIS OSGOOD TOPS the list of goaltenders drafted by the Red Wings who went on to have success with the franchise. It's a short list, and Osgood alone has helped the Wings win the Stanley Cup.

The decision to trade for Dominik Hasek in the summer of 2001 led to Osgood's departure from the club, and so the Wings went into the 2003 draft looking to strengthen their pool of goaltending prospects. They had no shot at the first guy on the Central Scouting Bureau's list of North American goaltenders: everybody knew Marc-Andre Fleury was a future superstar, and the Pittsburgh Penguins took him with the No. 1 pick, only the third time a goalie went in that coveted spot. (The first was Michel Plasse, drafted by the Montreal

Canadiens in 1968; the second was Rick DiPietro, drafted by the New York Islanders in 2000.)

The second guy on the list, however, was available when the Wings finally had a pick at No. 64.

Jimmy Howard was from Upstate New York, but he spent the senior year of high school at Ann Arbor Pioneer, playing for the U.S. National Team development program. His billet family were Wings season-ticket holders. Howard wanted to play at the University of Michigan, but when the Wolverines didn't show any interest in him, he turned down Michigan State University, Ohio State, and Boston University to play at Maine. He won 14 games as a freshman, catching the eyes of Wings personnel, including Jim Nill and Ken Holland. Howard's coach, Tim Whitehead, told scouts that the bigger the game, the more Howard thrived: "He doesn't play like he's under any pressure."

Wings scout Mark Leach saw the same thing, reporting to Nill that Howard "was in complete control" during big games.

Howard was a star at Maine, winning Hockey East rookie of the year honors and setting a school record for consecutive scoreless minutes (193:45). In his sophomore season, 2003–04, he led the Black Bears to the NCAA championship game, losing 1–0 to the University of Denver. In August 2005 Howard signed a three-year contract with the Wings, ending his college career after three seasons.

"I have no doubt that Jimmy is probably the best goalie with the most potential that we've ever drafted," Holland said at the time. That was quite a compliment, considering Chris Osgood, the Wings' pick at No. 54 in 1991, had backstopped the team to the 1998 Stanley Cup title.

The Wings had seen Howard as a potential starting goaltender in the NHL when they drafted him in June 2003. He made good on that prediction in 2009–10, when he started 61 games. He won 37 games in each of his first two seasons, and made the NHL's all-rookie team in 2010. By 2012 he was named an All-Star, a feat he repeated again in 2015 and 2019. Howard's performance faltered his last season with the Wings, but he won 244 games for them over a 10-season span and ended his career at 246–196–70 record, with a 2.62 goals-against average and .912 save percentage. He's the second winningest goaltending draft pick in team history, behind Chris Osgood.

Petr Mrazek caught the eye of Joe McDonnell, then a scout for the Wings, while playing in the Ontario Hockey League for the Ottawa 67s. Mrazek delivered a standout performance in 2012 when he represented the Czech Republic at the World Junior Championship in Western Canada. He led the Czechs to the quarterfinals, putting together a show-stopping, 52-save performance against the U.S. Even the Canadian fans were cheering for Mrazek by the end.

The Wings drafted Mrazek in the fifth round, at No. 141, in 2010. Within a couple years, there was talk within the organization that Mrazek would be the goaltender of the future, the one to succeed Howard.

Mrazek made good on that prediction, starting the majority of games in 2015–16 and 2016–17. But as good as he could be, he was prone to inconsistency—"up and down like a toilet seat"—as then general manager Ken Holland put it. The Wings exposed him in the 2017 expansion draft and ultimately traded Mrazek at the 2018 trade deadline. After finishing that season with the Philadelphia Flyers, Mrazek moved on to play for the Carolina Hurricanes and Toronto Maple Leafs.

Mrazek was drafted 10 years after Stefan Liv, whom the Wings traded up to get in the fourth round. He was part of a draft class that saw Holland and assistant general manager Jim Nill focus on Europeans. Liv was born in Poland but abandoned as an infant, and adopted at six months by Swedish parents. At 11, he lost his father, Jans, to cancer. The Wings were Liv's favorite team as a boy, and as soon as they drafted him, he called his mom, Anita. Liv never made it to the NHL, and his place in Wings history is a tragic one. After spending one season, 2006–07, in the organization playing in the minors, Liv returned to Europe to continue his career. Liv perished September 7, 2011, in the Lokomotiv Yaroslavl plane crash.

Mrazek, Howard, and Osgood played for the Wings at a successful time in franchise history, all part of the 25-season playoff streak. Tim Cheveldae came in as they were building toward that success.

The Wings drafted Cheveldae in 1986—like Howard, he was picked at the 64th spot, but back then that was in the fourth round, not the second, as in 2003. Cheveldae had not been a standout in juniors, posting a 4.88 goals-against average in 36 games in his draft year, and a 5.04 GAA in 23 games in 1983–84. But the Wings' system was low on goalies, and Cheveldae was a low risk at that point in the draft. He began his time with the organization with their AHL team in Glen Falls, New York, which is where he was January 30, 1989, when his phone rang. Cheveldae was napping when the Wings called and told him they needed him in Detroit that evening, because Greg Stefan's back was aching and there was no one to back up Glen Hanlon. Cheveldae didn't have enough gas in his car to make the 45-minute drive to the airport in Albany, arriving just in time to see his scheduled 3:40 PM flight taxiing down the runway. By the time he got on the next flight and landed, the game was 15 minutes underway. Police escorted Cheveldae to a helicopter, which ferried him from Detroit Metropolitan Wayne County Airport to downtown Detroit.

Cheveldae's next trip to the airport was more sedate: he was with his new teammates, accompanying the Wings on a trip through Western Canada. He made his NHL debut February 2, 1989, but only lasted two games. By 1990 the Wings viewed Cheveldae as their goalie of the present and future. He started 71 games in 1991–92, winning 38 of them. He was named an All-Star, joining Steve Yzerman and Sergei Fedorov.

Cheveldae was a workhorse, but fans berated the quality of his play if not the quantity. Ultimately, management didn't see Cheveldae as the goalie who would take them to the Stanley Cup, and so he was traded in March 1994, swapping him out for Bob Essensa. Cheveldae won 128 games in a Wings uniform, continuing his career with the Winnipeg Jets and, for a brief stint, the Boston Bruins.

The Wings had better success drafting Cheveldae than the guy he replaced, Greg Stefan. Stefan was one of the last draft picks by the franchise at a time it was in tremendous disarray. He was taken in the seventh round, at No. 128, in 1981, the year before Bruce Norris gave up and sold the team to Mike Ilitch. Stefan had a reputation for being tough and for handling pressure well. By 1984 he was considered the top goalie in the organization, and a leader in the locker room. But as the 1983 draft class—Steve Yzerman, Bob Probert, Petr Klima—came into full force and expectations for the Wings grew, Stefan's play was viewed as a weakness. When he was scratched after a couple brutal outings in the second-round playoff series against the Toronto Maple Leafs in 1987, Stefan sulked in the press box and refused to dress as a backup. Jimmy Devellano, the general manager, started looking around for better options. When he didn't find any at a price that was agreeable, Stefan stayed.

The physical style that had appealed to the Wings at the draft took a toll on Stefan, who nursed one injury after another late in his career. He played just seven games in the 1989–90 season, which would turn out to be his last.

The first goaltender the Wings drafted who made it to the NHL was Jim Rutherford, who they took at No. 10 in 1969. The draft was only just beginning to become a major source for teams to stock up on players. The Wings had drafted a goaltender in 1966, but Grant Cole never made it from the 24th pick to the NHL. Rutherford had three stints with the Wings, the longest of which came during the "Dead Wings" era of 1973–1981.

The greatest goaltender in Wings history was Terry Sawchuk, who won 350 games and three Stanley Cups for the franchise. He was near the end of his career when the draft came into existence. The Wings have chosen many a goaltender in the draft, but few became successful.

16

A TEENAGER AS
TOUGH AS NAILS

WHEN RED WINGS scouts sized up Bob Probert, they saw a man-sized teenager, they saw raw scoring power, and they saw revenue.

The 1983 draft was the first under Mike Ilitch and the regime he installed after purchasing the Wings in June 1982. The big pick was at No. 4—that's where general manager Jimmy Devellano knew he had to draft a difference-maker if the franchise was to rise from the miserable state it had been left in by the Norris family. But there were 12 rounds in the draft, and with the Wings finishing 17th out of 21 teams, that meant three picks in the top 50.

When the Wings were on the road, so was Devellano—scouting. One of the benefits of living in Detroit was being within driving distance of many of the teams that played across the Canadian border in Ontario. That's how Probert kept showing up in Devellano's scouting reports.

"Bob was my pick," Devellano said in 2021. "He played for the Brantford Alexanders, and on most Friday nights I would go to London, and of course he'd come there with Brantford. When he came into Windsor, I would see this big kid. He was tough as nails. But the other side of him, and the showbiz side of me, was that I wanted to draft a local kid, a Windsor kid, because I thought we'd draw people from Windsor. It was about selling tickets."

Probert put up average offensive numbers in his draft year, recording 12 goals and 16 assists in 51 games in the Ontario Hockey League. But he was 6'3" and even as a teenager weighed 206 pounds; and he had racked up 133 penalty minutes. That stood out as Devellano and Neil Smith watched Probert.

"I saw Probie quite a bit that year," Smith said in 2021. "He was so dominant. He was a power forward. The distracting part about Bob was his skating. He was a very awkward skater. It's one of the most amazing things I've ever seen— when he got to the NHL level, he found a way to improve his skating so he could keep up. He overcame whatever skating deficiency he had. And he always had great hands."

The Wings selected Probert in the third round, at No. 46, after taking Steve Yzerman with the fourth pick and Lane Lambert at No. 25.

Back then, NHL clubs didn't delve much into the makeup of a player off the ice. A top prospect might get invited to town for a short visit in the weeks before the draft, but once past potential first-round picks, scouting reports focused on what a player did on the ice. Had the Wings looked past Probert's performances, they would have seen a troubled teenager who at age 17 had lost his father, a former cop in Windsor, to a heart attack and who readily outdrank everyone around him.

In his book, *Tough Guy: My Life on the Edge*, Probert detailed when his craving for booze began:

> The first time I drank, I was 14. The family went to a party at my aunt's in Michigan, and my dad brought a cooler of beer home with us—American beer in cans, all different kinds. I was putting them away in the fridge, thinking, *I wonder what that tastes like?* So I opened one and knocked it down. Nothing was happening. I had another, and another. After drinking about five of them I started getting a buzz, then it really kicked in.… Having a couple of beers became a regular thing. I had a high tolerance. My dad would be downstairs watching TV and my mother would be sleeping, and I'd sneak up to the living room or into the back yard and drink by myself. I liked to have between four and half a dozen. I'd hide the cans and get rid of them the next day. I liked the buzz. I really liked it.

Probert also wrote he knew he had a problem with alcohol when he was 16 years old.

Probert's drinking problems would soon come to light, but in June 1983, he was a beacon of hope to a team craving excitement. "I was looking for size and talent and people who

Bob Probert serves a penalty during a game on April 1, 1988.

had the ability to play in the league," Devellano said. "He was a man at a boy's age. He was from Windsor. He was the son of a cop.

"After I drafted him, we brought him over to Detroit and took him, Lane Lambert, and Steve Yzerman to a Detroit Tigers game, got box seats. I took them to Carl's Chop House. I kept it light. We talked about their families and such. I saw nothing wrong with Bob Probert, nothing to indicate there was a problem. He tended to be quiet."

At the draft, Devellano said he hoped Probert would develop into a "Clark Gillies–type player" in three years. Gillies was a 6′3″, 210-pound forward who had provided the New York Islanders with offensive punch and a physical presence during their four-year run as Stanley Cup champions from 1980 to 1983. He was a scorer and an enforcer, renowned as one of the toughest guys in the NHL.

It was a bold mold to shape for Probert, but he had the size and skill to make form.

Probert stayed in Brantford in 1983–84 and more than doubled his production, recording 73 points in 65 games, along with 189 penalty minutes. His breakout performance earned him a spot in the 1984 OHL All-Star Game, held February 7 in Guelph, Ontario, about a three-and-a-half-hour drive from Detroit. It was further reinforcement for the men responsible for rebuilding the Wings through the draft.

"Our first and second picks, Yzerman and Lambert, are on our team already," Devellano said. "I remember I told Mike, 'Our first, second, and third picks are all going to make it.' I'm excited and bragging a little bit.

"Neil said, 'Let's go to Guelph, we can see Probert in the All-Star Game.' So we drive to Guelph, and I'm all excited to see this big kid. We get there, and I said, 'Neil, get us a lineup.' He knew all the coaches. He comes back and had a funny look on his face. He said, 'Jimmy, Probert is scratched.' I said, 'What do you mean, he's scratched? We drove 200 miles.' Neil said, 'Yeah, he broke curfew last night, after the All-Star dinner, he broke curfew.' I was really pissed. It spoiled my week."

Devellano and Smith drove back to the Detroit. The next day, Devellano was still upset. "I wanted to get to the bottom of the problem," he said. "I called the coach. He explained that Probert had been out drinking and missed curfew. That was the first sign. It wasn't good. I brought Bob to Detroit and scolded him, told him this can't go on. I said, 'This isn't what we expect from our young players.' I told him I'm a fair person, that he was going to get a second chance.

"Little did I know there would be 50 chances along the way."

In May, the Wings signed Probert to a four-year contract, and Devellano spoke again of Probert's potential at the NHL level: "If Bob puts his mind to it, he could be to the Red Wings what John Tonelli and Clark Gillies are to the New York Islanders."

Probert spent the first month of his final junior season, 1984–85, practicing with the Wings because he had been kicked off his junior team, the Hamilton Steelhawks. In November, he was traded to the Sault Ste. Marie Greyhounds. Probert recorded 73 points for a second straight season, but he did it in just 48 games. He also picked up 193 penalty minutes.

Probert split his first year of professional hockey between the Wings and their American Hockey League affiliate, the Adirondack Red Wings. He was sent to the minors out of training camp but was called up and made his debut November 6 in a game against the St. Louis Blues—Wings coach Harry Neale wanted more muscle in the lineup after a fight-filled 5–5 tie with the Blues four days earlier. But the promotion was short-lived. In eight games, Probert had 26 penalty minutes but no points, and he was sent down with a message to work harder and lose weight.

"He is a little bit of a lazy player, but I don't mean to criticize him," Neale said. "It's just that his enthusiasm and tenacity for the game aren't among his better pieces of equipment. And he'd probably be a little better if he was a little lighter."

Injuries prompted the Wings to recall Probert in mid-December. He recorded his first NHL point December 15 and his first goal December 21, scoring on a long shot from the top of the left faceoff circle in a game against the Chicago Black Hawks. After eight games this stint, Probert had three goals, five assists, and 26 penalty minutes.

The turn of the calendar year in 1985–86 was tumultuous for the Wings, as Neale was fired and Brad Park replaced him behind the bench. The Wings had won only eight times in 35 games under Neale. Park promised "intelligent hockey" when he took over but delivered the opposite. In a January 13 game against the Toronto Maple Leafs, Park told his players on the bench to go on the ice during a bench-clearing brawl—an absolute no-no, by hockey rules. The game was delayed 19 minutes. Probert's contribution was a head butt that left the Leafs' Bob McGill unconscious on the ice. (McGill was able to get up and skate off.) The NHL suspended Probert four games. Park got a six-game suspension. The NHL didn't like it, but fans did.

Probert didn't make it past his first year without needing another scolding over alcohol. In early April 1986 he was in his fourth stint called up from the minors when he was arrested on drunken driving and speeding charges in Windsor, where Probert lived with his mother.

Clocked at going more than 100 kilometers per hour in a 50 kph zone (more than 60 miles per hour in 30 mph zone), Windsor police described Probert's condition: "His eyes were bloodshot, he smelled of alcohol, and he staggered." Probert refused a breathalyzer test and then "got very snarky and snotty and made a real jackass of himself," police sergeant Harold Pinkerton said. Devellano—who had chastised Probert in 1984 over the OHL All-Star Game boozing incident—said it was "very, very disappointing, but it is not surprising to me. There have been indications of this kind of thing happening before."

Devellano added that "we don't want our players driving around drunk. It's a terrible example, and I won't allow it."

Probert appeared in 44 games with the Wings in his first year of professional hockey, piling up eight goals, 13 assists, and 186 penalty minutes. Added to his 152 penalty minutes with Adirondack, he totaled 338 penalty minutes. He was almost as busy racking up entanglements with law enforcement.

In July, Probert was arrested again. Windsor police said Probert had been asked to leave a bar at 1:25 AM by an off-duty police officer and refused. A scuffle ensued, and Probert was charged with assaulting an officer. Probert was supposed to be at Hazelden Foundation, a treatment facility in Minnesota, but his admission had been delayed because he had mononucleosis. In late July, Probert was admitted to the facility.

The 1986–87 season began with a new coach in Jacques Demers and a supposedly sober Probert. Sent to the minors, he was called up early in November and played excellent hockey. It didn't last long. Right before Christmas, Probert crashed his car into a utility pole in Windsor and was charged with drunken driving. It was his third arrest in 1986. The Wings suspended him without pay for five days.

January 1987 began with Probert losing his driver's license for a year. In February, he was sent to a treatment facility in Windsor, but he was granted permission to play games, including on the road, making the facility little more than a place he spent the night on occasion. In March, beer was banned from the Wings' dressing room as a gesture to help Probert with his alcoholism—but when the division title was in sight, Demers promised there would be champagne. Before the season ended, Probert was expelled from the Brentwood Recovery Center for violating rules, though he and Demers vowed Probert had not been drinking.

For all the troubles Probert got into, fans couldn't get enough of him. He fought, he scored, he received standing ovations. In the playoffs, playing on a line with Yzerman and Gerard Gallant, Probert scored the game-winning goal to tie the second-round series against the Maple Leafs at three games apiece. Those who had scolded, cajoled, and pleaded with Probert were relieved to have something so positive to parse.

"It's such a big thrill to see him come through for us like that," Devellano said. "We're glad we hung in there with him. He's such a good hockey player, really. He's big, strong. He's got good hands. In our style of hockey, he really fits the bill. I think we showed this series why we wanted to keep him."

Probert demonstrated in spades why he was so valuable the following season. There was his six-point performance November 14 against the New Jersey Devils, part of a six-game point streak. There was the big hit on Oilers superstar Wayne Gretzky December 2, which earned cheers and laughs from fans at Joe Louis Arena. There was his chemistry with Yzerman, which helped Yzerman thrive to the point he was named the NHL's player of the month for December 1988, the first time a Wings player had earned that distinction since the inception of the award in 1980–81.

The feel-good story of the season got a boost in mid-January. Probert was at a dentist's appointment when he found out he had been named to the All-Star Game. Probert was delighted, describing it as the biggest "up" after a rollercoaster couple of years. He was 22 years old and playing the kind of hockey that thrilled his employers and enthralled fans. He had 22 goals, 43 points—and a league-leading 253 penalty minutes.

Probert was hand-selected by Edmonton coach Glen Sather, who represented the Campbell Conference team. "I happen to think he's a hell of a hockey player," Sather said. "He's tough, he can score, he can handle the puck, and he gives a lot of guys some room out there. And look what else he's done. He's beat a problem that millions of Canadians and Americans suffer from. Whether he's going to beat it permanently or not, I don't know. But I thought this would be a great chance for him to get some recognition. He's worked hard at his game, and he's worked hard off the ice at his life."

This time there were no hang-ups—or hangovers. Probert assisted on Gretzky's goal, and kept a pile of All-Star Game posters as memorabilia. Once again, Probert looked like a brilliant draft pick.

In March, the Wings rewarded Probert with a three-year extension. He finished the season with 29 goals, 33 assists, and an NHL-leading 398 penalty minutes. His strong performance continued in the playoffs. In the Conference Finals, the Wings took on Gretzky's Oilers in a rematch of the previous year. Probert came through with a goal and an assist in Game 3, pulling the Wings to within a game. Two nights later, he scored twice in an overtime loss. Probert's 21 playoff points topped Gordie Howe's franchise record of 20 in one season, set in 1955.

One night later, Probert threw away everything.

Around 2:00 AM on May 11, technically the early morning hours of the day of Game 5, Smith and assistant coach Colin Campbell found Probert and a group of Wings that included Petr Klima and Joe Kocur at an Edmonton nightclub, the Goose Loonies. It was three hours past curfew. They were drinking alcohol. Klima and Kocur were injured and would not have played. Demers justified letting Probert play by saying to banish him would have punished the rest of the team, but Probert's play was as listless as the team's, and the Oilers advanced with an 8–4 score.

Accounts at the time claimed Klima encouraged Probert to go drinking. Probert may have been too pliable for his own good, but he willingly went out, he willingly tarnished all the good work of the season as he downed shot after shot.

The Wings urged Probert to enter an alcohol rehabilitation facility for a fifth time. But instead of signing into the Betty Ford Center, Probert signed a deed for a boat.

For all of Probert's misdeeds—he reported to camp in September, then disappeared, eventually rejoined the team but was overweight—the Wings wavered on how to deal with him. No matter how much he messed up—and he had messed up considerably—fans at Joe Louis Arena chanted his name when he wasn't in the lineup and gave him standing ovations when he was. Devellano had hoped in 1984 that he was giving a teenager a second chance after the incident at the OHL All-Star Game. It was only four years later, and it was hard to keep a tally of how many chances Probert had been granted. He had been arrested for drunk driving multiple times, he had gone out drinking the night before the most crucial game of the season, he showed up late, or overweight, or both.

On March 2, 1989, Probert hit a new nadir when he was arrested at 5:15 AM at the Canadian border, charged with smuggling 14.3 grams of cocaine into the United States. The packet of powder had fallen out of Probert's underpants when he was strip-searched by U.S. Customs agents at the Detroit-Windsor Tunnel. He was sentenced to three months in federal prison, threatened with deportation, suspended—he faced all sorts of punishment, but when he was back in a Wings uniform on March 22, 1990, the Joe Louis Arena fans cheered Probert like a lovable outlaw.

In the 1990–91 season opener, Probert elbowed Claude Lemieux in the face and fought Troy Crowder. In the home opener, Probert scored in overtime, and fans gave him the loudest ovation of the night. In 1991–92, Probert recorded

44 points and enjoyed one of the most illustrious rivalries of his pugilistic career. In February, Probert and Tie Domi, a 5'8" scrapper with the New York Rangers, went at it for 45 seconds. Fans at Madison Square Garden loved it. As he skated away, Domi used his hands to mimic buckling a belt. Domi explained it was a World Wrestling Federation move, meant to taunt Probert. Probert called Domi "a little dummy." Their rematch didn't happen until the following season, on December 2, again at Madison Square Garden. Probert, eager to get the fight out of the way, grabbed Domi and started pounding him. Domi didn't land many punches, but he still reveled before fans as he skated away—but the last laugh belonged solidly to Probert, whose old linemate, Yzerman, mocked Domi by mimicking his heavyweight belt taunt.

Probert turned 27 in 1992, and as tough as he was, his hard style of play and harder style of living was catching up him. He put up 43 points and 292 penalty minutes in 1992–93, but the following season, his points dropped to 17. (His penalty minutes didn't suffer: He racked up 275 and had a career highlight fight with Pittsburgh's Marty McSorley that lasted around 1 minute, 40 seconds. Probert said afterward it was the most tired he had ever been after a bout.)

As his effectiveness waned, so did tolerance for Probert's reckless behavior. On July 15, 1994, he got drunk and got on his motorcycle. He crashed into a car, catapulting through an intersection and landing on a slice of grass. His blood-alcohol level was three times the legal limit. He also tested positive for cocaine.

On July 20, five days after the crash and a little more than a month after his 29th birthday, the Wings severed ties

THE BATTLESHIP AND THE CANOE

In July 1991, general manager Bryan Murray signed Troy Crowder to serve as an enforcer alongside Bob Probert. Crowder was a Group I free agent, which meant the team that held his rights had to be compensated. The New Jersey Devils demanded Probert, but to his and the Wings' relief, NHL arbitrator Edward Houston nixed that request. "You can't expect to get a battleship for a canoe," he said. Instead, the Devils received forwards Randy McKay and Dave Barr.

"It would have been devastating if we had lost Bob Probert," Murray said. "Thank goodness it worked out."

Probert was on edge until the decision was announced. "I'm glad I'm still here," he said. "But I feel for the guys who have to leave. It's a shame."

Devils general manager Lou Lamoriello treated the arbitrator's ruling with aplomb, admitting he never expected to win, but figuring it made sense to try.

Probert was a battleship all right, but Crowder was more like a dinghy—he played just seven games during a three-year contract with the Wings.

with Probert. Publicly, they wished him well. Privately, they wondered what was next. "I drafted Bob 11 years ago in 1983," Devellano told the *Detroit Free Press*. "In my 12 years with the Red Wings organization, myself, the coaches, the ownership, we've never spent more time on one player and his issues and problems than we have on Bob Probert. I've had so many dealings with him that he's almost like a son to me. But I think that in the best interest of the team and Bob, it's important we part company and he try to get his life back together with someone else."

Probert played 474 games with the Wings, recording 259 points and 2,090 penalty minutes. He spent seven seasons with the Chicago Blackhawks, retiring in 2002 with 384 points and 3,300 penalty minutes in 935 career games. He was done being a tough guy on the ice, but not done getting in trouble with the law. The day after his 39th birthday, he listed his alias as "the Bad One" when he was booked for resisting arrest in Delray Beach, Florida. A few weeks after his 40th birthday, Probert was charged with assaulting an officer after an all-night booze binge.

Probert's popularity in Detroit never waned. He received yet another standing ovation on January 2, 2007, when he appeared at Yzerman's retirement ceremony. It's tempting to wonder if Probert's No. 24 might not have ended up in the rafters, too, had he been free from his addictions.

Probert died of a heart attack July 5, 2010, while boating on Lake St. Clair, one month past his 45th birthday. He was posthumously diagnosed with an enlarged heart and with chronic traumatic encephalopathy (CTE), a degenerative disease caused by repeated blows to the head. On April 9, 2017, the day of the last game at Joe Louis Arena, Probert's family, with assistance from Joe Kocur, his old Bruise Brother, spread some of Probert's ashes in the penalty box.

When they scouted Probert, the Wings saw a tenacious, skilled, supersized teenager who they judged could help restore respect to the franchise. He did. Fans cheered when Probert scored, reveled when he fought, forgave when he transgressed. He was captivating and confounding, caring and careless, and, ultimately, one of the most popular players of the 1980s.

"It was very, very unique to see a man that big, that tough, with such good hands," Smith said in 2021. "That's what really sat with you."

17

HE LIKES TO GET
THE DUKES UP

WHEN **JIMMY DEVELLANO** introduced Joey Kocur after drafting him at No. 88 in the 1983 draft, Devellano noted it was a sign that the Wings weren't "going to be pushed around much longer."

It was Devellano's first draft as general manager of the Wings, and Kocur's appeal was obvious: he was a beefy 6′, 204 pounds, and had racked up 289 penalty minutes in 62 games with the Saskatoon Blades in the Western Hockey League in 1982–83. He also had 23 goals among 40 points.

"He likes to get the dukes up and fight a little," Devellano said.

It was a masterful understatement of what made Kocur so valuable. Kocur was playing for the Adirondack Red Wings in

December 1984, when there was chatter in Detroit he might get called up to deter foes from directing cheap shots and big hits at prize 1983 draft pick Steve Yzerman. Kocur was just shy of his 20th birthday, and already one of the most feared players in the American Hockey League. His right hand was covered with scars and bruises, and there was a bucket of ice ready in the penalty box in Adirondack that Kocur could shove his fist into for relief. "There is a total awareness of him by every team in the league," Adirondack coach Bill Dineen said. (He wasn't just known in the minors, either. Earlier that year, Devellano had rejected an attempt by Vancouver GM Harry Neale to acquire Kocur.) That was shortly after Kocur had hammered Marty McSorley, then a minor-league player who would go on to forge a name for himself as an enforcer in the NHL, too.

Kocur had 125 penalty minutes in 29 games with Adirondack at the time.

"It's something I've done all my life," Kocur said. "Fighting shows you want to be in the games."

Kocur was called up to Detroit in early January 1985, but as luck would have it, he had been injured in his last fight, his 25th in 38 games. The skin on the back of Kocur's right hand split when he threw a punch, and it took 20 stitches to close the wound. Kocur ended up undergoing surgery on the hand when an infection developed, further delaying his NHL debut. The infection had spread to his elbow by the time it was discovered. When he recovered, Kocur was sent back to Adirondack for conditioning, under orders not to fight.

Kocur finally made his debut on February 20, 1985. He played 17 games, earning 64 penalty minutes. He started the following season in the minors but wasn't there a month before being called up. It was a turbulent time for the Wings—Brad Park replaced Harry Neale as coach mid-season—but Kocur was a bright spot. In January, he posted a two-goal, three-point game while playing on a line with Yzerman and Petr Klima, all picks from the '83 draft. The next day, Devellano referred to Kocur as "my goon turned goal-scorer."

"I love it," Kocur said. "The hardest part is just trying to catch up with those guys when they're carrying the puck."

Any offensive production from Kocur was a bonus. He had been drafted because he was a bruiser, and it was his fists that got him a spot in the lineup and a place in fans' hearts. "The fans in Detroit, they're great," Kocur said. "If we don't win, they still like us. They like to see what I do. They like a good fight."

Kocur led the NHL with 377 penalty minutes in 1985–86, despite playing in only 59 games. In 1986–87, his first full NHL season, Kocur led his team with 276 penalty minutes, including 42 minutes in one game alone, shattering the record of 30 set by Ted Lindsay in 1952 and equaled by Dennis Polonich in 1976.

Together with Bob Probert, whose toughness compelled Devellano to pick him at No. 46 in the '83 draft, the Wings had a formidable duo of tough guys. Nicknamed the "Bruise Brothers," the two were featured in a front-page story on hockey enforcers in the *Wall Street Journal* in April 1988.

Kocur proclaimed he loved fighting, but the price he paid was harsh. Every knuckle on his right hand had been broken. After fights in back-to-back games in 1990, doctors feared Kocur had injured a tendon.

Kocur played through the pain, but as the organization's frustration at falling short in the playoffs grew, he was deemed expendable. In March 1991, Kocur was part of a five-player swap, sent to the New York Rangers along with defenseman Per Djoos in return for forward Kevin Miller, defenseman Dennis Vial, and the rights to enforcer Jim Cummins, who was from the Detroit area. Wings general manager Bryan Murray wanted to add a bit more finesse to the lineup and believed Miller would bring that. Neil Smith, who had been a scout with the Wings at the '83 draft and had left in '89 to become GM of the Rangers, was happy to get Kocur.

"This shows we can get into the playoffs with toughness and physical strength," Smith said.

Kocur was sad to leave the only organization he had known but also excited about the opportunity. His former linemate, Steve Yzerman, lamented the trade. "Joey literally fought for guys like me and Shawn Burr, always there for this whole team," he said. "I'll always be grateful for that part of it. I know Joey went through a lot of soreness and problems in his hands just to give us some room on the ice."

The Bruise Brothers were now fearsome foes. On December 17, 1993, Kocur and Probert fought one another, sending 19,875 fans at Joe Louis Arena to their feet as the fists flew. Kocur left Probert with a bloody nose; Probert left Kocur without his helmet after slamming him into the boards.

Yzerman never forgot how tough Kocur was. In December 1996, still smarting from the way his team had been manhandled by the Colorado Avalanche in the Western Conference Finals, Yzerman suggested to Scotty Bowman that the Wings take another look at Kocur. By then he was 32 years old, out of the NHL, and nursing a right hand badly damaged from years of fighting. He still had that aura about him, though, that made the Wings want to draft him 14 years earlier. He still could get his dukes up.

In his second game back, on January 5, 1997, Kocur fought Probert, then with the Chicago Blackhawks, to a draw. Kocur wasn't the fighter he used to be (neither was Probert), but he added toughness and had won the Stanley Cup with the Rangers in 1994. He was just what the Wings wanted.

"He keeps people honest," Yzerman said. "What Joey brings is something that our team needed."

Kocur's comeback ended with a Cup celebration. He stuck around for two more seasons, retiring after 820 games. His 2,519 penalty minutes ranks third in his draft class.

18

BIGGER AND GRITTIER

SIZE AND GRIT were determining factors for the Wings in the 1992 draft, which is how they ended up with Darren McCarty.

Ken Holland was a chief scout at the time, and he hired a guy he used to play hockey with by the name of Paul Crowley to be a part-time scout. Crowley lived in Peterborough, Ontario, a convenient location for scouting the junior teams in the greater Toronto area.

Darren McCarty was from Leamington, Ontario—about an hour's drive from Detroit—and played for the Ontario Hockey League's Belleville Bulls. He was passed over as an 18-year-old in the 1990 draft, and again the next year, even though he posted 30 goals, 67 points, and 151 penalty minutes in 60 games in 1990–91. The following season McCarty parlayed his growing confidence into even better numbers, posting 55 goals, 127 points, and 177 penalty minutes in 65 games. Crowley kept a close eye on McCarty and sent Holland encouraging scouting reports.

"Paul probably saw McCarty play 20 times," Holland said in 2021. "As we got near the end of the year, Paul took me to watch Belleville. Paul told me to look at this guy, Darren McCarty. He said, 'His skating isn't great, but I've seen him play a lot. He's got a lot of will, a lot of compete.'

"I remember interviewing Darren one on one. It was the Wednesday before the draft. At the end of the meeting, Darren said, 'Mr. Holland, you draft me, I will do whatever it takes to play in the National Hockey League.' You hear lots of that from guys who are hoping to be drafted, but between Paul Crowley, who I trusted and who had seen him play 20 times or so, and then the interview, I liked Darren."

The mitigating factor for the Wings as they approached the draft was the entirely too fresh memory of how the team had been bowled over by the Chicago Blackhawks in the second round of the playoffs that spring, even though the team by then included Steve Yzerman, Sergei Fedorov, Nicklas Lidström, and Vladimir Konstantinov.

"I knew we had to get harder, bigger, stronger, tougher," Holland said. "Our first pick was out of Ottawa, a guy named Curtis Bowen—he didn't make it, but he was a big, strong guy. I wanted to have that draft influenced by big, strong wingers. We needed to get some of those players into our system."

Crowley pushed hard for McCarty, convincing Holland that at best, McCarty would be a very good pick, and at worst, he'd be a one-dimensional player who could fight. The Wings selected McCarty in the second round, at No. 46.

McCarty spent his first year of professional hockey with the organization's American Hockey League farm club in Glen Falls, New York. At training camp in 1993, McCarty impressed the Wings during an exhibition game when he pummeled Chicago's Cam Russell. McCarty skated to center ice, stripped off his sweater and shoulder pads and struck a pose like an old-time boxer. Fans roared, and management approved.

"I wanted to see McCarty in these kinds of situations," Bryan Murray said. "He certainly has a presence. There's no question he can be a player in this league because of his size, his strength, and his character, and he's big-time tough."

McCarty played 67 games his rookie year, his promotion overlapping with Scotty Bowman taking over behind the bench. It was a memorable time for McCarty, who capped 1993 by getting married.

McCarty's role with the Wings expanded in 1994–95, when chief tough guy Bob Probert's troubled tenure came to an end. Formerly Probert's tag-team partner, McCarty's toughness—which was the chief reason he was drafted—came into the spotlight. McCarty and Probert fought December 12, 1996, when McCarty took Probert, then with the Blackhawks, into the boards in front of the Wings' bench and the two squared off. It wasn't much of a fight, but McCarty landed the most punches.

That was the season McCarty really came into his own, recording a career-best 19 goals and 49 points while playing on a line with power forward Brendan Shanahan and playmaker genius Igor Larionov. McCarty racked up 126 penalty minutes, though only 11 of those were from the infamous March 26, 1997, game when he pummeled Claude Lemieux. (Officials did not count that as a fight. McCarty's fighting penalty was for boxing with Adam Deadmarsh.) McCarty capped the night by scoring in overtime.

That was a goal to remember for a lifetime—but not his best of the season.

That came June 7, in Game 4 of the Stanley Cup Final against the Philadelphia Flyers. When the Wings drafted McCarty, they worried his skating would limit his effectiveness in the NHL. But McCarty showed in that game just how much his skating had improved when the took a pass from Tomas Sandström and strode across the blue line. Flyers defenseman Janne Niinimaa tried to shadow McCarty, but McCarty put the puck on his backhand, pulled it to the outside, through Niinimaa's legs, and continued up the flank. Niinimaa fell, and attempted one last defensive maneuver by swinging his stick at McCarty. It was useless. McCarty powered toward Philadelphia's net, put the puck on his forehand, drew the goalie out, pulled the puck across his body and onto his backhand, and tucked it into the net.

"It's good to see a guy like that get a big goal in a game," Kris Draper said. "Everybody loves him in the dressing room."

Everybody loved McCarty in the dressing room and in Detroit. He had avenged Lemieux's cheap shot on Draper and then scored what would hold up as the Stanley Cup–winning goal.

McCarty had turned into a very good pick: at the time of the 1997 Cup, he led the second-round picks of his draft

SUCCESS IN THE
SECOND ROUND

Darren McCarty is one of the most successful second-round picks the franchise ever made—his 275 points second only to Reed Larson's 570—but the Wings have had made a slew of good picks in Round 2. Justin Abdelkader leads the franchise's second-round picks with 739 games played, joining the Wings after his third year at Michigan State. Abdelkader worked hard to establish himself with the Wings and, at his best, played on a line with Henrik Zetterberg and Pavel Datsyuk, where Abdelkader's role was to retrieve the puck and screen the goaltender.

Tomas Tatar turned out to be the best part of the 2009 draft for the Wings, becoming a regular 20-goal scorer (and falling one goal shy of 30 once) during his 407 games with the Wings, before he was traded at the 2018 deadline to acquire assets for the rebuilding process. Tatar recorded 222 points in 407 games for the Wings, his production just ahead of 2002 second-round pick Jiri Hudler's 214 points in 409 Wings games. Hudler was the third-ranked European skater by the NHL's Central Scouting Bureau, and the Wings didn't think he'd be available at No. 58. Hudler was undersized but deceptively creative, and was part of the 2008 Stanley Cup run with 14 points in 22 games. His career with the Wings was undermined when he accepted what was rumored to be a $10 million, two-year offer to play in Russia in the summer of 2009, while he had an arbitration case pending with the Wings. Hudler's stint in the Kontinental Hockey League only lasted one year, and he returned to Detroit to pay two more seasons.

The Wings found a good deal of use for their second-round pick in 1994, because under coach Scotty Bowman Mathieu Dandenault transitioned from forward to defenseman. "He looks like like he's really going to be a good player," Bowman said. "He's got a big reach with those real long arms. He seems to be a busy player. He's always on the puck and he goes to the net. And those feet. They're boats. I've never seen anybody with feet that big. It's amazing how he can pick 'em up and put 'em down. It's amazing how he moves."

Dandenault wore size 15 skates, and it was his ability to glide around the ice that led Bowman to use Dandenault on defense. He played 616 games for the Wings and was part of the 1997, 1998, and 2002 Stanley Cup championships.

McCarty, Larson, Abdelkader, Tatar, Hudler, and Dandenault highlight the franchise's success in the second round. A pair of later acquisitions are making their cases, too. In 2013 the Wings made a trade during the draft, flipping first-round picks with San Jose and, in the process, gaining a second-round pick, at No. 58. They used that to draft Tyler Bertuzzi, whose blend of grit and skill was a welcome addition to the Wings as they faced rebuilding in the aftermath of their historic 25-season playoff streak. Likewise in 2016, the Wings made a draft-day deal to unload Pavel Datsyuk's contract after he decided to leave with a year to go on his deal. The trade with the Arizona Coyotes netted the Wings a second-round pick that they used on defenseman Filip Hronek, who would become one of their workhorses. They are among multiple examples where the Wings have done better in certain years in the second round than in the first.

class with 48 goals and was second with 117 points. But his bruising style of play left him prone to injuries—sprained knees, broken ankles, and cuts to the face regularly sidelined him. In April 1998, McCarty missed games while dealing with vertigo, which was triggered when he was hit from behind during a game. He rebounded and was a part of a second straight championship that June.

McCarty was part of the Grind Line, the hugely successful trio composed of Kirk Maltby and Kris Draper, with either McCarty or Joey Kocur on right wing. In any iteration, the line lived up to its name, grinding down foes with relentless physical play. (In the 2002 playoffs, when Kocur had hung up his skates and worked as the team's video technician, Kocur helped McCarty break out of a scoring slump by banging McCarty's stick on the floor, putting what McCarty called a "voodoo hex" on the stick. McCarty had a hat trick the next night, in Game 1 against his hated rival, the Colorado Avalanche.)

McCarty won a third Stanley Cup in June 2002. As the many years of physically demanding hockey accumulated, his effectiveness waned, and that coincided with the NHL implementing a salary cap. Needing to shed salary coming out of the labor dispute that wiped out the 2004–05 season, the Wings placed McCarty on waivers to initiate a buyout. McCarty was 33 years old and had spent 11 seasons with Detroit. He had gotten married and started a family; battled alcoholism; started a cancer foundation in support of his dad, Craig; founded a rock band, Grinder; scored big goals, pummeled a hated foe, and hoisted the Stanley Cup.

McCarty spent two seasons with the Calgary Flames, but fittingly finished his career in the place he called home: Detroit. In the fall of 2007, he reached out to Draper, who arranged for McCarty to play with the Flint Generals, an International Hockey League team partially owned by Draper. McCarty had gone through a tough time—divorce, bankruptcy, treatment for alcohol abuse—but he was certain he had more hockey in him. It was like a repeat of that day before the draft in 1992, when McCarty told Holland, "I will do whatever it takes."

In January, Holland offered his former draft pick a professional tryout contract with the Wings' top farm team, the Grand Rapids Griffins. The Wings' AHL affiliate had been in Upstate New York when McCarty began his NHL career, but the path led to the same destination. By March 2008, he once again wore a Wings uniform. He played just three regular-season games, but was part of the playoff run that yielded his fourth Stanley Cup. The Wings had gambled a second-round pick on him in the draft, and he rewarded them with a memorable career.

1992

Swapping players from the 1992 draft with the Edmonton Oilers helped the Wings win four Stanley Cups.

Kirk Maltby came to the Wings on March 20, 1996, sought out for his grit as the Wings eyed a playoff run in the wake of being knocked around in the 1995 Stanley Cup Final. Maltby dated to the same draft as McCarty, taken at No. 65 by the Edmonton Oilers. He had left an indelible impression on the Wings when he put a hard hit on Paul Coffey that knocked the defenseman out of the lineup. The deal cost the Wings defenseman Dan McGillis, who was part of the "bigger, stronger, harder" draft class of 1992, where he was chosen in the 10th round, at No. 238. McGillis spent 12 seasons in the NHL, appearing in 634 games. He and McCarty were the only players from the 11 selected by the Wings that year who established themselves at the NHL level.

The 1992 draft is famous for being the site of the Eric Lindros trade. Lindros was the No. 1 pick in 1991, but he refused to play for the Quebec Nordiques. The Wings made an offer, but the Nordiques agreed to trades with the Philadelphia Flyers and New York Rangers. The case went before an arbitrator, who ruled in favor of the Flyers. Wings general manager Bryan Murray expressed displeasure at being rejected, saying, "We made a real good offer, and we had to be considered as a team that had an excellent chance to make the deal." Murray didn't specify who the Wings had offered, but reports in Detroit at the time named Steve Yzerman. It's unlikely that would have happened, as team owner Mike Ilitch would have had to agree, and he nixed other trade talk involving Yzerman.

19

HOW ABOUT THAT NICE VLADIMIR KONSTANTINOV?

THE RED WINGS were inordinately pleased with having drafted Sergei Fedorov in the fourth round of the 1989 draft, even though they weren't sure when or if he would get out from behind the Iron Curtain. Their attempt to draft Pavel Bure in the sixth round was thwarted, so they went for another Russian in the 11th round after chief amateur scout Neil Smith consulted with chief European scout Christer Rockström.

"The late-round Europeans at that point were always better than the late-round Canadians and Americans," Smith said. "It was like men and boys. There was no comparison. I asked Christer who he liked, and he answered, 'How about that nice Vladimir Konstantinov? You remember the fighter in Piešťany last year? The fighting captain of the Russian team.' And I did remember him from that tournament. That's the game where Canada and Russia got in the bench-clearing brawl, and they turned the lights out because the referees didn't know how to handle it. I remembered Konstantinov was tough."

The "Punch-up in Piešťany" was an all-out altercation between the Soviets and Canadians during the 1987 World Junior Championships. Both teams were disqualified from the tournament—it didn't matter much to the Soviets, who already had been eliminated from medal contention, but it mattered to the Canadians because they'd had a chance to play for the gold medal. Despairing of convincing the players to stop brawling, overmatched officials turned out the lights after about 20 minutes. Konstantinov's contribution was a head-butt that broke Greg Hawgood's nose.

Konstantinov was obstinate and he was tough. He was also a mobile, puck-moving defenseman who could make tape-to-tape passes. Rockström believed he could step right into the Wings' lineup and make a difference. The thinking at the 1989 draft was that if Konstantinov could be pilfered from the Soviets, the Wings might just germinate their defense corps with two potential high-end players in Nicklas Lidström, who had been selected in the third round, and Konstantinov.

Considering the astronomical odds that a North American player taken in the 11th round would ever make it to the NHL, taking a proven Russian was well worth the gamble, and the Wings bit on Rockström's suggestion.

"Konstantinov was all Christer Rockström," said Ken Holland, then an amateur scout, in 2021. "Christer was really big on him, really thought he would be a good fit for us. There was concern about how we would get him out, when he would be able to play for us. But we knew if that ever happened, he was an NHL player."

Konstantinov was 22 years old when the Wings drafted him and had a wife and daughter. The next year, in 1990, he was in Tacoma, Washington, for the Goodwill Games. It had been barely a month since Fedorov had left the Red Army after a game in Portland, Oregon, and defected to Detroit. Speaking through an interpreter, Konstantinov stated he had no intention of leaving his team, because his Red Army contract stipulated he couldn't go to the NHL until he was 28.

That was what had to be said publicly. Privately, the Wings did what they had done with Fedorov, and set about trying all possible avenues to get Konstantinov. In December, Jim Lites, the team's executive vice president, set up a meeting with Soviet officials to put out feelers for striking a deal. At the last minute, the Soviets called off the meeting. In April 1991, Nick Polano, the assistant general manager who had helped spirit away Fedorov and Petr Klima, went to Helsinki, Finland, for the World Championships.

"If we do anything at all, it will be aboveboard," Polano said at the time. "With the Russians, timing is everything, and they don't like to talk about losing a player to the NHL during major tournaments."

In August, there was hope that months of quiet negotiations would open a path for Konstantinov to come to Detroit.

In September, he signed a multiyear deal with the Wings. Team officials set about to secure his visa.

Securing Konstantinov's arrival in Detroit required lies, bribes, and the beginning of the end of the Soviet Union. Konstantinov lied about having a rare form of cancer, backed by doctors who had been bribed to fake documents. Irina Konstantinov convinced Red Army officials to let her husband seek treatment in the United States. Just as he was about to leave from Moscow's Sheremetyevo airport, Konstantinov found out he had been placed on a no-fly list. The plan changed: Konstantinov was to take the train. But then history intervened: In August 1991, a group of hardline Communist officials staged a coup. Tanks rolled through the streets of Moscow. Boris Yeltsin, president of Russia from 1991 to 1999, refused to blink, and the standoff ended within days. By the end of the year, the Soviet Union had dissolved.

During the demonstrations, thieves had broken into the car that Konstantinov had been using and stolen his medical records and passport. The Konstantinovs returned to their apartment. A man (suspected to be one of the thieves) called and offered an exchange. Konstantinov and Valery Matveev, a reporter who served as the Wings' facilitator in Russia, met the blackmailers at the Kosmos Hotel. Konstantinov and Matveev came armed with hockey sticks, a helmet, and a gun, but the exchange went smoothly. The thief took the hockey gear and handed back the documents.

Within a few days, Konstantinov and Matveev made it to Budapest, Hungary. They were met there by Lites and an immigration attorney, who traveled with Konstantinov

Vladimir Konstantinov in a game in April 1997. He was one of the Wings' fiercest defensemen. *Photo by Mary Schroeder*

to Detroit. Irina and the couple's two-and-a-half-year-old daughter, Anastasia, arrived in the U.S. a few days later.

Rockström had been right: "That nice Vladimir Konstantinov" was a great choice. He produced 34 points in 79 games his first year in the NHL, in 1991–92, along with 172 penalty minutes. It wasn't long before he was adored by fans and reviled by foes. He was every bit the tough player from the "Punch-up in Piešťany," but he was also every bit the skilled player Rockström had seen.

"I remember Christer telling us that Vladdie was really good with the puck," Smith said. "I had seen him play. When we took him, we knew it made sense to take a guy who, if we could get him, would come right in and play."

Konstantinov stood 6', 195 pounds, but played like a giant. He amassed 687 penalty minutes his first five seasons, while missing only nine games. He was as stoic as he was tough, and soon became a fan favorite. Dubbed "the Vladinator," Konstantinov appeared in sunglasses, vowing, "I'll be back," in clips on the Jumbotron at Joe Louis Arena. His theme song was George Thorogood and the Destroyers' "Bad to the Bone."

Konstantinov's fame grew when Scotty Bowman traded for Igor Larionov in the fall of 1995 and went on to form the Russian Five. With Larionov centering a line between Fedorov and Slava Kozlov and Konstantinov partnered with famed Russian defenseman Slava Fetisov, the group put on performances with the puck that dazzled.

In 1995–96, Konstantinov scored a career-best 14 goals among 34 points. He led the NHL with a plus-60 rating. "He was so competitive," Lidström said in 2021. "The way he played, you could tell he wasn't afraid of anybody."

Konstantinov fought Adam Deadmarsh during the famous March 26, 1997, game between the Wings and the Colorado Avalanche. When the teams met that spring in the playoffs, it was Avalanche coach Marc Crawford who wanted a piece of Konstantinov. Crawford spent an entire news conference on a day between games in the Western Conference Finals series whining about Konstantinov.

"We've got to play very physical against Konstantinov," Crawford said. "We have to expose the fact that he's clutching and grabbing all the time. He could get a penalty every shift he's on the ice.... He's really a very, very clever player at clutching and grabbing around the net. You have to really persevere and keep your feet moving and expose the fact he does that all the time."

In the Stanley Cup Final, Philadelphia Flyers coach Terry Murray described Konstantinov as "one of the dirtiest defensemen in the league. Every time he hits, he leaves his feet and his elbows are always up."

Konstantinov loved it. "I just start laughing and they start complaining," he said.

That May and the first 12 days of June 1997 were a fun, fabulous, and fulfilling time for Konstantinov. He was 30 years old and at the height of his career. He was a finalist for the Norris Trophy, and on June 7, he added Stanley Cup champion to his résumé. He, Irina, and Anastasia had a beautiful home in a swanky Detroit suburb. It had only been eight years since he was drafted, and six years since he bluffed his way from Russia to Detroit.

Konstantinov's career ended June 13, 1997, when the man hired to chauffeur Konstantinov, Fetisov, and team masseur Sergei Mnatsakanov from a golf outing to a private party fell asleep and crashed the limousine into a tree. Konstantinov lurched forward into the mini bar, into glass that splintered as the vehicle skidded to a stop. Doctors described Konstantinov as having "scrambled brain," a condition that can shear neurons and cause swelling. He lay in a coma for two months.

Konstantinov never recovered. He played six seasons in the NHL, recording 175 points, a plus-185 rating, and 838 penalty minutes.

Two of the men drafted with Konstantinov that day in June 1989, Nicklas Lidström and Sergei Fedorov, went on to have such transcendent careers they were inducted into the Hockey Hall of Fame in 2015, three years after retirement. The Wings won the Stanley Cup with both in the lineup again in 1998 and 2002, and with Lidström again in 2008. Those who were there at the 1989 draft, those who best remember that "nice Vladimir Konstantinov" are convinced that, had his career not been cut short, he would have been there for all of them, and more.

"Most of us in the Red Wings organization feel that the loss of Konstantinov left a Cup on the table," executive vice president Jimmy Devellano said in 2021." We won four. Most of us feel, had we had a healthy Konstantinov, somewhere along the line, we'd have won a fifth."

20

TAKE THE RUSSIAN

THE ADRENALINE RUSH from drafting Sergei Fedorov in 1989 lingered for a year. At the 1990 draft, the Wings had made a good, safe choice with their first pick, selecting a big center named Keith Primeau at No. 3. They didn't have a second-round pick because it was traded to the Calgary Flames for Brad McCrimmon.

The Wings were on the draft board again in the third round, at No. 45. Chief scout Ken Holland leaned toward Stu Malgunas, a defenseman out of the Western Hockey League with an outside chance to make it to the NHL.

General manager Jimmy Devellano leaned towards Vyacheslav Kozlov, a small Russian forward who had stood out three years earlier during an international tournament played in Lake Placid, New York. It was a treat to see players from behind the Iron Curtain, though the secrecy sometimes baffled.

"I saw this kid on the Russian team, with No. 13, but there was no name on the back," Devellano said in 2021. "They had given me a printed sheet that was a program, and there was no No. 13 on the program. And this kid kept coming out at me. He could skate, he could handle the puck. Was he ever good. I said, 'Who the hell is he?' It bugged me."

Eventually Devellano tracked down somebody who spoke Russian.

"I found out his name was Slava Kozlov," Devellano said. "But what startled me was, he was the youngest player on the team. He was 15. And he was playing against 18-year-olds.... I got on the phone to Mike Ilitch and said I thought I had seen the best 15-year-old player I had ever seen, and I had seen Wayne Gretzky play at that age."

When Kozlov was eligible for the draft, Devellano was ready to pounce. "I'm not losing this kid," he said. "Teams still weren't taking Russians, not early, not late. They didn't take Russians. But we did."

When Holland didn't want to take Kozlov as early as the third round, the matter was deferred to Jim Lites, the Wings' executive vice president. He didn't hesitate with his answer: "Take the Russian."

At 5′10″ and 172 pounds, Kozlov was on the smaller side. But for the second straight year, the Wings felt they had drafted the best Russian prospect available. "He's good enough to play in the NHL right now," Devellano said at the time.

The following January, Wings scouts were in Saskatchewan to watch Kozlov at the World Junior Championships. Holland and Nick Polano, the assistant general manager, gave Kozlov's feisty play rave reviews and described him as a can't-miss star in the NHL. In April, Kozlov represented the Soviet Union at the Word Championships. He scored three goals in a 12–2 preliminary-round rout against the U.S.

Every shift he played reinforced the Wings' decision to draft him. The question was how to get him to North America.

Kozlov's path changed in October 1991. The 19-year-old was driving to practice with Red Army teammate Kirill Tarasov in the front passenger seat when the car slammed into a bus. Early reports out of Russia indicated Kozlov had suffered severe head and facial injuries.

Tarasov did not survive.

Within days, it emerged Kozlov had suffered a concussion and a broken nose. He was released from the hospital and returned to playing hockey.

Kozlov arrived in Detroit in February 1992 under the auspices of being examined by Wings medical personnel to make sure he was recuperating properly. Higher-ups in the organization were confident Kozlov was ready to play in the NHL, and all that needed to be done was to negotiate his release from the Red Army.

Bryan Murray, the Wings' coach and general manager, raved about Kozlov's skills. "I've seen him play a number of times, and he certainly is a talented young guy," Murray said.

On February 19, 1992, Kozlov skated in his first Wings practice. Management wanted him to be around the team as much as possible, to be around compatriots Sergei Fedorov and Vladimir Konstantinov.

When negotiations with the Soviets stalled, the Wings filed suit in late February in Wayne County Circuit Court against the Red Army team and the NHL. Allegedly, Kozlov was one year into a five-year contract with the Red Army, and the Wings wanted it declared null and void.

A judge cleared Kozlov to play in early March. That ruling coincided with the NHL penalizing Bob Probert with a three-game suspension for hitting St. Louis Blues defenseman Garth Butcher with a stick. The suspension actually would span six games, because immigration problems prevented Probert from traveling to Canada. The three games would have to be served in the United States, but the Wings were about to embark on a six-game trip that featured three stops in Canada.

That ruling dismayed team officials, but the Kozlov one delighted. The Wings were convinced the Soviets would fold in their bid to keep him tied to the Red Army and weren't about to give in to demands for developmental fees.

"They always want to negotiate after the horse is out of the barn," Jim Lites said.

The Russians continued their court case before a federal judge but didn't get any better result. Red Wings attorney Michael Lewiston called that skirmish "a naked effort" to undo the judgment in circuit court and described Kozlov as "the badminton birdie" in a match that spanned the Atlantic Ocean.

After a turbulent and tragic six months, Kozlov was ready to move on. "I am very happy that this is over," he said, "and I am looking forward to starting my NHL career."

Kozlov made his NHL debut March 12, assisting on two goals by Fedorov. Soon, Kozlov was playing left wing on a line with Steve Yzerman.

The acrimony with which Kozlov departed the Red Army faded as Russia moved forward from the Cold War. When a labor dispute threatened the start of the 1994–95 season, Kozlov eyed a homecoming as a way to keep playing. The Red Army responded with a red carpet treatment. Kozlov was put up in a $200-a-night suite at the President's Hotel in Moscow. The club even agreed to pay a $9,000 insurance premium to protect Kozlov from financial losses in case of injury.

Kozlov did get hurt in his first game, suffering several broken teeth and a concussion when he was clipped with the blade of an opponent's stick. On the whole it was a positive experience for Kozlov, who notched seven points in 10 games before returning to Detroit when the NHL and the labor union forged peace.

In the mid-1990s, the Wings lineup was so populated by stars who commanded the spotlight—Yzerman, Fedorov, Primeau, Ray Sheppard, and Paul Coffey—that Kozlov sometimes was left in the shadows. "I just think maybe he's not getting headlines," teammate Doug Brown said.

Kozlov forced his play to the forefront. In the 1995 playoffs, he scored in double overtime in Game 5 against the Chicago Blackhawks, securing the Wings' advancement to the Stanley Cup Final.

"Everybody just screamed," Kozlov said.

Kozlov never grew as comfortable speaking in English as his fellow Russians, preferring to let his play speak for him.

"It's funny to watch him," Chris Osgood said in 1998. "He just likes to come out and say, 'I score goal,' or, 'I score winning goal, so good day.' He doesn't really like to talk. Maybe that's why he doesn't get as much credit as he should."

When Scotty Bowman assembled the Russian Five— Kozlov, Fedorov, Igor Larionov, Vladimir Konstantinov, and

Slava Fetisov—it was the other four who commanded the spotlight. But Kozlov's talent shone across the NHL, and when the Buffalo Sabres dangled six-time Vezina Trophy winner Dominik Hasek in the summer of 2001, it was Kozlov they wanted in return.

The forward without a name on his jersey had journeyed from the Red Army to the Red Wings. He spent nearly a decade playing for the Wings, winning Stanley Cups in 1997 and 1998.

"He never was as good in the NHL as he was when I saw him in Lake Placid, but there was the car accident," Devellano said in 2021. "When we made the Hasek deal, even Scotty said, 'Wait, do we want to give this player up?' It was a chance to get the best goalie in the world. But Slava Kozlov, he was a really good player for us."

21

NEIL SMITH

NEIL SMITH WANTED to be involved with the NHL, and
so, like many people with a passion, he didn't care how
he had to get his start, didn't care how small the role, how
much smaller the pay.

Smith met Jimmy Devellano in the early 1970s in Toronto
through mutual acquittances. In 1974, while a scout with the
New York Islanders, Devellano drafted Smith in the 13th round,
at No. 204. Smith went to Western Michigan and played there
from 1974 to 1978, serving as captain his sophomore season.
He went to training camp in the late 1970s, when the Islanders
were on the verge of winning four straight Stanley Cups, and
wondered to himself, *What am I doing here?* By 1980, he was
a former defenseman looking for work.

A hockey buddy's father owned a giftware company and
offered Smith a job. It was low-paying, but Smith got to live

in New York City. After a couple of months, Smith reached out to Devellano, who by then was the director of scouting and assistant general manager of the Islanders.

"I said to him, 'Is there anything I can do for the Islanders? Because I just want to be in hockey so bad,'" Smith said in 2021. He pitched sending the Islanders reports on Rangers games, essentially scouting opponents. Devellano thought it a swell idea and told his boss, general manager Al Arbour.

"Shaking like a leaf, I went to see Al Arbour, and he gave me these forms to fill out, and I started to go to all these Rangers games," Smith said. "Then Al asked me to go to Hartford games and Boston games, to do this and that. I wasn't getting paid, but I quit the other job because I wanted to be in hockey so bad.

"That was in '81. They won the Cup that year. The next year, I did it full-time, and the Islanders were now paying me. They won the Cup again in '82, and then that summer, Jimmy D. got the job with the Red Wings."

Devellano brought his young acolyte with him to Detroit, announcing Smith's hire as director of professional scouting on August 12, 1982. Smith's duties with the Wings focused on scouting opponents. He would sit in press boxes and fill out forms, including answering 25 questions regarding every goal. It was part of Devellano's approach to modernize the Wings and fulfill promises made when new owner Mike Ilitch made Devellano the first big hire after purchasing the franchise in June.

"I'm looking for patterns and individual traits," Smith said at the time. "That, along with videotapes, brings certain things to light for a coach. I watch how each goal was scored, all the line combinations, the defensive pairings, the forechecking. With the worst teams, you can't see any patterns." (Smith went on to say that, when watching the Wings, "it was hard to see anything.")

While he primarily was a pro scout, Smith also helped scout for the amateur drafts. In May 1985, Smith's duties were expanded, and he was named general manager of the Adirondack Red Wings. In his first season, the team won the Calder Cup as champion of the American Hockey League.

In 1986, Smith was 32 years old and the youngest chief scout in the NHL.

"It's weird how you get to these places," Smith said in 2021. "You get there because you're not worried about money. You're willing to do it no matter what. You start off humbly and prove yourself, and you move up and up. Jimmy put a bug in the year of Al Arbour. It was serendipity."

Smith traded traversing the greater New York metropolitan area for traveling the world. The Wings were front-runners in being willing to draft European players and in gambling on players behind the Iron Curtain. In the mid-1980s, Smith went overseas to watch Petr Klima, whom the Wings had drafted in 1983.

"If you were going to Czechoslovakia, what you did was, you flew to Vienna," Smith said in 2021. "You rented a car and then you went through the Austrian border. You passed the Austrian checkpoint, and then you drove up slowly to this Czech station, where you had to pull over, turn off your car, step out. You showed them everything—passport, how much money you had on you. They checked in the trunk, under the hood, under the car, all over. Once they let you go, after

Neil Smith worked his way up from scout to assistant general manager with the Wings. *Photo by Mary Schroeder*

taking $20 from you which they said was counterfeit, which it wasn't, then you'd drive up the road just a tiny bit. There'd be guys with machine guns and dogs and mirrors to put under your car. You'd look out to the left and there'd be barbed wire and towers. You'd drive past that, and there was Bratislava.

"The people didn't have anything. The people were poor, there was smog everywhere. I remember being in Prague and how dirty everything was, the buildings, everything was just so gray. The people looked miserable. Then you'd get back out of there and you'd try to explain to people, you don't know lucky you've got it. Those people are not allowed to leave."

Trips to what was then the Soviet Union were even scarier.

"In Russia they were really miserable," Smith said. "It was terrifying to be there and it was terrifying to get out because they went through everything when you were leaving to make sure you were the guy in the passport and that you really weren't a Russian trying to get out. You just felt, *They are in prison living there.* There were dollar stores, hard currency only, and Russian citizens couldn't go in them. Only tourists. It was a bizarre time. You were nervous the whole time you were there."

There were nerves domestically, too. In 1986 the Wings had the first pick in the draft, and they needed to get it right. Everybody in hockey had it pared down to two choices, and as it happened, both had ties to the Wings' backyard. Joe Murphy was a Canadian starring at Michigan State, and Jimmy Carson was a Detroit-area native starring in the Quebec Major Junior Hockey League.

It was Smith's first time announcing the top selection.

"Here was the pressure," Smith said in 2021. "Joe Murphy was playing at Michigan State, and playing with young men, against young men. And he was putting in some fabulous numbers. He could skate like the wind and he had hands that looked great. And Jimmy Carson was playing in the Quebec league. There was a lot of pressure on us to take Jimmy Carson because he was from Detroit, and Mr. Ilitch favored Detroit kids. But we believed that Murphy was a better prospect because of where he was playing and how he was doing it.

"That's basically how that decision was made. And I do believe if you polled the other 20 teams that year, 15 of them would have gone with Murphy and five others with Carson. The Quebec league was thought of as a softer league, there were so many points being scored. What Murphy did in going to Michigan State and doing what he did at 18 was amazing."

Murphy didn't turn out to be a great pick and eventually was used to acquire Carson, but neither made an impact on the Wings. Ultimately, Carson retired with 561 points compared to Murphy's 528, but Murphy played 779 games compared to Carson's 626.

The 1988 draft was a forgettable one for the Wings; the only player to make it to the NHL out of the 11 they selected was Sheldon Kennedy, whom they took in the fourth round. But the 1989 draft made up for it in spades, with selections including Nicklas Lidström, Sergei Fedorov, and Vladimir Konstantinov, all of whom played key roles in the 1997 Stanley Cup championship.

While Fedorov was a rising star with the Red Army when the Wings drafted him, Lidström was an unknown defenseman splitting time in Sweden's first and second divisions of hockey in his draft year. It was on one of Smith's trips overseas in the mid-'80s that he met Christer Rockström, the man who would introduce the Wings to their future Hall of Fame defenseman.

"Christer showed up at the airport in Stockholm to pick me up," Smith said. "He was driving a Mercedes, a stick shift, that was used as a taxi. He didn't speak very good English at all, but we hit it off almost right away—he was young, I was young, and he knew all the young players. He knew all the night spots to go out to afterwards to have fun in Stockholm."

Rockström took Smith to see Lidström play, and Smith knew right away the Wings had to have him.

No one in the NHL knew just how amazing the Wings' 1989 haul would be that summer, but Smith's role in raising the franchise from its "Dead Wings" era had garnered notice. In July, news broke that the New York Rangers had identified Smith, then 35, as the top candidate to replace the fired Phil Esposito. Devellano went on the record as saying it would take "only very, very mild" compensation to get Smith from the Wings. The promotion was announced July 17, 1989.

In less than a decade, Smith had gone from scraping by in New York as a salesman for a giftware company to running an Original Six franchise. When he had first started working for the Islanders as an advance scout, he made no money. Reports the day he was hired by the Rangers had Smith making $200,000 a year.

Smith was delighted, calling it "the biggest thrill of my life." Devellano described his emotions as mixed: "You hate to lose such a quality young hockey man and a personal friend as well, but that's what happens when you hire good young people and develop them. This is a great opportunity for Neil, to get the top job in the major market like that."

Privately, Devellano was upset at Smith's departure, and the two men, often reported by Devellano as having a father-son relationship, rarely talked after the split.

Smith made a substantial imprint on the Rangers, drafting star players in Alexei Kovalev, Doug Weight, and Sergei Zubov, and pulling off a blockbuster trade for superstar Mark Messier. In 1994, the Rangers won their fourth Stanley Cup in franchise history. It was fitting outcome for a man whose history played a significant role in the Wings' path toward glory. The first players Smith helped the Wings draft—Klima, Steve Yzerman, Bob Probert—reinvigorated the franchise, and the last ones—Lidström, Fedorov, Konstantinov—made them Stanley Cup champions.

22

CZECH MATE

JIMMY DEVELLANO AND his scouts spent as much time as possible during the 1982–83 season scouting for players who looked like they could help revive a franchise that had lost all its luster. New owner Mike Ilitch had hired them to rebuild the Red Wings, and there was tremendous pressure to have a good first draft. A couple international tournaments led the Wings to identify two players from the Czechoslovakian national team as possible targets.

When the 1983 draft began on June 8, the most important job was to get the first pick right. Steve Yzerman was a highly rated prospect, a safe—and as it turned out, spectacular—choice at No. 4. But as the rounds wore on, the choices became more of a gamble.

When Devellano got to the fifth round, the talk centered on the players who had stood out at the World Junior

Championships and the World Championships. The player the Wings really wanted, defenseman Frantisek Musil, was already gone—the Minnesota North Stars took him in the second round.

That left Petr Klima, a fast, strong, skilled forward who had impressed at the World Juniors, where he had recorded eight points in seven games. "I had a source in Czechoslovakia who said, 'Nick, this guy is the best player we have, but you won't like him, he's always in trouble with the authorities,'" Polano told the *Detroit Free Press* in 1988. "I thought to myself, *Hmm. Sounds to me like a good candidate for defection.* By the time we got to the fifth round, I was giving Jimmy the eye. Finally, Jimmy said, 'Okay, but now you have to deliver him.'"

Klima wasn't able to freely leave from behind the Iron Curtain, but there had been players before him who had done so. In the 1970s, Vaclav Nedomansky defected from Czechoslovakia to play in the World Hockey Association, and he later played five seasons with the Wings. In 1980, Peter Stastny defected from Czechoslovakia to Canada.

In August 1983, Ilitch had a trip planned to Europe. Part of the agenda was making contact with Klima in an effort to convince him to defect. Ilitch's outlook was simple: "Whatever it takes," he said at the time.

In November, the Wings sent Louis Jakub, a Czechoslovakian native who lived in the Detroit area, to Czechoslovakia as a representative in hopes of recruiting Klima. "It was impossible for him to come at that time because he was in the army, and the government could have punished his parents," Jakub revealed in 1985.

In September 1984 Klima played in the Canada Cup. (The Czechoslovakians, with future Wings goaltender Dominik Hasek in net, gained only one point at the tournament.) Klima had replaced Frantisek Cernik, who had been signed by the Wings in the summer of 1984 when he received permission to play outside his communist homeland after years of service. Eleven years younger than Cernik, Klima was expected to serve his country for some time.

"He's young and has a long future ahead," Czechoslovakian coach Ludek Bukac said.

Klima's future looked bright enough that, in January 1985, the Calgary Flames offered to trade for his rights. "They're not going to get them," Devellano said. "We still have high hopes of getting Klima out of the country ourselves."

In late August, news broke that Klima had left the Czechoslovakian national team while it was on a training assignment in West Germany. He failed to appear at practice at a facility near Rosenheim and was discovered to be missing from his team's hotel. The Associated Press reported Klima was seen having a drink with a teammate at the hotel restaurant the night before. West Germany hockey officials said Klima stood up and said he was going to the men's room. Instead, he got his luggage from his room and left.

The next day, Reuters reported that Xavier Unsinn, the West German national coach, said that Klima had left West Germany with a North American scout and was headed for Canada. (The story held such intrigue that the *Detroit Free Press* had a Europe-based correspondent write an article about the hardship of escaping to the West. The article told the story of 19-year-old Radek Struz, who convinced his dad,

Czechoslovak Air Force Major Bozej Struz, to take him and two friends on a short flight one Sunday afternoon in July 1985. Once aloft, the friends chloroformed Major Struz, and Radek, who often had flown with his dad in the four-seater single-engine plane, piloted the aircraft 125 miles south to Austria, flying at 300 feet above ground to avoid radar detection. The elder Struz regained consciousness, and the hijackers untied his right hand so he could land the plane in a clover field near Gaindorf, northwest of Vienna. Radek and his friends requested asylum; the major was driven back to his homeland.)

The Wings' scouting contact in the area was a guy named Mike Daski, a former coach from Winnipeg, Manitoba. On August 21, two days after Klima was reported missing, Daski said he had talked to Klima. "He does not know what to do," Daski said. "Should he defect? Naturally, any communist player would like to come to the States to play hockey. But there is a lot of pressure on their family and their loved ones."

Hours later, Daski changed his story and said he had talked with Klima's coaches, but not with Klima. Daski explained the Czechoslovakian officials were angry with him and accused him of persuading Klima to defect from Dukla-Jihlava, the Czechoslovakian Army team. "To defect from the army [he] would be a traitor," Daski said. "They could shoot him."

In September, Czechoslovakian officials conceded Klima had defected. A front-page article in the *Czechoslovakia Sports Daily* quoted Dr. Jan Starsi, coach of the national team: "Petr Klima was lured by money of the National Hockey League and betrayed the collective of his teammates." (The article

Petr Klima (left) is greeted by Wings executive Jim Lites upon arriving in Detroit September 22, 1985.

was translated for the *Detroit Free Press* by Voice of America broadcaster Pavel Pechacek.)

Klima was 20 years old and considered one of the top left wings in the world. His service with the army hockey team Dukla-Jihlava had ended, clearing one hurdle on his path to the NHL.

Jim Lites, the Wings' executive vice president, and Nick Polano, who had moved from coaching to being assistant general manager, had gone to West Germany to meet Klima and help him and his girlfriend defect. They kept a low profile and kept on the move, changing hotels from Rosenheim to Munich to Stuttgart to Koblenz to Wiesbaden to Frankfurt. Klima ran, swam, biked, and lifted weights to keep fit. As the weeks wore on, boredom set in. One day he rented a Mercedes 500 and crashed it on the Autobahn.

"No speed limit," Polano said later. "Petr thought it was funny."

In Detroit, future teammates eagerly awaited his arrival. Yzerman, who had played against Klima the previous year in the Canada Cup tournament, said, "He was the best player from Czechoslovakia, without a doubt. He can skate like the wind. He's definitely a sniper. Definitely a stickhandler. I shouldn't compare him to Wayne Gretzky, but he is speedy. I tell you, he's good. I was on the ice a couple times when he scored."

Training camp began with Klima still in Europe. His immigration paperwork was rushed through with the help of Attorney General Ed Meese and his Justice Department staff in Washington.

On September 21, a sporting goods employee showed up at camp with a white Wings sweater bearing Klima's name and No. 85. That was around 2:30 PM. Three hours later, Klima landed at Detroit Metropolitan Airport aboard a TWA flight from New York, the second leg of a flight plan that began in Frankfurt, Germany. Ilitch and Lites headed up the welcoming committee waiting at the gate. Klima was 20 years old and had just gained refugee status in the United States.

Speaking through an interpreter, Klima expressed gratitude for having made it and explained that he chose No. 85
because it represented the year he gained his freedom. He
also gained a hefty pay raise: his income soared from the
$7,000 he had made in the Old World to $200,000 in the New
World. Klima bought a house in the affluent Detroit suburb
Birmingham and a black Camaro IROC Z28. (He had a harder
time shopping for a replacement for a treasured Levi's jacket
generously detailed with pockets, zippers, and straps that had
been left behind; an excursion to Oakland Mall did not yield
a satisfactory imitation.) Klima owned two Great Danes and a
German Shepherd. In short order he was joined by his fiancée,
Irena Zelenak.

On opening night at Joe Louis Arena in October, fans
welcomed Klima with a five-minute standing ovation.

It looked so promising for both sides. The Wings chanced
a draft pick on Klima in 1983 because they saw his potential
as a scorer. On October 10, 1985, he reinforced their choice
when he scored in his NHL debut, one of 32 goals his rookie
season. He even served as acting captain briefly in March.
Klima was convinced he was doing exactly what the Wings
wanted him to do. When Harry Neale and Brad Park, who
split coaching duties during 1985–86, asked Klima to play
defense, he was defiant. "I never play defense," Klima said.
"I score goals."

(It was a matter of appreciation for Klima that he could
speak so freely. In his second year with the Wings, he told
the story of what had happened when he mouthed off to his
coach while with the Czechoslovakian Army. "Jail," Klima
said. "They put me two weeks in jail. I say something stupid

to my coach. They take my favorite center away, put him on another line. I tell coach I don't like it, I won't play." His superiors were livid at such insubordination, and punished Klima. "No food," he said, "just bread and water for two weeks." Klima returned to his team, lesson learned. "I keep mouth shut," he said.)

Klima posted 30 goals in 1986–87 and 37 goals in 1987–88. He was every bit the star the Wings thought he would be—complete with blond-streaked hair, a diamond earring, and an artificial tan—but as productive as he was on the ice, Klima was problematic away from it.

In May 1988, he was among the group of Wings who broke curfew and went out drinking at Goose Loonies, a night club in Edmonton, Alberta, the night before Game 5 of the Conference Finals against the Oilers. Klima would not have played, regardless, because he was sidelined by a broken thumb, but he violated team rules and encouraged Bob Probert, by that time an admitted alcoholic, to do the same. (The morning after, Brent Ashton walked up to a table of his teammates at their hotel in Edmonton and yelled something along the lines of, "Where's Petr Klima? I'm going to kick his ass. He took Probie out drinking last night." *Detroit Free Press* columnist Mitch Albom was seated at a nearby table and overheard the conversation, leading to the incident coming to light in the press.)

The Wings lost the game, and with it, the series.

Klima's reckless, selfish behavior was condemned by the team, but there was no indication he learned a thing. In October 1988, he was arrested for drunk driving. Klima was still on probation stemming from his arrest for alcohol-related driving in May 1987. He was also suspended by the team, for missing practices, flights, and curfews.

The Wings reinstated Klima later that month and sent him to the minors. He returned to Detroit in early November and apologized to his teammates. In December, he was ordered to work with kids at Children's Hospital of Michigan as part of his sentencing for violating terms of his probation for driving while impaired.

Klima was limited to 51 games in 1988–89, and still scored 25 goals. He was still productive—and still a problem. In May 1989, he was pulled over along Long Lake Road near Troy, north of Detroit. An eyewitness said that when police officers attempted to handcuff Klima after he failed dexterity tests, he broke loose and fled. Officers gave chase and overcame him. Klima was charged with driving under the influence, resisting and obstructing a police officer, escape from lawful custody, and driving with a suspended license. The Boys and Girls Club of Royal Oak, where Klima was supposed to perform 48 hours of community service following his conviction for an earlier alcohol-related driving offense, said he wasn't welcome.

Klima had worn out his welcome with the Wings, too. It was a tough time for the franchise: seven years had passed since Ilitch had bought the team, and six years since the 1983 draft that brought in Yzerman, Bob Probert, and Klima. There had been playoff successes, but no Stanley Cups. Rumors percolated that there would be a blockbuster trade with the Edmonton Oilers, and that Klima would be involved. Just as when he had crashed that Mercedes in Germany four years earlier, Klima thought it was funny.

"Nobody wants me, I'm a drunk," he said in October 1989. "Maybe I should start drinking again. If I get traded to Edmonton, I'll quit. Whoever trades for me is going to have trouble, big-time, because I won't go. I'll wait a year and go to Europe, play in Germany. Things are changing back home. I could play in Germany and be less than an hour from home."

Klima was right about that: by the end of 1989, the communist-backed government in Czechoslovakia had been peacefully deposed, and the country transitioned to a parliamentary republic. (Three years later, it would split into the sovereign states of the Czech Republic and Slovakia.)

The Wings didn't care about Klima's threats, and neither did the Oilers. On November 2, the sides consummated Devellano's biggest deal since taking the GM job in Detroit: Klima, Joe Murphy (the No. 1 pick in 1986), Adam Graves (the No. 22 pick in 1986), and defenseman Jeff Sharples went to the Oilers. The Wings got Jimmy Carson (the No. 2 pick in 1986), forward Kevin McClelland, and a fifth-round pick in 1991. Klima didn't take it well.

"They had no right to trade me," he said in November. "They took me from my home once. Then they took me away again. They came to me in '83 and said, 'We want you, Petr. Come to Detroit. Play hockey for us, and we will take care of you.' In '85, I leave my home, my family. I came and built a home here. Then they make me leave again."

Klima won the Cup with the Oilers in 1990. After four seasons with Edmonton, he went on to play for the Tampa Bay Lightning, Los Angeles Kings, and Pittsburgh Penguins. In the fall of 1998 he was back at Wings camp, invited to try out for a spot. He could have had one, too, but balked when contract negotiations stalled with the sides $50,000 apart. In January 1999, he signed a prorated $75,000 contract, and on February 14 he scored in his first game back with the Wings, just as he had done when he debuted in 1985. It was the only goal he scored in 13 appearances.

In 2001, Klima resumed his playing career after a two-year lull. It made for a fitting and full circle as he returned to the Czech Republic, playing for the same club he was with in his draft year, 1982–83. In two decades, Klima had gone from dreams of defecting to living the dream life of an NHL star. He had also become a father, in 1997, to twin sons Kelly and Kevin. They played briefly for Little Caesars hockey, and after attempting to forge professional careers in lower leagues in the United States, in their twenties they signed to play in the Czech Republic. After retiring, Klima resided in the metro Detroit area and participated in Wings alumni games.

Klima starred in the NHL for 786 games, recording 313 goals and 260 assists. He was a 30-goal scorer five times, and 40-goal scorer once. He helped revive the Red Wings and might have helped them become Stanley Cup champions had there been fewer problems off the ice. That he was a gifted skater and scorer is undebatable.

"We drafted Steve Yzerman in '83, but in the same draft we took the best 18-year-old in the fifth round when he we got Petr Klima," Devellano said in 2021. "The Iron Curtain was up, and you couldn't get him. Most people thought you were wasting a draft choice. It was up to us to get him, but if we didn't get him, it was a fifth-round pick blown. He became a big story. We got him to defect. He came in and was a star player, pretty much from day one."

23

BUILDING DOWN THE MIDDLE

SHAWN BURR HAD an irrepressible personality that delighted teammates and fans. He spent a decade with the Red Wings, working his way from the minors to the spotlight. He entertained with his hands and his wit, and steadily overcame the unreasonable expectations with which he first joined the organization.

In 1983 the Wings' first pick became an instant sensation, setting the bar high for the following year's first-round pick. Shawn Burr didn't get to Detroit as quickly as Steve Yzerman had, but Burr was an appealing pick on June 9, 1984. It was Jimmy Devellano's second draft as general manager of the Wings, and he didn't pick until seventh. That was the year Mario Lemieux was the No. 1 pick, and in succession, Kirk

Muller, Eddie Olczyk, and Petr Svoboda, all of whom would go on to become All-Stars. (It was an inauspicious beginning for Lemieux and the Pittsburgh Penguins: he refused to come down from the stands and put on a Penguins sweater because of stalled salary negotiations.)

Burr was a 6'1", 200-pound center who was from nearby Sarnia. He had 41 goals and 44 assists in 68 games with the Kitchener Rangers in 1983–84, and his 1.25 points-per-game average earned him rookie of the year honors in the Ontario Hockey League. Burr was known for being clever around the net, and possessing exceptional anticipation.

"We think we took the best player available, and you have to be strong down the middle in order to build a good team," Devellano said. "Last year we started with Steve Yzerman, and this year we're continuing to build down the middle with Shawn Burr."

Devellano's second pick in 1984, defenseman Doug Houda, played 172 of his 561 career games with the Wings and later served on the coaching staff. Milan Chalupa, a defenseman from the Czech Republic, appeared in 14 games with the Wings. None of the other nine picks made it to the NHL.

Such was Devellano's faith in Burr that in August, Burr was signed to a five-year deal similar to the one inked the year before by Yzerman. The next month Burr scored in his first exhibition game and entertained the crowd of 4,000 that had gathered at McMorran Arena in Port Huron with a Michael Jackson victory dance.

Burr didn't score in the nine games he played for the Wings that fall and was sent back to his junior team. He did have one very memorable outing, though, in his second game, when he lined up in the faceoff circle opposite Guy Lafleur, the Montreal Canadiens legend. Burr won the draw, and bumped into Lafleur. Larry Robinson took offense to that.

"He told me, 'Don't ever hit him again.' And I said, 'Then tell him to stay out of my way,'" Burr recalled in 1987.

It turned out Burr needed time to mature. He scored one goal in 14 games with the Wings spread over 1984–85 and 1985–86, but in 1987–88, he looked like he had ripened into the player Devellano thought Burr would be. He centered the second line (behind Yzerman), scored 22 goals, and was noted for being good at both ends of the ice.

"I'm proud of the way he's come on, but I'm not surprised," Devellano said. "He's got character and pride and heart. He's going to be a player for this franchise the way Bobby Clarke was for Philadelphia."

Burr didn't reach that stratosphere, but he made Wayne Gretzky see stars in the 1987 playoffs with a bone-rattling body check. It was the first game of the Western Conference Finals, and Gretzky had suffered a concussion the previous week. The hit was the talk of Edmonton, but Gretzky wasn't put out.

"I had my chest down and he could have hit me a lot harder," Gretzky said. "He hit me fair and square."

Burr's play declined when he suffered multiple concussions, but he still was signed to a three-year contract in September 1989. Devellano predicted Burr would "have his best year this coming season." It started out poorly for the former first-round pick, as he was put on waivers in October and told to go home and wait for instructions. Burr called it "embarrassing, for sure." It was a risky way for the Wings to send a message to Burr that he needed to play more like the sound defensive player he was early in his young career.

"He had not played that kind of bump-and-grind game," coach Jacques Demers said. "He used to have equal ice time with Steve Yzerman. The big players on the other teams were insulting him. They hated playing against him. For him to be successful, for the Red Wings to be successful, he has to play that way again."

Burr spent a brief stint in the minors, then returned to find himself on a line with Yzerman. Burr went on to record career highs with 24 goals and 32 assists in 1989–90, fulfilling Devellano's prophecy.

As his game rounded into form, Burr's personality bounded out the locker room and beyond. He once said of himself, "I have the perfect body—for a mailman." Curious if he ever stopped talking, he remarked, "I stayed up one night to see if I talked in my sleep, but I didn't." Observing himself being interviewed on TV one day, he said, "I can't believe I sound like that. It's like one of the Muppets is behind me, lip-syncing."

In 1991, Burr played on a line with Sergei Fedorov. (Burr was quick to embrace Fedorov when he joined the Wings in 1990. He invited the young Russian for a day of boating on Lake St. Clair. When Fedorov showed up wearing skin-tight briefs, Burr supplied him with swim trunks.) Burr scored 19 goals that season, the sixth straight season he had been at or near the 20-goal mark. Off ice, he continued to make team-mates laugh.

"My first game as a rookie, he put my name upside down on my jersey," Chris Osgood said. "He was the guy who kept

1984

The 1984 draft was one of the best in NHL history, yielding Mario Lemieux, Luc Robitaille, Brett Hull, and Patrick Roy, among many future Hockey Hall of Famers.

Two of those luminaries joined the Wings to help form the powerhouse that captured the 2002 Stanley Cup. It was a little after 7:00 in the evening on July 3, 2001, when general manager Ken Holland was on the phone with Robitaille. The day had begun with a news conference at Joe Louis Arena to introduce Dominik Hasek, the superstar goaltender acquired from the Buffalo Sabres. Like Hasek, Robitaille was chasing a Stanley Cup.

"First they get the Dominator, then they get me," Robitaille said on July 6. Drafted in the ninth round, at No. 171, Robitaille had spent 15 seasons in the NHL, recording 1,238 points in 1,124 games. He won the Calder Trophy as the NHL's rookie of the year in 1987.

In August, Brett Hull joined the roster. "Detroit just seemed like a perfect fit for me," he said. Drafted in the sixth round, at No. 117, Hull had banked 1,183 points in 1,019 games.

It was a perfect fit for both. Hull was so delighted to play with rookie center Pavel Datsyuk that he nicknamed their line with Boyd Devereaux "Two Kids and a Goat." Robitaille played with Igor Larionov and Tomas Holmström on what was the best fourth line in the NHL.

The two gems from the 1984 draft celebrated the following June, securing their legacies with a Stanley Cup championship. Robitaille retired in 2006 with 1,394 points in 1,431 games, second in his draft class only to first overall pick Mario Lemieux's 1,723 points in 915 games. Hull retired in 2005 with 1,391 points in 1,269 points, ranking third in the 1984 draft class.

everybody else relaxed. He did the dirty work for the team on the ice and then kept the guys relaxed in the dressing room."

Burr fell from favor under Scotty Bowman and was among the changes enforced after the crushing disappointment of the 1995 playoffs, when the Wings advanced to the Stanley Cup Final only to be swept by the New Jersey Devils. Bowman, coach and director of player personnel, traded Burr to the Tampa Bay Lightning in August, for defenseman Marc Bergevin and a little-known player named Ben Hankinson.

Burr recorded 362 points in 659 games with the Wings and retired from the NHL in 1999 with 440 points in 878 games. After stops in Tampa and San Jose, he briefly played in Detroit again with the International Hockey League Vipers in 1999–2000.

Burr was diagnosed with acute myeloid leukemia in February 2011. He passed away August 5, 2013, aged 47.

Former teammate Kris Draper summed up what Burr had meant to the Wings: "If you were in the same room with him, you knew you were going to laugh and you knew it wasn't going to be quiet," he said. "He was definitely a guy that had a lot to say, talked a lot, had some unreal one-liners. Very quick, very witty. Just a great guy to be around."

24

1985

THE PLAYER WHO had the most impact on the Red Wings from their 1985 draft class was a well-liked, hard-nosed defenseman they took in the third round.

It wasn't a particularly strong draft for the Wings, whose first pick came at No. 8. That put them out of reach of Craig Simpson, whose 84 points in 42 games in 1984–85 at Michigan State University had made him a top-ranked pick. (He went at No. 2 to the Pittsburgh Penguins, after the Toronto Maple Leafs took Wendel Clark at No. 1.)

The Wings selected Brent Fedyk, an 18-year-old right wing who had shown meteoric improvement with the Regina Pats in the Western Hockey League, going from 15 goals and 43 points in 63 games in 1983–84 to 35 goals and 70 points in 66 games his draft year. Wings scouts saw Fedyk as a versatile scorer who blended speed, balance, and agility.

With their second pick, at No. 29, they took Jeff Sharples, a defenseman from the Kelowna Rockets in the Western
Hockey League. It was eight spots into the third round, at
No. 50, that the Wings chose Steve Chiasson, an offensive
defenseman out of the Ontario Hockey League. Those were
the prospects management had the highest hopes for, though
the slow pace at which 1984 first-round pick Shawn Burr was
developing, those hopes were tempered by patience.

"This draft will not affect the Detroit Red Wings for three
or four years," general manager Jimmy Devellano said. "We
are not expecting our first pick to step right in. Although it
sure would be nice to be surprised."

The Wings drafted 12 players, including goaltender Mark
Gowans of Windsor in the fourth round, Detroit-born defenseman Chris Luongo in the fifth, and forward Randy McKay
of Michigan Tech in the sixth. Neither Gowans nor any of the
six picks made in rounds 7–12 appeared in the NHL.

At 6', 180 pounds, Fedyk combined size, skill, and skating
ability. At the draft, chief scout Neil Smith expressed surprise
he was available at No. 8. "Brent is a highly skilled player, the
type that depends on skills but is not afraid to use his body,"
Smith said. "We had him rated much higher than eighth.
When it was our turn, there was no doubt, absolutely cut
and dry, that we'd take him. It was as if he was dropped into
our lap."

Smith even drew comparisons to Mike Bossy, the New
York Islanders star right winger who won his fourth consecutive Stanley Cup championship in 1983. Fedyk, Smith posited,
"is a Mike Bossy type, a natural goal-scorer, and a very skilled
player with good determination."

Fedyk made his NHL debut December 27, 1987, earning an assist on a goal by Steve Yzerman. That was one of two NHL games Fedyk played in that season. It wasn't until 1990–91 that Fedyk was a full-timer with the Wings, and the Mike Bossy talk had been left behind. Fedyk was a productive player in the minors—he had 40 goals with the Adirondack Red Wings in 1988–89, but the best he did with the Wings was 16 goals in 1990–91. In October 1992, the former first-round pick was traded to the Philadelphia Flyers for a fourth-round draft pick in the 1993 draft.

By that time, Sharples already was gone from the organization. He appeared in 105 games over three seasons, and in November 1989 was part of the package of players the Wings sent to the Edmonton Oilers in the Jimmy Carson trade. (The Oilers received Joe Murphy, Adam Graves, Petr Klima, and Sharples). Sharples never made it to the NHL again. Luongo, the forward taken in Round 5, played four games for the Wings, logging most of his 218 NHL games with the Islanders and Ottawa Senators.

Of the players the Wings drafted that year, it was McKay who enjoyed the longest NHL career, retiring with 932 games, ranking eighth all-time in the 1985 draft class. But only 83 of those came in a Wings uniform. In September 1991, NHL arbitrator Edward Houston ruled in favor of the Wings by sending McKay and Dave Barr to the New Jersey Devils as compensation for the Wings signing Troy Crowder to a three-year contract. (The Devils had asked for Bob Probert.)

It was Chiasson who had the biggest impact on the Wings. At the time of his draft, the 6′2″, 202-pound defender was scouted as a punishing hitter. "I use my size to my advantage," Chiasson said. "That's always been my game."

Chiasson split his first two seasons between the Wings and their AHL affiliate, but by April 1988, it was clear the young defenseman was on a good developmental path. Coach Jacques Demers favored him in the playoffs over veterans Doug Halward and Harold Snepsts. Chiasson delivered big hits, killed penalties, and chipped in offensively.

"He's a smart kid," Demers said. "He's got a good feel for the play."

On December 1, 1988, Chiasson registered a goal and three assists in a game against the Quebec Nordiques. The 21-year-old had established his role in the defense corps. Chiasson enjoyed his best personal season in 1992–93, when he recorded 62 points in 79 games—21 points better than Nicklas Lidström posted in 84 games—and represented the Campbell Conference in the 1993 NHL All-Star Game. When the Wings determined that they needed to bring in a Stanley Cup–proven goaltender after the debacle of the 1994 playoffs, when young Chris Osgood gave up the puck on the goal that eliminated the Wings in the first round of the playoffs, it was Chiasson who was sacrificed.

On June 29, 1994, Chiasson was traded to the Calgary Flames for Mike Vernon, who had won the Cup in 1989. Bryan Murray hadn't been willing to relinquish Chiasson, but Murray was fired June 3, and Devellano and Scotty Bowman were in charge of player personnel. Bowman didn't hesitate.

"Vernon has been a No. 1 goalie for some time, and it's very difficult to find a No. 1 goalie," Bowman said. "This was

IGOR LARIONOV

Igor Larionov wasn't among the dozen players the Wings drafted in 1985, but he was the player from that draft year who played the most games in a Wings uniform and played a central role in three Stanley Cup championships.

Larionov already was a star in his native Russia when he was drafted in the 11th round by the Vancouver Canucks. It was something of a throw-away pick, given the unlikelihood at the time he'd ever escape the Iron Curtain.

It took four years, but in May 1989, Larionov was released from the Red Army. Larionov was 28 years old. He played three years for the Canucks, then spent a season in Switzerland, which prompted the Canucks to place Larionov on waivers. He was claimed by the San Jose Sharks and enjoyed an excellent first season there in 1993–94, recording 56 points in 60 games.

Larionov came to the Wings in October 1995, in a trade that only Scotty Bowman could have explained. Larionov was a 5'9" center approaching his 35th birthday. Ray Sheppard, the player sent to the Sharks, was a 6'1" right wing who had turned 29 a few months earlier and had recorded 52 goals in 1993–94. In the lockout-shortened 1994–95 season, Sheppard put up 30 goals in 43 games—a number that extrapolated to 57 goals in a normal season.

On paper, the deal looked skewed. But in the mind of Bowman, the coach and director of player personnel, it was a steal. "This is a real class player,"

Bowman said. "He won a couple series almost sin-
gle-handedly for his team." In the spring of 1994,
Larionov had helped the Sharks upset the Wings in
the first round, contributing 10 points in the seven-
game series.

In Detroit, Larionov was reunited with Slava Fetisov, whom the Wings traded for in April 1995. The
two had helped forge a path to the NHL for Soviet
hockey players by standing up to Viktor Tikhonov.
Larionov had Olympic and World Championship
gold medals, but the silver of the Stanley Cup had
eluded him in four years in the NHL.

"It's a joy for me to play with this organization,"
Larionov said.

It became a joy for fans—and a pain for opponents—to watch as Bowman put Larionov on a line
with Sergei Fedorov and Vyacheslav Kozlov, and
paired them with Fetisov and Vladimir Konstantinov
on defense. The Russian Five debuted October 27,
1995, in a road game against the Calgary Flames.
Larionov and Kozlov each scored, and Fedorov had
two assists in the Wings' 3–0 victory.

Larionov added Stanley Cup champion to his
honorific in 1997, and again in 1998 and 2002.
He spent the better part of eight seasons with the
Wings, recording 397 points in 539 games. The
Wings didn't get anything out of the six players they
chose after the sixth round in 1985, but a savvy
trade 10 years later yielded the player from that
draft class who would leave an indelible imprint on
the franchise.

the only way to plug the gap because we weren't going to do it with a free agent."

Chiasson had 267 points in 471 games with the Wings. He wasn't who they were most excited about when they left the draft at the Toronto Convention Centre on June 16, 1985, but Chiasson developed into an All-Star and landed the Wings the goaltender who would help end a 42-year drought.

Chiasson spent two-and-a-half seasons with the Flames, finishing his career with the Hartford Whalers/Carolina Hurricanes franchise. He logged 305 points in 751 career games in the NHL.

Chiasson died on May 3, 1999, while driving under the influence. Leaving a team party just a few hours after the Hurricanes had been eliminated from the playoffs, Chiasson's pickup ran off the road. His old teammates in Detroit were devastated.

"For myself, guys who played with him, and everybody around the league, it's really sad what happened," Yzerman said. "He was a great player to have on your team, he played hard and fit in well. He played through some serious injuries, broken bones and whatnot. He was a guy who was always accountable. He never complained too much about anything.

"One thing he always used to say, and I always thought it was probably the best thing you could say when things weren't going good, was, 'Shut up and play.' That was it—don't worry about anything else, just go out and play."

25

DILEMMA AT NO. 1

IN 1985-86 THE Red Wings were a team in turmoil. They were a disappointment to their owner, Mike Ilitch, who had bought the team in 1982, and to their general manager, Jimmy Devellano. They had made the playoffs in 1984 and 1985, but instead of making progress, they regressed. Harry Neale lasted 35 games as coach, replaced by Brad Park. The Wings won eight games under Neale, nine under Park. As the season wore on, it was an open secret that the best thing that could happen to the Wings would be to finish last among the NHL's 21 teams, because then at least they'd get to draft first.

Park's decision in mid-February to keep veteran Danny Gare on the roster and send Chris Cichocki, a college free-agent signing who had shown some promise, to the minors drew some raised eyebrows from opposing general managers. Park also drew attention for what players called "tax-free, wife-free" extra cash they could earn—reportedly, players would get $1 for a "hit" and $5 for a "crunch." Park told reporters that "it's just a game—a way to have a little fun" and denied there was money involved.

The bottom line was that the Wings finished 17–57–6. At 40 points, they had 14 less than the 20th-place Los Angeles Kings.

The talk going into the draft was which player would go first: Joe Murphy, a forward from Vancouver, British Columbia, who had moved to the U.S. to play hockey at Michigan State University; or Jimmy Carson, a forward from the Detroit suburb of Grosse Pointe Woods who had moved to Canada to play junior hockey in Montreal, Quebec? "It had to do with the glamor of the Canadiens and the excitement of playing in Montreal," Carson said in 1986.

Carson recorded 70 goals and 83 assists in 1985–86 for Verdun, totaling 153 points in 69 games. That is a staggering number, but Carson wasn't even the leading scorer in the Quebec Major Junior Hockey League. Luc Robitaille—who would go on to play for the Wings from 2001 to 2003 and was part of the fabled 2002 Stanley Cup championship team, playing on the fourth line with Igor Larionov and Tomas Holmström—was tied with Guy Rouleau for first place, with 191 points.

Murphy's numbers—24 goals, 37 assists in 35 games—look sedate by comparison. Murphy, however, was convinced he had made the right decision in choosing college over junior hockey.

"It's been hard hockey to play," he said in February 1986. "It's challenging hockey. I like playing it. And I think it prepares you better for the NHL. This teaches you defense. You play more of a physical game. There's no fighting, but there's lots of hooking, clutching, grabbing, and hitting."

Devellano had signed five college free agents the previous season but expressed reservations about drafting one with such a coveted pick. "It's a crapshoot, because you never know what you're going to get," Devellano said at the time. "And the one thing I can't tell about college kids is how tough they are, because there is no fighting."

Michigan State coach Ron Mason downplayed that dimension of the game, saying, "Fighting isn't toughness. Toughness is a willingness to go into the boards and take a hit to make a play. And Joe Murphy is tough."

Wings scout Neil Smith didn't question Murphy's toughness. "He's got a mean streak in him," Smith said. "He'll get even with somebody who gives him a shot."

Mason cautioned that Murphy would be best served by another season of college hockey. But after seeing Murphy play at the 1986 International Ice Hockey Federation World Junior Championship, where Murphy's 14 points tied for the tournament scoring lead, Smith deemed Murphy ready for the NHL. "He was great," Smith said.

There was speculation the Wings would be willing to trade the pick in exchange for another first-round pick and a defenseman. In March, Devellano described himself as "very, very unhappy with the way the season has gone. I'm not happy with the defense, which was on a 400 goals-against pace." But Devellano, taking direct aim at management under previous owner Bruce Norris, also noted, "Unlike past regimes, I never gave up a draft pick to try to improve our team."

Still, Devellano was willing to listen to offers for the first selection. The Edmonton Oilers called him. So did the Minnesota North Stars. Both tried to tempt Devellano with established players. The offer from the Oilers included a goaltender, and while Devellano didn't reveal a name, it was believed to be Stanley Cup champion and NHL All-Star Grant Fuhr.

Devellano didn't bite. The day of the draft, he was all smiles. "My phone didn't ring at all last night," Devellano said, "and am I ever glad of that."

The Wings delegation on June 21, 1986, at the Forum in Montreal numbered Devellano, the scouting staff, new coach Jacques Demers, and several members of the Ilitch family. They were surrounded by a dozen television cameramen.

Shortly after 10:00 AM, Smith made the announcement. "The Detroit Red Wings are pleased to announce the first time a college player has been taken first in the draft. From NCAA champion Michigan State University Spartans, a center, Joe Murphy."

Murphy was 6'1", 190 pounds, and 18 years old. He was billed as a very good skater with excellent speed, a heavy slap shot, accurate wrist shot, and above-average passing skills. "Joe Murphy doesn't do anything poorly, and he does nothing excellent," read Smith's scouting report. "I love his involvement level and that little mean streak he has."

(Smith's report on Carson was less rosy: "Jimmy Carson has excellent offensive skills, but he adds nothing defensively. May be a defensive liability. And he does not body check.")

Murphy showed off another of his attributes soon after being drafted: his sense of humor. Asked how he liked his

Joe Murphy (left) was drafted No. 1 in 1986 and Brent Fedyk was drafted No. 8 in 1985. Pictured on the eve of the 1989–90 season. *Photo by Mary Schroeder*

pizza, Murphy smiled and replied, "Any way I can get it, as long as it's Little Caesars."

Murphy was surrounded by family and friends at the Forum when he was drafted. Bill Jamieson, the team's publicist, handed him a Wings sweater with Murphy's name on the back and the No. 1. Murphy's mother, Jane, had tears in her eyes. His father, Pat, tried to put the feeling into words.

"We're so proud of him," he said. "Joe has worked so hard for this."

Murphy slipped the jersey on over his sportcoat. "It's great, really great," Murphy said. "It's been building the whole year, but I still can't believe it. I'm really happy it's Detroit." Slowed by a throng of media, Murphy made his way to the Wings table, where he posed for pictures with Devellano and Demers.

The Wings did not agree with Mason that Murphy would be best served by returning for a second year at Michigan State. Devellano was confident he could get Murphy signed in time for training camp, because "he's going to get a bundle of money."

The Wings bundled up Murphy with a four-year contract worth nearly $1 million. Devellano made room for Murphy on the roster by trading centers Claude Loiselle and Kelly Kisio. But Murphy still had to convince Demers to put him in the lineup, and that audition didn't go smoothly. Murphy looked good in exhibition games, posting four assists in six games, but a lack of discipline led to a demotion to the American Hockey League's Adirondack Red Wings in Glens Falls, New York.

"Murphy has a very promising career, but he needs to understand that he has to mature," Demers said in early October. "He missed a curfew, he was late for a bus, and he missed a plane. It's totally unacceptable for an 18-year-old to do that."

Murphy explained he had missed the team flight to Dallas because he had driven to City Airport first, and by the time he realized his mistake and made it to Metro Airport, he was too late. He didn't like the demotion, but understood it.

"I'm not mad at them," Murphy said. "They just want to get the players playing by the rules."

Murphy was recalled 10 days later, in time for the Wings' home opener on October 11. Repentant, Murphy said he would "just stick to hockey. I'm not going to be breaking the rules, that's for sure."

Murphy earned his first NHL point October 15, in a game against the Kings. But it was Carson—the guy whom the Wings passed over in the draft that summer—who looked like a star, scoring two goals and assisting on another in the 4–3 Los Angeles victory. Afterward, he was asked about the draft. "They felt he was the guy they needed, and I respect their decision," Carson said.

Murphy lasted five games before the Wings felt he would be better off getting more playing time in the minors. It was a disappointment, but deemed a temporary demotion for a player who was still maturing. Murphy turned 19 on October 16.

"There is no question Joe Murphy is going to be a very important part of the Detroit Red Wings' future," Demers said. That was at the end of October. At the start of December, the Wings and Murphy both sounded sour. Management was upset Murphy had reported to the minors two days late. Murphy was upset he had to be in the minors.

"I was really down in the dumps," he said.

His game showed it. He wasn't practicing or playing hard. People around him tried to do damage control, pointing to his age, to the crippling expectations placed on a teenager. Murphy's parents traveled from Vancouver to Glens Falls to visit him.

February brought signs of improvement. Murphy registered several multiple-point games in the minors, showing off that offensive skill set that made the Wings choose him over Carson. But at the start of March, Murphy was in trouble again, this time for goofing off in practice. Bill Dineen, coach of the farm club, suspended Murphy for three games. The team won every game.

There was chatter at the trade deadline that the Wings might be better off to unload Murphy. The Canadiens were interested. But it was only nine months since the Wings had left the draft table raving about Murphy's potential—too soon to give up on him.

The Wings' patience looked like it would be rewarded during training camp in 1987. Demers raved about Murphy, describing his play and attitude as phenomenal. His work ethic had improved, but he still disappointed. By Christmas 1987, Murphy had five goals and five assists in 30 games. Trade talk resurfaced. There was chatter about the Edmonton Oilers offering defenseman Paul Coffey for Murphy, Shawn Burr, and two No. 1 draft choices—but that would have fleeced the Wings.

The Wings tried benching Murphy. After a 6–3 loss to the Penguins in Pittsburgh on December 26, the Wings next traveled to Minnesota. On the way to the airport, Demers ordered the bus driver to pull into a roadside restaurant parking lot, and Demers placed a call to Dineen. The upshot was that Murphy didn't play the next two games.

"What I think Joe does to us, he gives us some sugar and then takes it away," Demers said. "We'd like him to play hard every game. There's been times where we've been very impressed with his play. There's been times when he's not there at all."

On January 8, 1988, the Wings played the Kings. It marked the first time since the 1986 draft that Murphy and Carson faced one another. Since that day, Murphy had six goals and 13 points in 37 NHL games. Carson had 61 goals and 130 points in 122 games.

"There's no use getting down on me so soon," Murphy said. "Some guys come in and do it right away, and it might take some guys a little longer."

By January 1989, the Wings were irrevocably down on Murphy. The hope that he would become a cornerstone of a Stanley Cup team was extinguished. He no longer fit into the team's plans.

"When it comes to Joe Murphy, I have a very, very clear conscience," Devellano said. "Joe Murphy has been given every opportunity to win a spot. But there comes a time when you have to produce. When it doesn't happen, you have to make decisions."

Murphy was sent to the minors. Again.

The Wings sent Murphy away for good on November 2, 1989, in a blockbuster trade with the Edmonton Oilers. The six-player swap saw Murphy, Petr Klima, Adam Graves, and Jeff Sharples go to the Oilers for Carson and Kevin McClelland. (This was the second blockbuster trade for Carson; the Kings had traded him to the Oilers as part of the August 9, 1988, deal that saw Wayne Gretzky become a King.)

It was the biggest deal Devellano had orchestrated since being named general manager of the Wings in July 1982. His prize pick in 1986 had recorded just 14 goals and 32 points

1986

Of the dozen players the Wings drafted in 1986, 10 went on to appear in the NHL.

The Wings used their first two picks to take local stars, selecting Joe Murphy from Michigan State at No. 1 and fellow center Adam Graves from the Windsor Spitfires at No. 22.

The other picks were defenseman Derek Mayer (third round, No. 43), goaltender Tim Cheveldae (fourth round, No. 64), forward Johan Garpenlov (fifth round, No. 85), defenseman Jay Stark (sixth round, No. 106), defenseman Par Djoos (seventh round, No. 127), defenseman Dean Morton (eighth round, No. 148), forward Marc Potvin (ninth round, No. 169), goaltender Scott King (10th round, No. 190), forward Tom Bissett (11th round, No. 211), and defenseman Peter Ekroth (12th round, No. 232).

"After we got Adam Graves, they could have escorted us out of the Forum and we could have gone away with smiles on our faces," Neil Smith, the team's chief scout, said on June 21 at the event in Montreal. "We got two guys we had rated in the top 10 overall. We should be ecstatic, and we are."

The scouting report on Graves rated him as physically strong in addition to having a lot of puck handling and play-making skills. Introduced to the Detroit media at a luncheon at Joe Louis Arena in August, Graves sported spiked hair and an attitude of gratitude. "All through the season I knew where I was rated," Graves said. "I was hoping in some way that maybe I could get a chance to play with the Red Wings. I played right across the river, and I've kind of found a home in Windsor."

Graves would go on to play 1,152 games in the NHL, though only 78 for the Wings. In November 1989, he was part of the trade between the Wings and Edmonton Oilers that saw Murphy and Jimmy Carson swap teams. Graves played two seasons for the Oilers, winning the Stanley Cup in 1990, and won a second Stanley Cup in 1994 as a member of the New York Rangers. He finished his career with the San Jose Sharks, retiring in 2003.

Mayer (17 NHL games) never played for the Wings. Morton made his lone NHL appearance in a Wings uniform in 1989–90, and King appeared in two NHL games, both for the Wings. Bissett's five games came with the Wings in 1990–91. Stark and Ekroth never made it to the NHL.

Cheveldae made a significant mark on the team, rising to be the No. 1 goalie from 1990 to 1993. He played 72 games in 1991–92 and was named to the 1992 All-Star Game. (Back then, such news was delivered via fax. Cheveldae, Steve Yzerman, and Sergei Fedorov were on the sheet that arrived at Joe Louis Arena on January 7, marking the first time the Wings sent three players to the game since Gordie Howe, Frank Mahovlich, and Carl Brewer were named to the 1970 game.)

At a time the roster included Yzerman, Fedorov, and Nicklas Lidström—all future first-ballot Hockey Hall of Famers—Cheveldae's playoff struggles left him to serve as scapegoat. In 1993–94 he lost the starting job to newcomer Chris Osgood. On a cold morning in early March, general manager Bryan Murray knocked on Cheveldae's hotel room door. Cheveldae met him in the lobby 10 minutes later to find Murray had traded Cheveldae to the Winnipeg Jets for goalie Bob Essensa. Just like that, Cheveldae had gone from rising star to discarded. He appeared in 264 regular-season games in a Wings uniform, posting a 3.40 goals-against average and .883 save percentage.

Garpenlov lasted 609 games in the NHL, but his tenure with the Wings was short. Debuting with 18 goals in 1990–91, he was traded in March 1992 to the San Jose Sharks for Bob McGill, a hard-nosed defenseman and frequent sparring partner of Wings forward Bob Probert.

Potvin played 121 NHL games, but he was another one who didn't spend much time with the Wings. He played 14 games between 1990 and 1992 before being part of the trade that sent Jimmy Carson to the Los Angeles Kings for defenseman Paul Coffey.

While several of their selections from the 1986 draft played for the Wings, it was, ultimately, not a very good one for them. Murphy was a bust; their desire to unload him necessitated losing Graves, and Cheveldae wasn't the man to lead them to the Cup. Murphy played 90 games for the Wings, and Graves, 78. The smiles and ecstasy from the draft dissipated into disappointment and regret.

in 90 career games with the Wings. "I guess I erred in picking Joe Murphy instead of Jimmy Carson," Devellano said.
"I don't mind admitting my mistakes."

Murphy would go on to win the Stanley Cup with the
Oilers in 1990. It was during a game against the Wings, on
January 9, 1991, that Murphy suffered the first of a series of
concussions. Murphy came around the back of the net at Joe
Louis Arena when Shawn Burr rammed into him. Murphy
went airborne, and his head slammed into the railing. He was
helped off the ice.

"I was spewing blood everywhere," Murphy said.

A contract holdout that lasted well into the 1992–93 season soured things there, and Murphy was dealt to the Chicago
Blackhawks in February 1993. In July 1996, Murphy signed
as a free agent with the St. Louis Blues. They dealt him to
the San Jose Sharks the next season. Murphy was very briefly
reunited with Neil Smith, the man who so proudly had called
Murphy's name with the No. 1 pick in 1986, in November
1999, when Smith, then the general manager of the New York
Rangers, offered Murphy a tryout. But Murphy signed with
the Boston Bruins, after accusing the Rangers of sawing his
sticks. Murphy's erratic behavior—he yelled at Bruins coach
Pat Burns and openly criticized teammates—landed him on
the waiver wire after 26 games, and the Washington Capitals
decided to give him a chance. He played sparingly for them
for two seasons, and on December 1, 2000, Murphy played
his last game in the NHL. He recorded 233 goals and 528
points in 779 games. The former first overall draft pick had
earned approximately $13 million.

As his NHL career faded into the distance, Murphy's life unraveled. In 2018, he was found in Kenora, Ontario. Murphy was 50 years old and homeless. In an October article, the *Detroit Free Press* described Murphy as a lost soul, a man with a weathered and scarred face who went barefoot and wore a winter coat full of holes. Murphy slept on a small patch of grass near a gas station, wrapped up in a blue blanket.

"It's crazy," he said, "but I love my life and this place."

He conceded he had mental health problems, and admitted he had done crystal meth. "I've had some depression and I've had some anxiety," Murphy said. "I think it's a combination of things that have happened to me. Maybe a brain injury from concussion, for sure, and from some other things that have happened to me in my life, and I think it's affected me emotionally with anger. I've gotten very good…. The anger is a sin, and in the temple, Christ displayed how he got rid of the anger and how you cannot sustain the anger."

In a moment of lucidity, Murphy remembered that June day in 1986 in Montreal.

"My grandfather came to the draft," he said. "It was just a big deal for me. They watched a lot of games, my grandpa and grandma."

JIMMY CARSON

"This is exactly like I wanted it."

That was Jimmy Carson's response when, three and a half years after the Wings had passed him over in the draft, he finally became a member of his hometown NHL team. On November 2, 1989, Carson was introduced as a Wing in the Olympia Room at Joe Louis Arena. Coach Jacques Demers presented Carson, who was born in Southfield and grew up in Grosse Pointe Woods, a white Wings sweater bearing No. 10. (That number previously had been worn by Alex Delvecchio, but would not be retired until November 10, 1991.)

"I'm ecstatic," Carson said. "I've waited a long time to put this jersey on."

As a little kid, Carson used to attend games at Olympia Stadium, where his dad, Chuck, ran the parking lots. In 1986 Carson was a highly regarded prospect, but the Wings deemed Joe Murphy a better all-around player and chose him with the first pick in the draft. Carson went second, to the Los Angeles Kings.

He outplayed Murphy right away, quickly becoming one of the best young players in the game, recording 55 goals and 107 points in his second NHL season. That led to his inclusion in the blockbuster trade of the decade, on August 9, 1988: Carson, Martin Gelinas, the Kings' first-round draft picks in 1989, 1991, and 1993, plus $15 million in cash, went to the Edmonton Oilers for Wayne Gretzky, Marty McSorley, and Mike Krushelnyski.

Carson, who had just turned 20, was shocked. "I think going to Edmonton will mean a lot of pressure," he said. "If people think I'm going to replace Wayne Gretzky, absolutely not."

Carson had an excellent first season with the Oilers, recording 100 points in 1988–89. But he wasn't happy there; the Oilers had a passionate fan base, but the city left Carson cold. "I'm an American kid," Carson said in February 1989. "I'm used to big cities. Edmonton is a very small city, very small. I think everybody in the world knows I'd love to play in Detroit. It's been my dream since I was five years old. I was heartbroken when they didn't take me."

Rumors of a trade swirled, but the Wings players involved were Bob Probert and Petr Klima, guys whose alcohol-fueled troubles led Edmonton hockey media to refer to them as "The Booze Brothers."

As a second season in Edmonton got underway, Carson grew so disenchanted he didn't show up for practice in mid-October, leading to a suspension. It was clear the relationship between Carson and the Oilers—and the city—was over. "Yankee Go Home," read a headline in one Edmonton paper.

Talks with the Wings revived. Finally on November 2, the sides struck a deal: the Wings got Carson, Kevin McClelland, and a fifth-round draft pick in 1991 for Murphy, Petr Klima, Adam Graves, and Jeff Sharples.

Carson debuted in a Wings uniform November 4, making a fast and favorable impression on his new teammates. "He's a real smart player," Steve Yzerman said. "He knows how to get into position for a shot."

Demers, the coach, said Carson, "did the things we're used to seeing from Steve Yzerman."

Carson played for the Wings nearly four years, but he never was the star. The first season he played behind Yzerman, and the next season Sergei Fedorov joined the lineup, making Carson the third center on the depth chart. Carson's best season was in 1991–92, when he tallied 34 goals and 69 points in 80 games.

"Sometimes I think about being somewhere else," he said in early January 1993. "But I'm not the kind of guy who looks back."

At the end of January, Carson was part of another blockbuster trade. This time he went back to the Kings in a multiplayer deal that netted the Wings Paul Coffey, at that time the highest-scoring defenseman in NHL history. Once again, Carson was shocked.

"That's the only word I can think of to describe it," Carson said.

Carson's NHL career lasted 626 games, yielding 561 points. He finished his playing days in Detroit with the Vipers, winning the International Hockey League Turner Cup championship in 1997 and retiring after the following season.

26

WHY NOT DETROIT?

FOR YEARS, THE NHL Draft was held in Montreal, and if not Montreal, somewhere else in Canada. It was an event held by Canadians, largely for Canadians.

Soon after he was named general manager of the Red Wings in 1982, Jimmy Devellano set about to change that. When he attended NHL Board of Governors meetings, he would bug his cohorts: Why not someplace else? Why not Detroit?

The Queen Elizabeth Hotel housed the draft from its inception in 1963 until 1972. In 1973, it was held at the Mount Royal Hotel, and from 1974 to 1977, at the NHL offices in Montreal. The Queen Elizabeth played host again in 1978 and 1979.

The event was private until 1980, when the general public was admitted to the Montreal Forum. It wasn't until 1985, when the draft went head-to-head with the Montreal Grand

Prix, that it was moved elsewhere—and then it was just to Toronto, to the Convention Centre. By next year, it was back at the Montreal Forum.

Finally in 1987, the draft moved outside Canada. On June 13, Joe Louis Arena was filled with general managers and scouts, with players and their girlfriends and parents and grandparents, and with about 5,000 fans. They were served soda pop and free Little Caesars pizza to nourish them through the 12-round event. Marian Ilitch, secretary-treasurer and wife of owner mike Ilitch, watched as day unfolded.

"I love the draft," she said. "But in the last rounds, I start feeling badly for the kids who aren't going to be picked."

Seeking to make the most of the event, the NHL staged a Hockey Hall of Fame exhibit at neighboring Cobo Hall, and celebrated the induction of 10 men to the Hall of Fame, including John Ziegler, the Michigan native and NHL president who got his start in hockey as a lawyer for the Wings.

The Buffalo Sabres finished with a league-worst 28–44–8 record, earning the right to make the first selection. They chose Pierre Turgeon, a 6'3", 217-pound center who would go on to be an NHL All-Star and Lady Byng Memorial Trophy recipient.

The Wings held the 11th pick. While Devellano and chief scout Neil Smith waited their turn, the New Jersey Devils selected a player with the second pick who would become a major piece in the Wings' Stanley Cup championship 10 years later—Brendan Shanahan, a left wing out of the Ontario Hockey League.

Smith rated the top seven players available as: 1) Turgeon, 2) Shanahan, 3) Dave Archibald (right wing), 4) Glen

Wesley (defenseman), 5) Jimmy Waite (goaltender), 6) Wayne McBean (defenseman), and 7) Chris Joseph (defenseman). Smith was only slightly off: Wesley went at No. 3 to the Boston Bruins; McBean at No. 4 to the Los Angeles Kings; Joseph at No. 5 to the Pittsburgh Penguins; Archibald at No. 6 to the Minnesota North Stars; and Waite went at No. 8 to the Chicago Blackhawks.

The player who would end up leading the 1987 draft class with 1,641 points in 1,378 games, Joe Sakic, was taken at No. 15, by the Quebec Nordiques.

The Wings were only a year removed from using the No. 1 pick in 1986 on Joe Murphy, who already had made that choice look like a poor one. Murphy's lackadaisical approach to professional hockey pushed people within the organization to be extra careful in doing research on potential prospects. So, when coach Jacques Demers was asked about the player the Wings would take with their first selection in that year's draft, he said, "I talked with the boy's parents, his coaches, everybody. He's a good kid."

The kid was Yves Racine, a defenseman who had put up 50 points in 70 games with Longueuils in the Quebec Major Junior Hockey League. Racine was one of 13 players the Wings drafted that day at the Joe. Gord Kruppke, a defensive specialist, was taken in the second round, at No. 32, and Bob Wilkie, an offensive-minded defenseman, was taken in the second round, at No. 41, with a pick acquired in a trade with the Philadelphia Flyers.

"This was a draft for the future," Devellano said.

There wasn't much to that future. Kruppke appeared in 23 games spread over three seasons and washed out of the

NHL by 1994. He never registered a point. Wilkie appeared in 18 games, eight of them with the Wings in 1990–91.

Racine was in the stands at the Joe with his parents and sister among a crowd of about 5,000 when Smith announced the selection. Racine kissed his mother, shook hands with his father, and posed for pictures. "I feel very happy," he said. "It was a surprise for me to be selected in the first round of the draft. Detroit is a good organization."

The NHL's Central Scouting Bureau had Racine pegged to go in the middle of the second round. But Smith had scouted Racine some 15 times and viewed him as a player who just needed to grow stronger. He had a powerful and accurate shot and was considered an excellent passer.

Racine lasted a little more than three seasons with the Wings. On October 5, 1993, he was traded to the Philadelphia Flyers for defenseman Terry Carkner, who was the sort of hard-nosed player deemed necessary for a team that kept coming up short in the playoffs. Flyers teammates had nicknamed Carkner "Norman," after Norman Bates of the *Psycho* movies because of the way Carkner responded when challenged by opponents.

"He's not very fancy, but he's strong and major-league tough," general manager Bryan Murray said.

It was a trade almost three years to the day that finally brought the Wings the player they needed to get to the Stanley Cup. In the years since his name had been called by the New Jersey Devils on the draft floor at Joe Louis Arena, Shanahan had gone from the Devils to the St. Louis Blues and onto the Hartford Whalers. He impressed everywhere he went, but Shanahan was not impressed with Hartford. He craved more than a small-market team with an unstable future and sought a trade.

Enter the Wings. Murray had been fired in June 1994, and Devellano and Scotty Bowman shared responsibility for player personnel. It was now a decade and a half since the Ilitches had bought the team, and still the Stanley Cup was elusive.

After much talking back and forth between Wings management and Whalers general manager Jim Rutherford, the Wings acquired Shanahan and journeyman defenseman Brian Glynn for Keith Primeau (who had been holding out in a contract dispute), defenseman Paul Coffey, and a first-round pick in the 1997 draft. Shanahan was everything the Wings desired—big (6'3", 220 pounds), tough (he had roughly 50 fights to his credit), and skilled (599 points in 634 games).

"Hockey-wise, I think everybody knows he's a hard-nosed player," Scotty Bowman said. "I don't know how many players are like him in the league, a power winger that can score."

They were so eager to get him into their lineup they dispatched team owner Mike Ilitch's private jet to pick up Shanahan in Hartford and bring him to Detroit in time for the home opener, on October 9, 1996. He arrived at the Joe at 6:44 PM and was on the ice 11 minutes later wearing a No. 14 sweater with an alternate's captain A on his shoulder.

"I am joining a spectacular hockey team, and I hope to be a major piece," Shanahan said that night. "The one thing you can say about the Detroit Red Wings, it's very difficult to get them off their game. Obviously, their game plan is to win the Stanley Cup. That's my goal as well. There is pressure. I welcome it. It's what I want. I like being in the big game, big moments of a game."

Shanahan had a big game October 21, when he scored his first two goals in a Wings uniform. He scored twice again the next game. On November 27, he scored his 300th career goal while recording his eighth career hat trick. He and linemate Steve Yzerman had such chemistry they were both named to the 1997 NHL All-Star Game, in San Jose, California. But the Wings hadn't gotten Shanahan for what he could do in the regular season. He already had proven he could score 50 goals. Twice.

It was what he could do for them in the playoffs that made the Wings flip for the former No. 2 pick. Shanahan delivered the series-winning goal in the first round of the 1997 playoffs, dispatching the Blues when he went to the net and stuffed a rebound on Grant Fuhr in Game 6. (Pierre Turgeon, the No. 1 pick in the '87 draft, was in uniform for the Blues by then. He scored a goal in the second period that would have tied the game, but officials waved it off because of the skate-in-the-crease rule.)

Shanahan scored only once in the second round against the Mighty Ducks of Anaheim, but it was one for the history books: at 17:03 of the second overtime in Game 4, Shanahan put away another series.

"We felt we deserved to win," he said. "We didn't want to be flying across the country anymore."

Shanahan scored nine times in the 1997 playoffs, packing 17 points into the 20 games it took the Wings to end a 42-year drought. On June 7, 1997, Shanahan hoisted the

LOCAL FAVORITE

The crowd favorite at the 1987 draft was defenseman Adam Burt, a Detroit native whose family history had a connection to Gordie Howe. He was selected in the second round, at No. 39, by the Hartford Whalers, who employed Howe as their director of player development.

Burt's dad, Harry Burt, worked at Olympia Stadium for four seasons in the maintenance department back when Howe was a player. Some nights that included scraping octopus off the ice.

Harry Burt was among family members at the Joe who started chanting Adam Burt's name when the Wings passed on him to select Yves Racine at No. 11. When the Wings passed on Burt in the second round twice—first selecting Gord Kruppke, then Bob Wilkie—fans booed.

"We do feel some pressure," general manager Jimmy Devellano said. "But I can't let the fans influence me. We're the ones who see the game and watch these kids play."

The fans may have been onto something, though. Burt played 737 NHL games—more than Racine (508), Kruppke (23), and Wilkie (18) combined.

"I think Hartford got the better player," Harry Burt said. "The Wings thought they were drafting a better player. That's their job. They get fired if they make mistakes."

Stanley Cup in the same arena in which he had been drafted 10 years earlier.

When Devellano first asked, "Why not Detroit?," it was about the draft. Then Shanahan wanted a place to thrive, and why not Detroit?

Shanahan played for the Wings for nine seasons, winning three Stanley Cups. When he departed in the summer of 2006, sensing it was time to move on when Yzerman retired, Shanahan had recorded 633 points in 716 games wearing a Wings uniform.

27

THE BIG
CANADIAN CENTER

WHEN THE RED Wings made their first pick in the 1990 draft, they went the traditional route and chose a Canadian. There was a Czech player available who would turn out to the best of the class, but the Wings had their eyes on Keith Primeau, with visions of playing him on a line with Bob Probert and Jimmy Carson. At 18 years old, Primeau already was 6'5", 220 pounds, and had paced the Ontario Hockey League with 127 points in 65 games with the Niagara Falls Thunder. Primeau was a center, but early on the Wings saw his appeal in a different position.

"We think he could be a better left winger on a major league roster," general manager Jimmy Devellano said. "He would be a tremendous asset roaming up and down that left side."

Nick Polano, then the assistant general manager, raved about Jaromír Jágr after scouting him at the World Championship in Switzerland, but there was hesitancy to take a European with the first pick.

"I don't feel we can take a boy and teach him a new language and go through all the other adjustments that are required," Devellano said. (The Pittsburgh Penguins took him at No. 5. Jágr was far and away the best of the draft class—his 1,921 points crushed the 1,065 points recorded by Keith Tkachuk, the second-most productive player of the 1990 draft.)

Primeau did everything he could to reinforce the selection that fall. There hadn't been a junior-age player to stick with the Wings since Yzerman in 1983, but Primeau showed such strides in becoming an NHL player, higher-ups in the organization were smitten. "His work ethic has been outstanding," coach Bryan Murray said in October 1990.

In early November, Murray tried Primeau on the left wing next to Sergei Fedorov in an effort to generate more scoring throughout the lineup. But a five-game losing streak left Primeau on the outside looking in, and he was sent to the minors for a conditioning stint in mid-November. By mid-December he was back in Detroit and back to making the Wings look smart for drafting him. He scored his first goal December 11 and added two assists the next game.

"It's starting to happen for him," Murray said.

It started, then stalled. The Wings urged their big rookie to play with more physicality, but it only came in spurts. His play with the puck wasn't much better—from mid-February until his season was cut short in late March because of hemorrhoids, Primeau registered just one point, an assist. This wasn't what the Wings envisioned when they drafted him.

That the organization might be better off trading him became a conversation topic in his second season. It wasn't a good look for the Wings, who had had to give up on their prize pick from the 1986 draft, Joe Murphy, trading him to the Edmonton Oilers in November 1989. In September 1991 it emerged that Primeau was the main part of what the Oilers wanted in a potential Grant Fuhr trade. No thank you, Murray told his counterpart in Edmonton, Glen Sather.

"What he wanted was unbelievable," Murray said. "I wouldn't do it."

Nor would the Wings put Primeau in the lineup, however. He didn't impress in practices, and in late October, he was assigned to the minors. "He's got to play, he's got to get some ice time," Murray said. "He has to become an important member on a team." Primeau was a few weeks shy of his 20th birthday.

His name came up in trade rumors again in February 1992, this time stoked by talks of Eric Lindros coming to Detroit. (The asking price by the Quebec Nordiques, who had drafted the disgruntled center at No. 1 in 1991, was absurd: Primeau, Sergei Fedorov, and Nicklas Lidström.)

Primeau reappeared in the Wings' lineup on a line with Steve Yzerman and Ray Sheppard. Primeau registered 16 points in 35 games in his second year, and inconsistency remained his calling card.

It seemed encouraging when Primeau showed up at his third camp hungry to show he belonged in the lineup, eager to prove he could be the left wing the Wings had drafted him

Keith Primeau at his home with his Mickey Mouse collection, October 4, 1994.
Photo by Steven R. Nickerson

to be. He played assertive, physical hockey and said all the right things. "This summer I did a lot of thinking," he said. "It's time to do something."

So the Wings hoped. Two years isn't much to judge a draft on in the big picture, but the fact was the two guys picked immediately after Primeau already had established themselves as stars. Mike Ricci, taken at No. 4 by the Philadelphia Flyers, had 97 points in 148 games. Jágr, the fifth pick, already was leading the draft class with 126 points in 150 games.

Primeau had 31 points in 93 games.

Primeau's thinking didn't match his performance as the season progressed. He was moved from left wing to center in November. In December, his name came up when the Wings were in pursuit of Winnipeg defenseman Phil Housley. In January, it was a purported trade involving Oilers forward Esa Tikkanen.

"It seems like there's bigger deals and different players mentioned every day," Primeau said.

The Wings kept holding onto Primeau because they kept seeing hints of the big power forward he could be. Players with his size and skill weren't easy to come by, and hope remained that he just needed to mature—that one day it would click, and he'd be the best pick in the draft.

Fans were not as patient. When Primeau was introduced before the home opener on October 13, 1993, he was greeted by boos. The result was a dismal performance from the 21-year-old. "I'm an emotional guy, maybe too emotional," Primeau said. "I take to heart what people say. When it's a compliment, I'm ecstatic. When it's the opposite—well, I took it personally. I was petrified the whole night. I didn't want to touch the puck."

It was a tenuous time for Primeau. Scotty Bowman had been named head coach, a sign of ownership's frustration with the lack of playoff success. Bowman was renowned for being quirky, was renowned for knowing how to push players' buttons to get the most out of them—and if that wasn't possible, for moving on from them.

Primeau responded by scoring 31 goals and 73 points in 78 games in 1993–94, earning top marks from Bowman. "Keith has become very dependable," Bowman said in March 1994. He's one of only five big centers in the league. Keith is a nice commodity to have."

The trips to the minors were over. Primeau played like a high-end draft pick. His confidence had never been higher. "Detroit never backed down from my development process, and I owe them a lot," Primeau said. "It had been tough not performing as well as I, the fans, and the organization expected. Now, the way things have transpired, I can sit back and laugh."

The laughter didn't last. The start of the 1994–95 season was delayed until January because of a labor dispute between the NHL and the Players Association. Primeau turned up at training camp out of shape. Fans went back to booing him.

On draft day in 1990, Devellano had overruled his scouts who wanted Jágr because Primeau looked like the type of player who could turbocharge a contender. When it didn't happen with Murray as coach, Bowman was brought in. But the Wings were ousted in the first round in the 1994 playoffs and swept in the Stanley Cup Final in 1995. In 1996, they lasted three rounds.

Meanwhile, Primeau had tired of his time in Detroit. He wasn't the star center—Yzerman and Fedorov absorbed that spotlight. As training camp neared in the fall of 1996, Primeau, just a few months shy of his 25th birthday, wondered if he'd be a better fit elsewhere.

"I guess a part of me would like to move on," he said in September. "It seems as though I'm not wanted by so many people."

It was a messy situation. Primeau was under contract for one more year, at $800,000. Negotiations to rework his contract stalled after he rejected a six-year, $10.2 million deal. He could hold out and hope that would force a resolution. Primeau knew the Wings had dealt with other malcontents— Shawn Burr, Ray Sheppard—by trading them.

"I think that's ultimately the card I play, force their backs against the wall," Primeau said. "Anytime you do that, most people are going to come out fighting. That could be the culmination of what happens in that scenario."

Primeau may have felt unwanted, but he had one very influential player in his corner: the captain. "I want Keith Primeau on my team," Yzerman said. "Our team, to win a Stanley Cup, people talk about being bigger, being physical. I want Primeau on my team. He's a good player. He can help us win a Stanley Cup. You want to win a Stanley Cup in Detroit, you need guys like him."

Still, Primeau wanted out.

"Primeau didn't like the way we used him," Devellano said in 2021. "He wanted to be a center. We wanted him to be a left wing. I said, 'Keith, we've got Fedorov and Yzerman. If you want to be the third or fourth center, you're not going to be happy with the minutes. By playing wing, you get top-six minutes.' Well, he wasn't happy about it. He was unhappy."

When Primeau didn't report to camp, the Wings suspended him.

While Primeau held out, management holed up. Bowman and Devellano shared player personnel duties. They had a roster loaded with star players, but there was no sparkle from a Stanley Cup. Devellano and Bowman evaluated the roster. Primeau was coming off a poor playoff performance, with one goal and five points in 17 games.

The Wings were ready to let go of their prize pick from 1990, but he wasn't the only change Devellano and Bowman considered. Paul Coffey was an All-Star defenseman who had won his third James Norris Memorial Trophy in 1995, the season he led the Wings in scoring with 58 points in 45 games. He had put up 14 points in the 1996 playoffs, but the lasting memory of that run came in Game 1 of the Western Conference Finals against the Colorado Avalanche, when Coffey accidentally scored into his own net.

Bowman had inherited Coffey, had inherited Primeau when he was named coach in 1993. He was ready to move on from both.

"I have a disgruntled Primeau and a disgruntled coach who wants me to make a move," Devellano said. "It just so happens we got lucky. Out it comes, out of Hartford, the word comes that Brendan Shanahan wants out. He doesn't want to play in a small market, he wants to be in a big market, play for a good team. Scotty didn't give a care about

Primeau. He said we can live without him. He didn't care for Coffey."

Still, there was some hesitancy.

"We vacillated a bit because it might have turned into a deal that didn't look so good," Devellano said. "What if Primeau blossomed? Coffey had a Norris. Shanahan had already been a bunch of places. But Brendan was a big, strong power forward, and we had an Yzerman or a Fedorov he could play with. So we made the deal."

In order to make the trade work, the Wings had to first sign Primeau. He agreed to a three-year deal worth $5.2 million in early October, but reneged when he found out Petr Nedved, who the Vancouver Canucks had taken one spot ahead of Primeau in 1990, had received a one-year, $2 million contract. Then Coffey announced he wouldn't report to the Whalers.

On October 6, Bowman told reporters the deal was dead. He said the same thing the next day and the day after that. But on the evening of October 8, Bowman spoke with Whalers general manager Jim Rutherford, and on October 9, the sides ironed out the details of the deal. Primeau hadn't agreed to terms, and Coffey hadn't agreed to report, but both sides were eager to rid themselves of disgruntled players.

"You have an unsettling situation, and it's going to fester over time," Rutherford said. "And there wasn't a better deal to be made."

Primeau never did become the dominant player befitting someone drafted at such a stratospheric spot. He spent three seasons with the Hartford franchise and finished his career with the Philadelphia Flyers. His 619 point in 909 games ranks 13th among the 1990 class, behind the Wings' third-round pick, Slava Kozlov (853 points in 1,182 games). Primeau was booed in his first game back at Joe Louis Arena on November 4, 1996. He had spent six forgettable years with the franchise that drafted him, and his biggest contribution was landing them the player who on June 7, 1997, helped the Wings win the Stanley Cup.

28

NIKLAS KRONWALL

WHEN NIKLAS KRONWALL was a teenager playing hockey in his native Sweden, his juniors coach used to suggest he eat two liters of ice cream as often as he could, in the hopes such an intake of calories would add to Kronwall's slight frame.

Kronwall was eligible to be drafted in 1999, but even the Red Wings, not usually deterred by a player's lack of size, passed on him that year. "We kind of liked him, but he was a small guy, a really small guy," Jim Nill said in 2021. "We didn't think he was very developed."

The 2000 draft was Nill's fifth as director of amateur scouting for the Wings. He didn't know it then, but he had drafted what would turn out to be bona fide stars the previous two years, selecting Pavel Datsyuk in 1998 and Henrik Zetterberg in 1999. They, too, were undersized Europeans, but they were late-round picks.

Håkan Andersson, the Wings' director of European scouting, had seen Kronwall more than anyone else in the organization, but he wasn't sure where to rank him as the draft approached. He was 5′11″, 165 pounds, and had recorded five points in 37 games with Djurgårdens IF in his draft year. Was Kronwall a first-round pick? A mid-round pick? Andersson had trouble deciding and consulted Joe McDonnell, one of the Wings' amateur scouts.

"He had a better overall picture," Andersson said. "I was just doing Europe, and he was doing North America and coming to Europe. So we watched Kronner play, and he wasn't very big, but he was mobile and he competed. He was good with the puck.

"We were going over a list of players we liked, and Joe said, 'I don't know many defensemen who are better than Kronwall. I know he's small, but I think he'll get stronger. I think he's a first-round pick for us.' That changed my perception a little bit, because I had a tough time putting 5′11″ defensemen down as first-round picks. You're always thinking about who else is going in the first round. But Jim Nill, Joe, and myself, we all liked him. So we decided to take him."

The Wings' first pick was at No. 29. Kronwall was one of nine players from outside North America the Wings drafted in 2000. Ken Holland, the general manager, explained the scouting staff's philosophy: "What we tried to do was take as many skilled players as we possibly could—lots of Europeans. We feel if you're going to get lucky, for the most part in the draft, you're going to get lucky with Europeans, because they're not seen as much. They're playing in little, out-of-the-way places. You hope one or two surprise you."

Andersson remembers that a scout for a rival NHL team told him that, when he tried to bring up Kronwall's name, his bosses laughed at him. But when the first round of the draft ended on June 24, Andersson was approached by Dave Conte, a longtime scout for the New Jersey Devils. "He came right over after we had picked Kronwall, when the first round had closed up and everybody was walking out," Andersson recalled in 2021. "He said, 'You took our player.' I said, 'What do you mean?' He said, 'We thought for sure we were getting Kronwall early in the second round. We didn't think anybody was going to touch him in the first round.'"

Kronwall was the second-to-last pick made before the draft paused for the day. "I remember it was a controversial pick," Nill said. "People wondered what we were doing. We used to talk about how you'd like to draft guys that you have to look up at when they stand next to you. This was a guy we looked down at, he was that small."

It was a controversial pick, but it was the right pick. Kronwall became a major player for the Wings and a key component of their 2008 Stanley Cup championship. He never looked physically imposing—in his prime, he was listed as 6′, 194 pounds—but he had impeccable timing and gained fame for his open-ice hits. He was so adept at delivering bone-rattling hits that the term "Kron-walled" became part of hockey parlance.

Even as a teenager, Kronwall was laying out opponents with crunching hits.

"A very good friend of mine was the captain of Kronwall's team, and he said they had a blast, all the other players," Andersson said. "Kronwall came in and was still a junior player, and he would hit guys and they would have to be carried off the ice. Some of them woke up and said, 'Who did that?' and the other players would say, 'Oh, it was that little junior kid over there.' And that was embarrassing for a lot of guys, that a little junior guy could level them."

Soon after drafting him, Andersson arranged to meet with Kronwall. The two went to a grocery store and walked down every aisle, with Andersson pointing out to Kronwall what he needed to eat to get into the shape it would take to make the NHL.

"We knew he was a skilled player, but he had to get bigger and stronger," Andersson said.

Kronwall remained in Sweden for three years after being drafted. In 2002–03, he tallied five goals and 13 assists in 50 games in the Swedish Elite League, leading the Wings to sign him to a two-year contract in July. He was still only 5'11", 174 pounds, but it was time to bring Kronwall to North America. At training camp in September, Kronwall was paired with countryman Nicklas Lidström.

"He was good moving the puck and looks like he has good vision," Lidström said. Kronwall began the season in the American Hockey League, but he was called up in mid-December when injuries decimated the Wings' lineup. Kronwall impressed in little ways—the way he used his body to separate foes from the puck, the way he handled the puck, and how adept he was at getting his shot through from the blue line. On January 14, two days past his 23rd birthday, Kronwall celebrated his first NHL goal, dropping to his right knee and pumping his right arm when his wrist shot sank into the Chicago Blackhawks' net.

HE GOT...KRON-VALLED?

The year 2006 spelled relief for Niklas Kronwall. That was when the Swedish Academy decided to include the letter *W* in the 13th edition of its dictionary. The letter had been included under the *V* section because *W* is pronounced *Double-V* in Swedish. That mattered to Kronwall because his family had spelled the last name with a *w* for a couple of generations, but his passport listed his name as *Kronvall*, which caused problems with immigration officials.

"On my airline tickets, it says *w*, so they're like, 'Hey, what's all this about?'" Kronwall said at the time. "I have to be careful."

Ten days later, his season ended. While skating in warmups before a game at Los Angeles, Kronwall hit a rut, fell, and suffered a broken right leg. He played just 20 games for the Wings, but looked like a building block.

When the 2004–05 NHL season was wiped out by a labor dispute between the NHL and the NHL Players Association, Kronwall starred for the Grand Rapids Griffins. In April 2005, he became the first European to be named the AHL's outstanding defenseman of the year, taking home the Eddie Shore Award. Those who had drafted Kronwall were eager to see him full-time in the NHL.

"He's not imposing to other players until he hits them," Nill said. "Then he's imposing. He hit a guy in center ice, with his shoulder, a clean hit. The guy had his head down, and he ended up with a broken jaw and a concussion. He's tough. He's got good offensive skills. He's good defensively, has great mobility, and is strong on his skates. He's one of our best young players."

Once again, Kronwall's path was derailed by injury. This time it was during an exhibition game, when he suffered cartilage damage in his left knee. Kronwall wasn't able to play until February 1, more than halfway through the season.

Kronwall played three games before leaving for Torino, Italy, where he was part of Sweden's gold-medal-winning performance.

Two years later, Kronwall won the Stanley Cup. He had missed all of the 2007 playoffs after suffering a fractured sacrum in March of that year, leaving him with just six playoff games worth of experience in 2008. Kronwall was magnificent in the Wings' run to the Cup. Partnered with Brad Stuart, the duo was devastatingly effective behind the top pairing of Lidström and Brian Rafalski. In addition to delivering highlight-reel hits, Kronwall was so productive he led all defensemen with 15 points and a plus-16 rating when everything was over.

Kronwall punished foes, but his play was also hard on himself. In the twilight of his career, he sought stem-cell therapy for his ailing body, especially his permanently damaged left knee. He retired in 2019, having appeared in 953 games, all with the Wings. His 432 points ranked second among all defensemen in his draft class. Over two decades Kronwall had proven the Wings right: he was worthy of being a first-round pick.

29

THE MULE

HÅKAN ANDERSSON HAD seen no evidence of it, but friends kept telling him the big Swede who played like a defensive expert had offense in him, too. They told him that Johan Franzén had been a really good scorer when he was young, but when he made it to the top Swedish league, his team's coach had told Franzén to focus on not letting opponents score.

Andersson, who started scouting Europe for the Wings in 1990, had seen Franzén play for Linköping, rising from the club's junior league to the Swedish Hockey League. Franzén was eligible in 1998, but despite his being 6′2″, 230 pounds, NHL teams hadn't shown interest. Still, Andersson kept hearing about Franzén.

"A friend of mine was a coach on that team and said, 'You should take a look at this guy. He's better than people think. Watch him,'" Andersson said in 2008. "I did, and I realized he's a very solid player. I looked at him more as a third-line big guy who can skate well and work hard and plays really good defense.

"Then, just by accident, I had some other friends who lived in southern Sweden, and they were from Franzén's hometown, Vetlanda, which is a small town, and they said to me, 'Do you know how he is as a junior player?' and I said I have no idea. They told me he was a hell of a scorer. He played for a third-level team, with older guys, when he was a junior, but he was their best forward a couple of years in a row, before he moved on to other leagues."

It was hard for Andersson to believe that the guy who averaged six points in 30-odd games in the SHL was once an offensive dynamo. But the statistics backed up what his friends said: in lower divisions, Franzén had been a 30-goal scorer. Andersson saw potential for Franzén to regain that form, and in the months leading up to the 2004 draft—when Franzén was 24 years old—Andersson kept talking him up to his bosses in Detroit.

The Wings didn't have a pick until the third round. Their first-round pick had been traded to the Washington Capitals as part of the package to acquire Robert Lang for a hoped-for long playoff run. The second-round pick had been involved in a 2003 trade for Mathieu Schneider.

Jim Nill, the director of amateur scouting, had to wait until No. 97 to make his first pick. The Wings were planning to take Alexander Edler, a 6'4" defenseman out of Sweden, but were undermined. Edler played in Jämtland, roughly a seven-hour drive north of Stockholm. Andersson wanted to scout Edler in one more game, and to make sure he wasn't making the drive in vain, before he left, he called Edler's coach to make sure Edler would be playing. The coach was friendly with an agent and tipped him off. The result was that at the draft, the Vancouver Canucks traded up to No. 91 and grabbed Edler.

The next name on the Wings' list was Franzén's.

"He was a late bloomer, worked his way up," Nill said in 2021. "We were watching him. He was playing well in pro games. We thought there was something there, but we never dreamed he'd become the goal scorer he was. He was a third-line guy in Sweden. We never dreamed he'd set a record for scoring in the playoffs."

Franzén arrived at camp in 2005 expecting to be sent to the minors to adjust to North American hockey. He made an immediate impression on Wings captain Steve Yzerman, who bequeathed Franzén a nickname that stuck with him for his NHL career. "He was just so big and powerful," Yzerman said in 2008, "and I just thought, *That guy is a mule.*"

Franzén's mulish play earned him a spot in the lineup, and then came encouragement to rediscover his offensive side. Usually it's the other way around—players want to score, and team personnel stress defense, but it was the reverse with Franzén.

"He would take the face-off and then drop back between the two defensemen," Andersson said. "So we would say to him, 'Johan, when you have a chance to get the puck, don't start thinking defense. You're going to be good anyway. Try to score. Go for the net, and if you lose the puck, that's when you go back—not before you lose the puck.'"

Franzén took the advice and ended up scoring 12 goals—not bad for a rookie playing on the fourth line. The 16 points he had his first season nearly doubled to 30 in his second season.

Freed from the mindset the coach in Sweden had imposed, Franzén became a force. In March 2008, he scored six game-winning goals, breaking the record of five shared by Gordie Howe and Henrik Zetterberg. Franzén scored 27 goals in 2007–08, his third season.

Franzén had a quiet opening to the playoffs that season, scoring twice in six games against the Nashville Predators. He made up for it against the Colorado Avalanche. Franzén wasn't with the Wings when the Wings-Avs rivalry was at its peak in the late 1990s to early 2000s, but he stoked simmering resentments between the clubs with three points in each of the first two games. He recorded his second hat trick of the series in Game 4, topping Howe's record of seven goals in one playoff series set over seven games against the Montreal Canadiens in 1949.

Franzén missed all but one of the six games it took the Wings to advance past the Dallas Stars in the Western Conference Finals. He was suffering from post-concussion symptoms, an ailment that would eventually claim his career. He scored his 13th goal of the playoffs in the Stanley Cup Final against the Pittsburgh Penguins, and soon after celebrated with the Stanley Cup. He had had a terrific run, but his health had suffered. On June 7, three days after the Cup-clinching game, Franzén revealed he had had "a collection of blood between the skull and the brain. It was a little bit scary. I couldn't do anything because that would have been dangerous. When it's the head, you get scared."

Franzén returned to score 34 goals in 2008–09. In April of that season, he signed an 11-year contract extension. "They drafted me, and I had some good times here," Franzén said. "We won the Cup. I really wanted to stay here."

Franzén had made himself a home in Detroit and enjoyed close friendships with several teammates. One of them, fellow Swede Niklas Kronwall, described Franzén as the type of guy who "likes to go into nature and come back with a bucket of blueberries."

He was good at picking spots to score, that's for sure: Franzén's 12 playoff goals in 2009 led the team, and his 23 points was one behind team leader Zetterberg, but the Wings came one victory short in their quest to repeat as champions. The calendar year would grow more challenging for Franzén in October 2009, when he suffered a torn anterior cruciate ligament in his left knee. He was limited to 27 games in 2009–10, but still scored 10 goals among 21 points and led the Wings with 18 points in 12 playoff games.

Franzén scored 28 goals in 2010–11 and had an especially productive outing February 2, 2011, when he scored five times on the Ottawa Senators. He was the first Wings player to do so since Sergei Fedorov's five-goal night December 26, 1996, and the third after Syd Howe to do so in franchise history.

As 2013 came to a close, Franzén was again sidelined by a concussion, the third of his career. In January 2014, he complained of dizziness after attempts to practice. He had to forego representing Sweden at the Sochi Olympics. Franzén was able to resume playing in late February and recorded his third career hat trick in his second game. Franzén appeared in 54 games in 2013–14, producing 41 points.

Franzén played 33 games in 2014–15. The head injuries had left him feeling debilitated. In April 2015, Franzén revealed the struggles he was dealing with, especially having to turn down his sons, four-year-old Eddie Bo and two-year-old Oliver Gunnar, when they wanted to play.

"To see the disappointment in their eyes breaks your heart," Franzén said. "For months, not being able to pick up your kids, or be able to play with them for more than two minutes—it makes you think. I was in a really dark place."

Franzén's attempt to play the next season was scuttled after two games. Approaching his 36th birthday, he had suffered at least four concussions in his 10 seasons in the NHL. In 2018, Franzén's wife, Cissi, revealed he continued to struggle with after-effects from the head injuries he had suffered.

Franzén's career with the Wings proved the people who had tipped off Andersson were right: he did have offense in him. Franzén scored 187 goals and 370 points in the regular season, and had 81 points in 107 playoff games. The Wings thought they were getting a good defensive player when they drafted him, and they did. But they also got a player who would go on to break a scoring record set by Gordie Howe.

30

JIM NILL

BEING THE DIRECTOR of amateur scouting in back-to-back years that yielded star players in late rounds would fashion an enviable wreath of laurels for anyone, but Jim Nill's career in the Red Wings hockey operations department is rich beyond drafting Pavel Datsyuk and Henrik Zetterberg.

Nill was named director of amateur scouting in August 1994. He had played nine seasons in the NHL, the final two and a half with the Wings. He came to Detroit's front office after two years with the Ottawa Senators, where he served as the team's assistant director of player personnel. It was a great move for Nill. "I'm excited," he said in September 1994. "Nothing against Ottawa, but I'm back with an NHL contender. In this business, you want to win the Stanley Cup, and that could happen here."

That came true in 1997, when the Wings won the Cup on June 7. The championship did make for an uneventful draft for Nill, though, because the Wings had traded their first-round pick to the Hartford Whalers as part of the enticement to obtain Brendan Shanahan. Giving up Keith Primeau and Paul Coffey wasn't nearly the hardship it was to surrender a first-round pick, especially for general manager Jimmy Devellano, who vowed to hold onto draft picks when he came to Detroit in 1982. "It was very tough," Devellano said. "We had a lively discussion on the trading of the pick. I didn't like the idea."

The deal turned out to be well worth it: Shanahan was exactly the dominant power forward the Wings needed. But it meant not having a draft pick in 1997 until the second round, at No. 49.

Nill painted an optimistic picture ahead of draft day on June 21. "Good players come out every draft, and they're not always the No. 1 picks," he said. "You should always be able to get two or three picks to the NHL. It doesn't matter where they are projected."

None of the seven players drafted turned out to be NHL-caliber players—the one taken in the second round, Yuri Butsayev, only lasted 99 games.

Nill had a penchant for drafting skilled European players, because he believed there was an advantage. "We feel if you're going to get lucky for the most part in the draft, you're going to get lucky with Europeans, because they're not seen as much," he said. "They're playing in little, out-of-the-way places. You hope one or two surprise you."

The 1997 draft was Nill's third at the Wings' table. In 1995, the Wings used their first pick, at No. 26, on Maxim Kuznetsov, a defenseman who had been playing in Russia. He played in 136 NHL games, 117 of them with the Wings. Ultimately, that year didn't yield much. Second-round pick Philippe Audet appeared in four NHL games, and third-round pick Darryl Laplante, in 35. (Audet all but prophesied that he would not succeed in the NHL when, shortly after being drafted, he admitted his biggest weakness was intensity. "Sometimes I play like a ghost," he said.)

Nill's second time heading up the Wings' draft table bordered on an optical illusion. Nine players drafted in 1996, only one of whom ever made it to the NHL. Jesse Wallin had been rated to go in the mid-teens, but he was available to the Wings at No. 26. A series of serious injuries—a broken foot, a broken arm—prevented his NHL career from ever really taking off.

Just how difficult it is to discern how a teenaged player will develop, especially early on in the draft when the hopes that the player will pan out are highest, really came into focus for Nill when he looked at his own family. "I have three kids," Nill said in 2021. "At 17 to 18 years of age, I didn't know what they were going to turn out to be, and I'm with them every day. I didn't know what they're going to turn out like at 22, 23.

"Now you start talking about players, some of whom you might only see two or three times. And especially when you go to watch players in Europe, if they're on men's teams, they might get a shift or two a period. So now you're trying to figure out what they can become. At 18, the full product might be there, but it might not be. You just don't now. They're still kids. They're 5'10", 150 pounds, and you don't know what they'll end up being. And then the mental part of it—some kids at 18 are mature. Some are not.

"Some players are ready for the NHL at a young age. Some aren't ready 'til they're 23 or 24 or 25. Zetterberg and Datsyuk came over when they were in their early to mid-twenties. If we'd brought them over when they were 18, 19 years of age, they'd have never made it. They'd have failed and gone home and might never have made it back again."

In 1998 the Wings were Stanley Cup champions again. It meant waiting until No. 25 to make the first selection, but at least Nill had a first-round pick. As he prepared to make a selection, Nill remarked, "This draft has a lot of depth. Center is what we'd like to address. It's our strongest position at the NHL level right now. But five years from now we might have some concerns."

That wasn't the position that was addressed with the first pick, however. When it came to their turn and Jiri Fischer was still available, the Wings pounced. The 6'5", 210-pound defenseman had been projected to be a top 10 pick by the NHL Central Scouting Bureau. "We're shocked he was on the board," Nill said at the time. "Shocked. We're very happy we got him. We're not saying we're smarter than everybody else, but that's why some teams are good at scouting and some are bad. We're confident we made the right pick."

Nill and his team of amateur scouts had hoped to steal Nikolai Antropov, a 6'6" center, but by the late 1990s the Wings were no longer unique in scouting Russia, and the Toronto Maple Leafs grabbed Antropov at No. 10. (He was a good pick, too, playing 788 games and recording 465 points.) Fischer was big and skilled, and established himself in the

Wings' lineup in 1999–2000. His career ended in November 2005 when he suffered cardiac arrest during a game, and he transitioned to a front-office role with the team.

The Wings drafted a center, Carl Steen, in the fifth round, but he didn't pan out. (Eight of the players the Wings drafted in 1999 never made it to the NHL; second-round pick Ryan Barnes appeared in two games.) It was in the sixth round, at No. 171, that the Wings found Datsyuk. When Håkan Andersson, the Wings' Sweden-based scout, first saw Datsyuk, he immediately called Nill and told him that Datsyuk "'reminds me so much of Igor Larionov,'" Nill recalled in 2021.

"Håkan said the same thing at the draft. Pavel was probably around 5′9″, 140 pounds. We knew he hadn't been seen by other scouts, so we knew we could take him a little bit later. We got to that part of the draft and decided to take him."

Datsyuk turned out to be one of the best of his draft class. He ranks third overall with 918 points in 953 games, and his .96 points-per-game average ranks first. He starred on the "Two Kids and a Goat" line with Brett Hull and Boyd Devereaux as a rookie, and won the Stanley Cup in 2002 and 2008.

As the 1999 draft approached, Nill had an unenviable task. Seeking a third straight Stanley Cup, Ken Holland, who had been promoted to general manager the month after the 1997 championship, had traded so many picks the Wings didn't have one until the fourth round. Even worse: the trades hadn't even yielded the desired result.

"It's one thing if you win the Cup and you don't pick 'til the third or fourth round," Nill said in 2021. "But we had lost in the second round. So you're disappointed and you go to the draft, and we had no picks."

Jari Tolsa, a forward out of Sweden, was Nill's first pick at No. 120. He never played in the NHL. The second pick, at No. 149, was a forward out of Russia, Andrei Maximenko. He never played in North America, either. Kent McDonell, a Canadian forward taken at No. 181, appeared in 32 games.

It was at pick No. 210 that the Wings struck gold.

"We had seen this guy, Zetterberg, play in Sweden," Nill said in 2021. "We liked a lot of guys ahead of him. Finally we decided, this is the time to take him."

Zetterberg joined the Wings in fall 2002. He would go on to succeed Nicklas Lidström as captain in 2012 and play more than 1,000 games in a Wings uniform.

Zetterberg and Datsyuk top the list of players the Wings drafted from 1994 until Nill left in 2013, when he was named general manager of the Dallas Stars. But it's a list that also boasts defenseman Niklas Kronwall (first round, No. 29, 2000), who played all 953 of his NHL games for the Wings and was a key figure in their 2008 championship; forwards Jiri Hudler (second round, No. 58, 2002) and Valtteri Filppula (third round, No. 95, 2002), both of whom established long and successful careers; and forward Johan Franzén (third round, No. 97, 2004), a late bloomer who became a power forward. Others include Gustav Nyquist (fourth round, 121, 2008) and Tomas Tatar (second round, No. 60, 2009), who became top-six forwards; and goaltender Jimmy Howard (second round, No. 64, 2003), who played 543 games in a Wings uniform.

"One player who really turned out better than I thought was Tomas Tatar," Nill said. "We really liked him. We did a lot of research on him. He turned out to be a pretty good

JESSE WALLIN

The Wings were thrilled in 1996 when Jesse Wallin was available to them at No. 26: he was a 6'2", 203-pound defenseman who had put up 24 points in 70 games with Red Deer in the Western Hockey League. He had been projected by hockey pundits to be a mid first-round pick.

"I thought he'd be a sure-fire thing," Nill said in 2021. "Jesse had high-end character, was a smart kid, he could really play."

Wallin exuded maturity, forced upon him when he came home one day in April 1994 to find his father dead of a self-inflicted gunshot wound. Wallin, then 16, discovered the body. He had watched his dad, Brian, battle mental illness.

"The only way you can get through something like that is to try to find something positive out of it," Wallin said at Wings training camp in the fall of 1996. "My dad was basically a victim. It wasn't what he wanted, but it's like any other illness. He couldn't help himself."

Born in Saskatoon, Saskatchewan, Wallin spent part of his youth in North Battleford, Alberta, where his dad was a farm implement dealer. "He taught me the game," Wallin said. "He coached me. He never pushed me, but he was always there to help. All my father ever told me was that if I wanted it and worked 100 percent all the time, he would look after me. All he asked was that I give it my best effort."

Wallin's playing career was cut short by a series of misfortunes. He suffered a broken right knee and left arm in an auto accident just before the start of the 1997–98 season, forcing him temporarily to use a wheelchair. He returned in time to captain Canada's team at the World Junior Championships only to suffer a broken left foot blocking a shot.

"I was in a state of shock," Wallin said in July 1998. "I couldn't believe it happened again."

Wallin made it to the NHL in 1999–2000, but his debut was his only appearance that season. He played 49 games over four seasons, unable to establish a foothold at a time the Wings were one of the best teams in the league. In August 2003, he signed with the Calgary Flames as an unrestricted free agent.

"We had good hopes for him," Wings general manager Ken Holland said at the time. "We're disappointed for him that things didn't work out."

Wallin suffered a concussion in his first game in the Flames organization and was forced to retire. He eventually returned to Detroit in a role that completed the circle begun in 1996 when it was his name that was selected by those at the Wings' draft table: under general manager Steve Yzerman, Wallin was named chief amateur scout.

player, exceeded what we thought he'd become. Another one is Jiri Hudler, [who] turned out to be a really good player. There was a small guy that people thought would never play, but he defied all the odds.

"Val [Filppula] was another guy that turned out to be really special. When we drafted him, he was small and weak, but had a great head. He's a guy you feel good about drafting, seeing his development."

On the other side of the ledger, there's one name in particular that Nill rues: Igor Grigorenko, a Russian forward drafted in the second round, at No. 62, in 2001. He was scouted as a playmaker, scorer, and a tough competitor. In May 2003 he suffered a broken hip and leg when he lost control of his car and crashed in Russia. A few days after the crash, it emerged he had an infection in his left lung and was heavily sedated.

Grigorenko recovered and went on to build a career in Russia. When the Wings brought him over for training camp in 2007, he showed up out of shape. He refused to report to the AHL affiliate in Grand Rapids and returned home. That was it for the Wings.

"The most disappointing player I remember, because I think he really would have been something, was Igor Grigorenko," Nill said. "That one stunk. We did our research on him, we really liked him. We really dug in on him. He was a bit of a late bloomer. I think he would have had a major, major impact with the way he played—he was heavy, had great skills. But he was in a car accident. He was never the same. If he didn't have that accident, we thought he was going to be a game-changer. He was the real thing."

Nill oversaw 18 drafts for the Wings, finding the real thing in rounds early and late. He joined the franchise as it climbed to peaks of success in the late 1990s, and his picks helped the team to Stanley Cup championships again in 2002 and 2008.

31

REED LARSON

WHEN JIMMY DEVELLANO was giving his prized draft picks a tour of Detroit in the summer of 1983, he took them past Olympia Stadium, site of the Red Wings' glory years in the 1930s, '40s, and '50s. Devellano told Steve Yzerman, Lane Lambert, and Bob Probert that the Big Red Barn was where Gordie Howe played on "the Production Line" with Sid Abel and Ted Lindsay, and where the Wings had won seven Stanley Cups.

"It didn't do anything for them," Devellano said in 1984. "I could see it in their eyes. I guess any teenager today is unlikely to know what Olympia means to some of us older hockey folks."

For Yzerman, Olympia meant one thing: "Lars and his big slap shot in the 1978 playoffs. I saw it on TV."

Reed Larson was a star defenseman for the University of Minnesota Gophers in the mid-1970s. He played for Herb

Brooks, who in 1980 would gain immortal fame in hockey circles when he coached the U.S. men's team to an upset of the mighty Red Army team en route to the gold medal at the 1980 Lake Placid Games. In 1975–76, Larson ranked fifth on the Gophers with 42 points in 42 games, and went on to win the NCAA championship. On June 1, 1976, the Wings drafted Larson in the second round, at No. 22. When no contact materialized, Larson returned to the Gophers.

The mid- to late 1970s were a tumultuous time for the Wings: the coaching job was a turnstile, management was in turmoil, and ownership was restive. Larson dove into the mess in the spring of 1977, after the Gophers suspended him for shoving a referee to the ice during a game against Michigan Technological University in January 1977. Brooks met Larson outside the arena and told him, "I think it's time."

Two weeks later, Larson was in the Wings' lineup. He was limited to 14 games that season, but he was soon a source of excitement. Larson led team defensemen and was third overall with 60 points in 1977–78, helping the Wings advance to the playoffs for the first time in eight years. The playoff run lasted only seven games (there was a preliminary round where the Wings won the best-of-three series against the Atlanta Flames in two games, followed by a five-game, first-round loss to the Montreal Canadiens), but the appearance and Larson's solid play was a ray of light in a dark decade for the franchise.

Known for his supersonic slap shot, Larson continued to carry the team with his strong play, consistently producing in the 60-point range and representing the Wings at the All-Star Game in 1978, 1980, and 1981. He served as captain from January 1981, when he was voted in by teammates, until he resigned the role before the start of the 1982–83 season, the first under new owner Mike Ilitch and new general manager Jimmy Devellano.

"They're changing everything," Larson said, "and there's some people better qualified than me. I'm not a big talker in the dressing room."

Larson was 26 years old and was, since entering the NHL, the Wings' second-leading scorer with 312 points in 406 games, trailing only Dale McCourt, a first-round pick from 1977 who had 337 points in 341 games. Larson considered leaving the Wings as the miserable final years under owner Bruce Norris careened toward a nadir, but reconsidered when Ilitch infused the franchise with his money and his energy in June 1982. The changes, Larson said, "make the blood rush through you. The teams we've been on for the last three or four years, it got pretty depressing. The organization was dying."

His decision to let the new regime name a captain went over well. "Reed Larson is a smart guy," Devellano said. "I'm really impressed with him. He was perceptive enough to see what we were doing, and he said, 'Let everything be new.'"

There was talk that the need for fresh faces might lead to trading Larson, but he was one of the better players on a team that didn't have many. In September 1983, Devellano signed Larson to a four-year deal worth a little more than $1 million.

"I wouldn't have come back under any circumstance if the previous management was still here," Larson said. "But now it's a whole different ballgame. They're going in the right direction."

Led by Yzerman—who had looked at Olympia Stadium and thought of Larson on that tour of Detroit in the summer of 1983—the Wings made it to the playoffs in 1984, only their second appearance during Larson's tenure. He was still a top player, leading team defensemen with 62 points, and still wielded that slap shot that made goaltenders cower. (In 1985, it was clocked at 136 mph by a radar gun at Joe Louis Arena.) Harry Neale, who had replaced Nick Polano in 1985, shifted Larson to play forward in an effort to spark offense. Larson had recorded 534 points, more than any other U.S.-born player, but that was as a defenseman. Neale was fired in December.

The 1985–86 season was particularly horrible for the Wings, who struggled so much they won only 17 games. Devellano had no choice but to deal at the trade deadline, and he sent Larson to the Boston Bruins for defenseman Mike O'Connell on March 10. It was the end of Larson's 10 years in a Wings uniform.

"People here have treated me nice and I've been paid well," Larson said. "I think if I had thought about how bad it really has been over the years, I don't think I would have made it. I'm crazy enough as it is without having to go completely bonkers."

Larson had 188 goals and 382 assists in 708 NHL games when he left the Wings. In January 1987 he became the first U.S.-born player to score 200 goals. Larson played in the NHL until 1989–90, retiring with 685 points in 904 games, ranking third in his draft class behind Bernie Federko (1,130 points) and Kent Nilsson (686). Larson was inducted into the U.S. Hockey Hall of Fame in 1996.

A 15′ x 10′ canvas of Larson was still hanging from the rafters just inside one of the entrances to Joe Louis Arena the season after he was traded. In November 1987, team officials debated replacing it with a picture of Steve Yzerman.

32

DALE McCOURT

AS THE 1970S progressed, the Red Wings franchise plummeted into disrepair. They were known as the "Dead Wings," as well as the worst team money could buy. In 1976–77 they failed to advance to the playoffs for a seventh straight year. The one benefit to being so awful was that finishing last gave the Wings the first pick in the 1977 amateur draft.

Dale McCourt's appeal was enormous. In 1975–76 he posted 55 goals and 84 assists in 66 games for the Hamilton Fincups in what was then the Ontario Major Junior Hockey League (renamed the Ontario Hockey League in 1980). McCourt captained the Fincups to the 1976 Memorial Cup, recording 28 points in 14 playoff games. In 1976–77, the year he was draft eligible, he posted 60 goals and 79 assists in 66 games, producing back-to-back 139-point seasons. He was voted the 1977 Canadian Hockey League Player of the Year.

At the 1977 World Junior Championships, he led all players with 18 points in seven games.

That was all too good to pass up for Ted Lindsay, the former Wings player who had been named general manager March 16, 1977, replacing his former teammate, Alex Delvecchio. On June 14, at the Queen Elizabeth Hotel in Montreal, McCourt's name was the first to be called.

(Among the hockey operations personnel at the event was future Wings general manager Jimmy Devellano. He was the director of scouting for the New York Islanders, and chose Mike Bossy at No. 15. Bossy would go on to lead the 1977 draft class with 1,126 points in 752 games.)

The Wings drafted McCourt June 14. A week later he was introduced to local media in Detroit, described as a sensational scorer. At the time, Lindsay said the World Hockey Association—he called it the "scum league"—had resorted to Watergate-like tactics to warn McCourt from signing with the Wings, suggesting he might get shot in Detroit. McCourt said one WHA official, whom he declined to name, told him that "when you are going downtown [in Detroit], if the light's red, don't stop. Drive through them."

McCourt wasn't worried. "I lived in Hamilton [Ontario] for three years, and that was supposed to be a crime city," he said. "I go in with an open mind."

If anything, McCourt was eager to seize the opportunity he eyed with the Wings. He was 20 years old and saw himself ready for the NHL. "I think I can make it this year, and I think we can make the playoffs," he said. "We have to get on an upward swing and stay on it."

McCourt made his debut October 13, wearing Alex Delvecchio's old No. 10. The Wings had honored Delvecchio for his 23 seasons in uniform before the November 24, 1974, game against the Los Angeles Kings, a little more than one year after Delvecchio had retired as a player. Unlike other ceremonies held to honor one of the franchise's all-time greats, his number was not retired. That was the way Delvecchio wanted it.

"It's just too pretty of a number to be retired," he said. "I'd rather see somebody wearing the number. It looks nice on the ice. I think it will be a bigger honor for me if the number is kept active and somebody wears it again." (The Wings finally retired No. 10 on November 10, 1991. Jimmy Carson was wearing it then and swapped it for a No. 12. That was Sid Abel's old number, which was retired April 29, 1995.)

McCourt did look good wearing it as he embarked on his NHL career. He reinforced the decision to make him the No. 1 pick by leading the team in scoring in 1977–78 with 72 points, leading them to their first playoff appearance in eight years. McCourt finished fourth in balloting for the Calder Trophy (rookie of the year) behind Bossy, who led the class with 91 points in 73 games.

There was a stretch where it looked like his rookie season might be McCourt's only one with the Wings. In the summer of 1978, Lindsay signed goaltender Rogie Vachon. Vachon was a restricted free agent with the Los Angeles Kings, and as compensation, an arbitrator awarded McCourt to the Kings. McCourt fought the decision in court, suing the Wings, the Kings, the NHL, and the NHL Players Association.

"I simply wanted to stay in Detroit and win the Stanley Cup," McCourt recalled in 2002. "It would have been different if the Wings didn't want me."

The case was headed to the U.S. Supreme Court when the dispute was settled.

The Wings appeased the Kings with Andre St. Laurent and two first-round draft choices. (The Kings used one of those picks, at No. 4 in 1980, to draft defenseman Larry Murphy. He would go on to play a key role in Wings history late in his career, helping them win Stanley Cups in 1997 and 1998.)

McCourt stayed with the Wings and continued to look like a worthy draft pick. He scored 28 goals in his second season and led them in scoring with 81 points his third season, during which he served as captain. In 1980–81, he recorded 86 points. McCourt was off to a terrific start in his fifth season, 1981–82, with 27 points in 26 games when he was traded on December 2. Jimmy Skinner, the general manager at the time, sent McCourt and two other former first-round picks, Mike Foligno and Brent Peterson, to the Buffalo Sabres for veterans Danny Gare, Jim Schoenfeld, and Derek Smith. Gare would go on to captain the Wings, but on the whole, it was a bad trade for the Wings.

The early 1980s were a bad time for the Wings. The team was reeling, and in 1982 reached a nadir in disarray that led Bruce Norris to sell the franchise after 50 years in his family. New owner Mike Ilitch brought in Devellano, who, after an 0–5–1 start, realized he needed to prop up the roster beyond the free agents he had brought in during the summer. He spoke to the Sabres about McCourt, who was out of favor with Buffalo coach Scotty Bowman for reporting to camp overweight. Nothing came of those talks, but McCourt's name resurfaced in Detroit in October 1983, when he was available in the waiver draft after being cut by Bowman. McCourt had been nearly a point-per-game player in Detroit (337 points in 341 games), and the new regime grudgingly considered bringing McCourt back, though they knew his reputation.

"I don't like him," coach Nick Polano said. "He's pretty slow and nonchalant. He's not my kind of player on a permanent basis. But temporarily speaking, he might be."

The Wings passed. McCourt finished his NHL career with the Toronto Maple Leafs in 1983–84. His 478 points ranks ninth in his draft class, but his .90 points-per-game average ranks second behind Bossy's 1.50. McCourt's impact on the Wings was brief, but his legacy was the lawsuit, which led to changes in the collective bargaining agreement that benefitted future players.

33

JOHNNY O

IN 1979, THE Red Wings drafted the second-best fourth-round selection in franchise history.

John Ogrodnick was a productive forward with the New Westminster Bruins in Western Canada. He scored 59 goals in 1977–78 and 48 in 1978–78, putting together back-to-back seasons in the 80-point range. The Wings were desperate for someone they thought could come in and help turn around a franchise that had become the laughingstock of the NHL.

Ogrodnick joined the organization in the fall of 1979, starting the season with the Adirondack Red Wings before his strong play earned a promotion. In his first full season with the Wings, 1980–81, Ogrodnick paced the team with 35 goals and ranked second with 70 points, 16 behind Dale McCourt.

Ogrodnick was everything the Wings hoped for when they drafted him and then some. From 1980–81 to 1982–83, he led the team with 104 goals and 209 points and did not miss a single game. He was also good defensively, something that pleased Jimmy Devellano when he was named general manager in July 1982, a month after the Ilitches bought the team.

"We'll hammer out a deal that will please John Ogrodnick," Devellano said in March 1983. "He is a good hockey player, and we're very appreciative of the work he's done."

Ogrodnick scored 41 goals that season, and followed up with 42 in 1983–84. In January 1984, he became the first Red Wing since Gordie Howe and Frank Mahovlich to be voted to a starting team in the NHL All-Star Game. Ogrodnick had also played in the 1981 and 1982 All-Star Games.

Another All-Star appearance followed in 1985. That was the season Ogrodnick became only the third player in Red Wings history to score 50 goals in a season. He reached that milestone and then surpassed Mickey Redmond's club record of 52 goals in a season, set in 1972–73, with 55 goals. It wasn't just a piece of franchise history that Ogrodnick earned; Mike Ilitch, less than three years into his ownership, wrote Ogrodnick a check for $50,000 in March 1985, shortly after he scored his 50th goal.

"Since I've had the team, that's the biggest accomplishment I've seen for our type of team," Ilitch said. "It just fired me up."

The Wings signed Ogrodnick to a five-year deal in October 1985. Things were changing under Ilitch—Steve Yzerman was the focal point of the franchise, and Devellano's other draft picks from 1983 were tabbed to be major parts of the team's future—but Ogrodnick was a star scorer and someone fans wanted to see.

He was also someone other teams wanted. There were rumors almost from the start of Ogrodnick's NHL career—the Winnipeg Jets wanted him, then it was the Calgary Flames, then the Washington Capitals.

The 1985–86 season was a miserable one for the franchise. They switched coaches midway through, and won just 17 games. Ogrodnick did what he could, pacing the team with 38 goals and 70 points, and earned a fifth All-Star appearance, at age 26. But ownership and management saw a need to shake things up, and counting on ample goal production from Yzerman and Petr Klima, Ogrodnick was deemed the best available bargaining chip.

On January 17, 1987, Ogrodnick was the centerpiece of a six-player deal between the Wings and Quebec Nordiques. The deal was consummated during the second intermission as the Wings played the Nordiques at Joe Louis Arena, when Devellano and counterpart Maurice Filion shook hands. The trade sent Ogrodnick, Doug Shedden, and Basil McRae to Quebec for forwards Brent Ashton and Mark Kumpe and defenseman Gilbert Delorme. Ashton was 26 and had 25 goals and 19 assists in 46 games. Delorme was 24 and had played for Wings coach Jacques Demers, who'd played a role in the trade negotiations, in St. Louis.

Ogrodnick was in tears as he packed his gear after the game. He had led the team in goals from 1982–83 to 1984–85, and his scoring had dipped because he had bought into Demers's more restrictive style.

"We're gonna miss Johnny O's shot and his work along the boards," Yzerman said.

At its core, the trade was Ashton for Ogrodick. Ashton scored 15 goals for the Wings to reach 40 on the season in 1986–87, but his output dropped to 26 goals the following season, his last with the Wings. Ogrodnick spent less than a season in Quebec, moving on to play for the New York Rangers. He had two productive seasons on Broadway, scoring 43 and 31 goals, but after scoring just 17 goals in 1991–92, the Rangers bought out Ogrodnick's contract and left him looking for a job at age 33.

Ogrodnick wanted to return to the team that drafted him and persuaded Wings coach Bryan Murray to extend an offer to come to camp on a tryout. Ogrodnick received a one-year deal, but the 1992–93 Wings were a deep team, and Ogrodnick struggled to get playing time. He recorded six goals in 19 games in what would be his final season.

Ogrodnick retired with 827 points in 928 games. He ranks second among fourth-round picks in Wings history with 265 goals, 546 points, and 558 games, trailing only 1989 fourth-round pick Sergei Fedorov. Fedorov being available in the fourth round had everything to do with him being behind the Iron Curtain, but why Ogrodnick was available in the fourth round in 1979 was baffling, given what a good player he was as a teenager. It worked out for Ogrodnick—he ranks 10th in scoring among 1979 draft picks, but seeing his name slip on August 9, 1979, rankled the 20-year-old.

"I was disappointed because I wasn't drafted until the fourth round," Ogrodnick said. "My junior coach and agent built my hopes up at the time. Was told I wouldn't go any later than the second round."

34

THE FIRST
18-YEAR-OLD

THE 1980 DRAFT marked a turning point in NHL history, setting the event on course to becoming what it is today. It was the first time it was a public event, held at the Forum in Montreal. Before then, the draft had taken place behind closed doors in various venues in Montreal, most often the Queen Elizabeth Hotel (from the first draft in 1963 to 1972 and from 1978 to 1979).

The other big change in 1980 was that the minimum draft age was lowered from 19 to 18.

The Canadiens had the first overall selection and chose Doug Wickenheiser. The Wings' first selection didn't come until No. 11, because of a move made by Ted Lindsay during his reign as general manager from March 1977 to April

1980. In the summer of 1978 Lindsay signed free agent goal-tender Rogie Vachon, which led to an arbitrator awarding Dale McCourt to the Los Angeles Kings as compensation. McCourt challenged that decision in court, and the dispute was settled when the Wings gave the Kings forward Andre St. Laurent, the first pick in 1980 and the first pick in 1982. The Wings' first pick in 1980 came at fourth, and the Kings used it to select defenseman Larry Murphy. He would go on to play a significant role in Wings history in the late 1990s and was inducted into the Hockey Hall of Fame in 2004, his first year of eligibility.

The Wings' pick in the first round, and the reason they didn't have a pick in the second, dated to a move Lindsay made in March 1978, when he acquired forward Errol Thompson, a second-round pick in 1978 and the 11th pick from the Toronto Maple Leafs, in exchange for Dan Maloney and the second-round pick in 1980.

By the 1980 draft the Wings were under the management of Jimmy Skinner. He did not take advantage of the expanded age group with his first pick, selecting Mike Blaisdell, a right wing out of the Western Hockey League. He was 20 years old and had turned heads starring for the Regina Pats, recording 71 goals and 38 assists, totaling 109 points in 63 games in 1979–80. In 18 playoff games, Blaisdell tallied 25 points.

By the third round, holding the 46th pick, Skinner was ready to gamble on an 18-year-old. He chose Mark Osborne, a forward who had put up 43 points in 52 games with the Niagara Falls Flyers in what was then called the Ontario Major Junior Hockey League. Osborne was at his parents' home in Etobicoke, Ontario, when an official from the Wings called.

"Some of my friends went to Montreal, but it wasn't suggested to me to go," Osborne said in 2021. "I hung out by our phone. I got a phone call, it must have been from Jimmy Skinner. That's how it was done—you waited by the phone."

Osborne attended Wings training camp in the fall of 1980, where he was greeted by coach Ted Lindsay, but left with the disappointment of not even appearing in any exhibition games. Back in Niagara Falls, Osborne dominated. (He would finish the 1980–81 season with 39 goals and 41 assists in 54 games.) Management in Detroit noticed.

"I knew I was going to get called up by the Red Wings because I was told that near the end of December," Osborne said. "But the night before I was supposed to go up, I broke my arm. So that quashed that whole idea. I was out for a couple months, then came back for the playoffs. Then I got to go to Adirondack. That was a great learning experience for me. Going from junior right to the NHL, that's a huge stepping stone. Going to Adirondack and playing in those American Hockey League playoffs for a team that ended up winning—it was really a valuable lesson for me. It was a really positive experience."

Osborne came to camp in the fall of 1981 ready to make the Wings. He had just turned 20, and had the confidence earned from winning the Calder Cup. In addition to being the first 18-year-old drafted by the Wings, Osborne was with the franchise at a historic time. On a personal level, he had a terrific rookie season, leading the team with 67 points in 80 games in 1981–82. But his accomplishments were overshadowed by the turmoil roiling the organization. The 1970s had been a disaster: Gordie Howe quit in anger after 25 years; the

Wings failed to make the playoffs from 1971 to 1977; the team cycled through 10 coaches and was known throughout the NHL as the worst team money could buy. (Under Lindsay's management, the payroll for the 1979–80 season ballooned to $5 million, the highest in NHL history to that point.) The start of the 1980s wasn't much better, with the Wings failing to qualify for the playoffs in 1980 and 1981.

In March of 1982, owner Bruce Norris mulled a spring cleaning of the front office. That was right after Skinner had bungled an attempt to lure Fred Shero, who coached the Philadelphia Flyers to the Stanley Cup championship in 1974 and 1975, to Detroit. When those discussions became public, it muddled finding a replacement for Wayne Maxner, who had replaced Lindsay as coach in 1980. At the time, the Wings were in 20th place in the 21-team league and on pace to miss the playoffs for the 13th time in 15 seasons. Maxner was fired a few days later, replaced on a temporary basis by Billy Dea.

Despite the upheaval and troubled times, Norris went through with a ceremony at Joe Louis Arena to celebrate 50 years of Norris family ownership. But fans weren't interested and let Norris know. They booed him, and that was that. Norris decided to sell.

"We're tired of listening to this," he said at the time.

In June 1982, Norris sold the Wings to Mike Ilitch, a Detroit-born pizza baron, whose first big hire was bringing in Jimmy Devellano to manage the team. "There were grumblings that the team was going to be sold, and Mike bought it just as I had ended my first year, and Jimmy D. came in as GM," Osborne said. "I knew right away that Mr. Ilitch was really ambitious and successful. He was determined to turn things around in Detroit. That was certainly a memorable time. There were a lot of positives right away."

The change in ownership injected excitement into the franchise and the city, but the results on the ice were the same. The Wings went winless through their first seven games of the 1982–83 season. When they played the Buffalo Sabres on October 23, 1982, Ilitch took in the game from the aisle directly behind the Wings' bench, meaning players couldn't help but see the man who signed their paychecks when they would come off the ice after a shift. Osborne scored his first goal of the season that night.

"I had to look twice," he said at the time. "I didn't know what it was like to score again."

The positive vibes didn't linger for long. After a 7–0 loss to the Boston Bruins on November 7, Devellano charged into the visitors' dressing room at Boston Garden and confronted Osborne and Blaisdell. Devellano ordered them to report to his room at the Parker House Hotel. Blaisdell had been on the ice for all seven of the Bruins' goals, Osborne for six.

"They were embarrassing," Devellano said at the time. "I blasted them like they've never been blasted before." Devellano told the players that they had let him down and that they were "stealing Mr. Ilitch's money."

At the time, Osborne had just three goals and two assists after 16 games. "He sort of left the onus on me to see what I can do to improve my play out there," Osborne said.

Devellano was adamant that something change. "They are never going to embarrass me again."

Osborne finished with 19 goals in 1982–83. His time with the Wings came to end end on June 14, 1983, when

Devellano traded him, Blaisdell, and defenseman Willie Huber to the New York Rangers for goalie Ed Mio and forwards Eddie Johnstone and Ron Duguay. It was Devellano's biggest move in his first year as general manager, but while they were excited to land a charismatic goal scorer in Duguay, Duguay was inconsolable at having to leave the New York nightlife. "I don't see much future in Detroit," he said. "They're not a contender. They haven't had much success in the past.... I'm not very happy. I'm very depressed. I had a good thing in New York. I really enjoyed it. A lot of stars come into New York and go to the clubs, and I run into a lot of stars. I went out with Cher. No big deal."

The trade was a big deal for Osborne. His career with the Wings had begun with such promise. "It was disappointing at the time," he said in 2021. "I was quite surprised to get that call. Here I thought Jimmy was calling to tell me about having drafted Steve Yzerman. He called and told me, 'We drafted Steve Yzerman, we think he's going to be a good player.' That's how the conversation started. And then he said, 'And we made a deal and you're involved.' That's how it happened."

Osborne was the only player lost in the trade ultimately deemed of value by Devellano. He described Osborne as "a good solid hockey player for the New York Rangers, and that doesn't surprise me. But without giving up Osborne, we would not have been able to make the deal."

Ultimately, the Wings did not get much from their 1980 draft. In addition to Blaisdell and Osborne, they drafted forward Mike Corrigan (fifth round, No. 88), forward Wayne Crawford (sixth round, No. 109), defenseman Mike Braun (seventh round, No. 130), defenseman John Beukeboom (eighth round, No. 151), forward Dave Miles (ninth round, No. 172) and forward Brian Rorabeck (10th round, No. 193). Of the eight players selected, Blaisdell and Osborne were the only ones who made it to the NHL. Osborne spent only two seasons with the Wings, but he enjoyed a career that lasted 919 games.

35

GERARD GALLANT

THERE WAS LITTLE fanfare for the Red Wings at the 1981 draft. They didn't have a first-round pick because of the 1979 trade for goaltender Rogie Vachon, which, after a debacle involving Dale McCourt, was settled with the Los Angeles Kings at a price that included a first-round pick two years later. It was a badly executed move and robbed the Wings of the second overall pick, which would have given them a shot at drafting future luminaries such as Ron Francis, Grant Fuhr, and Al MacInnis.

The Wings used their first pick, at No. 23, on forward Claude Loiselle. He had a solid career in the NHL with 616 games, but he only played 128 games for the Wings, as he was traded to the New Jersey Devils after the 1985–86 season. Corrado Micaleft, a goaltender taken at No. 44, and Larry Trader, a defenseman taken at No. 86, combined for 204 career NHL games.

It was the guy the Wings drafted in the sixth round, Gerard Gallant, who would have the biggest impact on the team. Gerard Gallant was playing in the Quebec Major Junior Hockey League with the Sherbrooke Castors in 1980–81, when his abrasive style and 101 points in 68 games appealed to Wings scouts. Gallant continued to play junior hockey through 1982–83, finishing his career in the QMJHL with the Verdun Juniors, where his teammates included Pat LaFontaine, a highly touted prospect from the Detroit area whom the New York Islanders drafted at No. 3 in 1983, one spot before the Wings were hoping to get him. Gallant posted 33 points in 15 playoff games for Verdun in 1983, and that same spring was signed by the Wings.

Gallant transitioned to professional hockey, spending the 1983–84 season with the American Hockey League's Adirondack Red Wings. He had a solid year, with 31 goals and 33 assists in 77 games. He began the following season in the AHL, too, but was called up by the Wings in January 1985. Gallant scored in his debut on January 22, flipping the puck behind New York Islanders goaltender Billy Smith to spark a 5–4 victory that ended an 0–10–2 skid, and produced six goals and 12 assists in 32 games.

The season ended miserably for the Wings, who lost 9–5, 6–1, and 8–2 in the opening round of the playoffs in a best-of-five series against the Chicago Black Hawks. When it was over, general manager Jimmy Devellano vowed there would be changes the following season. "We'll be leaning more on the younger players," he said. Gallant was told he would be a bigger part of the future.

A month into the 1985–86 season, Gallant led the Wings with seven goals and 12 assists. He was a pest on the ice and a pleasure off it, humble and polite and the pride of Summerside, Prince Edward Island, where Gallant grew up the ninth of 11 children.

His season suffered a setback in early December, when he incurred a broken jaw during a fight in a game against the Minnesota North Stars. At the time, Gallant shared the team lead with 13 goals with John Ogrodnick. By Christmas, Gallant had lost seven pounds because his jaw had been wired shut. While Gallant recuperated, the Wings made a coaching change, firing Harry Neale after 35 games (he had replaced Nick Polano in the summer of 1985) and promoting Brad Park, who had retired after the previous season.

Gallant finally returned in early February, after being sidelined three months. He scored seven goals the remainder of the season, finishing his second season with 20 goals and 19 assists. For the Wings, the season was one best forgotten: when they lost 5–3, to the North Stars on April 5, they assured themselves of their worst season in the franchise's 60-year history. The next night they won their season finale to close their record at 17–57–6 and 40 points.

As bad as things were going with the team, Gallant continued to reinforce the Wings' decision to draft him. He signed a three-year contract in June and got married in July. (Lane Lambert, a second-round pick in the '83 draft, was his best man.)

The 1986–87 season began with fresh hope: Jacques Demers was installed as coach, and one of his first actions

Gerard Gallant (left) and Wings teammate Claude Loiselle pose after a practice on November 6, 1985.

was to name Yzerman captain. Gallant, at 23, two years older than Yzerman, was named an alternate.

That abrasive style that had first endeared the Wings to Gallant continued to be his trademark. Gallant forechecked, back-checked, hit, fought—and scored. On New Year's Eve in 1986, Gallant led the Wings with 16 goals, and his 30 points was second behind Yzerman's 37.

"He's one of the best all-around players in the league, as far as I'm concerned," Yzerman said. "He certainly is the best all-around player on our team. He's also quite a character. He's pretty popular with the guys." Demers described Gallant as "a coach's player. He'll do anything to help win a hockey game. He'll check, he'll fight, he'll score a goal—anything you ask of him. He just keeps coming and coming. And he's not a gifted athlete. It's all hard work and pride and determination. He's your money-maker type of player.... I get carried away with guys like that. But they make me smile."

Gallant finished the season with a team-best 38 goals. The Wings placed second in the Norris Division, one point behind the St. Louis Blues. Gallant delivered in the playoffs, too: His eight goals was a team high, and his 14 points were four behind team leader Yzerman.

Gallant scored at least 30 goals four straight seasons for the Wings, through 1989–90. When Yzerman suffered a season-ending injury March 1, 1988, it was Gallant who was chosen to wear the captain's C on his sweater during Yzerman's absence. In 1988–89, Gallant played on Yzerman's left wing and recorded career highs with 39 goals and 93 points. Gallant's old teammate from Verdun, Islanders center Pat LaFontaine, was effusive in a March 1989 interview, saying, "I played with Gerard Gallant on left wing in juniors, and here's a guy who is an unsung hero—probably the most underrated player in the league."

The following month, Gallant was invited to join Team Canada at the World Championships, held that year in Sweden. "It's nice to see him finally get the recognition he deserves," Yzerman said.

CHRIS CHELIOS

One of the best players to come out of the 1981 draft, and one who would have a significant impact on the Wings, was Chris Chelios. The American defenseman was selected by the Montreal Canadiens, at No. 40. He won the Stanley Cup with them in 1986, won the Norris Trophy in 1989, and served as co-captain in 1989–90. In June 1990 he was traded to his hometown Chicago Blackhawks, where he won his second and third Norris Trophies, in 1993 and 1996, and once again served as captain, from 1995 to 1999.

In March 1999, the Wings were under the management of Ken Holland and eager to load up the team to pursue a hoped-for, third-straight Stanley Cup championship. Still reeling on defense from losing Vladimir Konstantinov to a limousine accident after the 1997 Cup, the Wings cast their eyes to Chelios. They had committed $16 million to Uwe Krupp the previous summer, but back problems limited him to 22 games, and there was deep concern about his future effectiveness. (Krupp would, in fact, not play again until 2001–02 and totaled 30 games over four seasons with the Wings. He was on the roster for the 2002 championship, but his name was not engraved on the Stanley Cup.)

Chelios was 37 years old, but still played big minutes. He was a leader and Cup champion.

"When you get a chance to acquire a player like Chris Chelios, you get pretty excited," Holland said on March 23. "I'm really happy to be able to add Chris to our hockey club. He's one of the premier defensemen in the league. We thought it was a move we had to make."

It was the first time the Wings and Blackhawks, longtime Original Six rivals, had struck a deal in nearly a quarter of a century. The Wings gave up defenseman Anderson Eriksson, their first-round pick from 1993, and first-round picks in 1999 and 2001.

The 1999 playoffs ended in disappointment, as the Wings were eliminated in the second round. But Chelios had been a worthy addition, stabilizing the Wings' defense. He won the Cup with them in 2002 and again in 2008. He played 28 games in 2008–09, the season in which he celebrated his 47th birthday. Chelios finally had to retire in 2010, ending a playing career that spanned three Original Six teams and totaled 948 points in 1,651 games. Of those, Chelios played 578 games in a Wings uniform, recording 152 points and a plus-158 rating.

In September, the Wings recognized Gallant's importance by signing him to a deal that doubled his salary to around $450,000 a year. Gallant's abrasive style was hard on his body, and back pain began to limit his effectiveness. He played only 45 games in 1990–91, the first season after Bryan Murray replaced Demers as coach. When Murray scratched Gallant from the lineup in November 1992, Gallant requested a trade, although nothing came of it. Gallant returned to the lineup and was put back on a line with Yzerman. In January, Gallant scored his 200th career goal.

It would turn out to be Gallant's last season with the Wings. In July 1993 he signed as a free agent with the Tampa Bay Lightning. Gallant played 563 games for the Wings, recording 207 goals and 260 assists. His 467 points were at that time tied with Nick Libett for eighth among the Wings' all-time leading scorers. Gallant didn't find happiness in Tampa, where he was rarely used. In 1995, he attempted to continue his career with the Detroit Vipers of the International Hockey League, but back pain forced his retirement after just three games.

Gallant played 615 games in the NHL, and ranks ninth in his draft class with 480 points. He helped turn around the Wings and ranked as the franchise's best sixth-round pick until Pavel Datsyuk was drafted in 1998.

36

TRADING PICKS
FOR PLAYERS

IN 1979, THE general manager of the Red Wings was so
desperate to improve the team, he gave up two first-round
picks. Ted Lindsay, who had followed fellow former Wings
great Alex Delvecchio in going from player to manager, tried
to improve the Wings' fortunes by signing free-agent goaltender Rogie Vachon in the summer of 1978. It was a messy move
that ended with an arbitrator awarding Dale McCourt, whom
the Wings had drafted at No. 1 in 1977, to the Los Angeles
Kings as compensation. McCourt objected, and the dispute
was settled when Lindsay appeased the Kings with a package
that included the Wings' first-round pick in 1980 and 1981.

Lindsay's gamble didn't pay off: he signed Vachon to a
five-year, $1.725 million contract, but the Wings played poorly

in front of Vachon, and after two disappointing seasons, he was traded to Boston. Vachon's lasting impact on the Wings was being in goal when they won their first game at Joe Louis Arena, making 30 saves in their 4–2 victory over the New York Islanders on December 30, 1979. The Kings used the pick they got from Detroit in 1980 to draft Larry Murphy, who would surpass 20 seasons in the NHL and factored into the Wings' draft history late in his career. The Wings did have Toronto's first-round pick from a 1978 trade, but by the 11th spot, they had missed out on Murphy, Paul Coffey, and Denis Savard, all of whom went into the Hockey Hall of Fame. Not having a first-round pick in 1981 meant the Wings missed out on, among others, Ron Francis, Grant Fuhr, and Al MacInnis, another trio of Hall of Fame inductees.

The Wings missed out on Brian Bellows, Scott Stevens, Phil Housley, and Dave Andreychuk in 1982 because Jeff Skinner, whose titles included director of player personnel and hockey operations, had let himself be swindled by Minnesota North Stars general manager Lou Nanne. In August 1981—nearing the nadir that would lead the Norris family to sell the Wings after 50 years of ownership—Nanne convinced Skinner to swap first-round picks in exchange for defenseman Greg Smith and forward Don Murdoch—neither of whom made an impact. (The player the Wings chose at No. 17, Murray Craven, had a long career, appearing in 1,071 games, but Stevens, Housley, and Andreychuk became Hockey Hall of Fame inductees.)

It was to this mess that Jimmy Devellano arrived in July 1982, hired by new owners Mike and Marian Ilitch to revive the Wings. Having been a part of building the New York Islanders into a multiple Stanley Cup–winning franchise, Devellano surveyed the Wings and, at his introductory news conference, vowed he would not trade "a first pick, a third pick, a sixth pick, a 10th pick." He pointed to his success as proof that Stanley Cup contenders are built through the draft, not through trades.

Devellano got the Wings on the right track—and by the time he started trading first-round picks, fans had forgotten his 1982 proclamation. The Wings' 1997 first-round pick was traded to the Hartford Whalers in the Brendan Shanahan deal, and nobody bemoaned that on June 21, 1997, because two weeks earlier Shanahan had helped the Wings end a 42-year drought and brought the Stanley Cup back to Detroit.

The other trade made to bolster their Cup contender status in 1996–97 didn't even cost the Wings any draft picks. The Toronto Maple Leafs needed to shed salary, and the Wings bolstered their team by taking on 36-year-old Larry Murphy, then the fourth-highest scoring defenseman in NHL history. On March 18, the Wings agreed to absorb the remainder of Murphy's contract, which ran through 1997–98. Murphy won back-to-back Cups with the Wings.

The tragedy that befell the Wings six days after the 1997 championship led to the decision to gamble with first-round picks at the end of the decade. Vladimir Konstantinov, the fiercest competitor on the team, had suffered career-ending injuries when the limousine he, fellow defenseman Slava Fetisov, and team masseur Sergei Mnatsakanov were riding in crashed into a tree. Konstantinov was 30 years old at the time of the accident and a Norris Trophy finalist.

"That was such an awful, awful loss," Jimmy Devellano, by then senior vice president, said in March 1999. "We are still feeling it."

The first attempt to fill the void had been a disaster and a distraction—Uwe Krupp. Signed to a four-year, $16 million deal in 1998, Krupp appeared in just 22 games before claiming a back injury prevented him from playing. The Wings didn't know they would not have Krupp's services again at all at the 1999 trade deadline, but they were hopeful for another Cup and saw a solution in veteran defenseman Chris Chelios.

"Chelios was signed to help try to fill that hole again, the hole left by poor Vladdie," Devellano said.

Chelios cost the Wings their first-round pick in 1999 (No. 23, Steve McCarthy) and in 2001 (No. 29, Adam Munro), as well as defenseman Anders Eriksson, whom the Wings had drafted in the first round in 1993. The Blackhawks didn't get much out of the draft picks, and Eriksson was gone from the organization within two years, while Chelios played 578 games and won two Stanley Cups with the Wings.

It was a busy time for then–general manager Ken Holland, who also traded a 1999 second-round pick and a 2000 third-round pick to the New York Rangers for Ulf Samuelsson, as well as another 1999 second-round pick (previously acquired from San Jose) to the Tampa Bay Lightning for Wendel Clark.

When a first-round pick yields a player who helps win the Stanley Cup, it's a well-rewarded price. But at the 2004 deadline, Holland traded a first-round pick as part of the package to acquire Robert Lang. Lang was a 20-goal scorer, but he only lasted two full seasons with the Wings. The Washington Capitals converted the trade into the No. 29 pick in 2004, where they chose Mike Green—an offensive defenseman the Wings came to covet and signed as a free agent at the tail end of his career.

The trade involving a first-round pick that really came to hurt over time was the one at the 2012 trade deadline. The Wings still had Nicklas Lidström, Henrik Zetterberg, Pavel Datsyuk, and Niklas Kronwall, and the onus was on Holland to bolster the roster. A slew of injuries had decimated the defense corps, and Holland gambled in reacquiring Kyle Quincey, a former Wings draft pick (No. 132, 2003) who had been lost on waivers in 2008. It was a three-team deal involving the Colorado Avalanche and Tampa Bay Lightning, where Steve Yzerman had been named general manager in 2010. Yzerman got the Wings' first-round pick, at No. 19, which was used on Andrei Vasilevskiy. Vasilevskiy became the Lightning's franchise goaltender and a Stanley Cup champion; Quincey stayed with the Wings for four more seasons but was little more than a depth player.

By the late 2010s, the Wings had gone from buyers to sellers at the trade deadline, and the focus shifted to trading players for draft picks. Tomas Tatar yielded a 2018 first-round pick, a 2019 second-round pick, and a 2021 third-round pick at the 2018 deadline. The following year, the return on Gustav Nyquist included a second-round pick in 2019. Andreas Athanasiou yielded two second-round picks in 2020.

The Wings' history is rich with examples of the gamble involved in trading first-round picks. When a team is not in playoff contention, it has not been worth the risk—but when the Wings were chasing the Stanley Cup, the majority of the time those trades paid off with the ultimate reward.

37

MORE TALK
THAN ACTION

THE 2015 DRAFT is most memorable to the Red Wings for leading to a conversation between two men who had not spoken in two decades.

The draft class itself was a bust: first-round pick Evgeny Svechnikov was as personable as they come, but a knee injury set him back, and he never developed into the high-end forward the Wings hoped they'd gotten when they chose him at No. 19. The third-round pick, defenseman Vili Saarijarvi, washed out of the system, too, as did the fourth-round pick, Joren Van Pottelberghe. Van Pottelberghe was a Swiss goaltender who appealed because of his work ethic. He never made an impression at the NHL level—but his agent sure did.

Kris Draper was retired by 2015 and worked for the Wings in the hockey operations department. Part of the scouting staff, he was at the draft, which took place at the end of June in Sunrise, Florida. Draper was in the lobby of his Miami hotel with his family when he saw his wife do a double-take at the man who was approaching them. It was Claude Lemieux.

The two were the centerpiece of the incident that sparked the famous Red Wings–Colorado Avalanche rivalry, ignited when Lemieux hit Draper from behind during Game 6 of the 1996 Western Conference Finals, smashing Draper's face into the boards and leaving him with a broken jaw and shattered orbital bone. Darren McCarty made Lemieux pay the following season, in the epic March 26, 1997, game at Joe Louis Arena, pummeling him while he turtled on the ice, but Lemieux never apologized for what he did. For all the times the teams met, for all the times players shook hands at the end of playoff series, Draper and Lemieux never spoke.

That changed because of the 2015 draft. Lemieux was Van Pottelberghe's agent, and that was why he approached Draper in the hotel. "It was weird," Draper said in 2016. "My wife and kids, they obviously know everything about it, and they weren't quite sure. My son was just looking. His eyes were bugging out. He wasn't sure what was going to happen. Julie wasn't quite sure. She went through the whole process with me. We sat there and talked. He said it was great meeting everybody. He walked away, and I was just like, 'Wow.'

"It was probably a four- to five-minute conversation. Nothing was mentioned about the game, the hit, the rivalry. It was just basically an agent talking to someone in management. And that was it."

Generally, drafts end with team personnel talking excitedly about the players selected. The 2015 draft was an important one for the Wings, who knew their playoff streak was nearing its end. (That happened in 2017.) But none of the guys worked out, and instead 2015 joined the list of bust drafts for the franchise.

The 1960s had mixed success, because the draft was only beginning to take shape. The desperation, and disarray, in which the Wings found themselves during the 1970s had an impact on the draft, too, and led to management at times trading picks in hopes of adding players who could have an immediate impact on the team. That's why, for example, the Wings did not have a first-round pick in 1981.

Under the direction of Jimmy Devellano, installed as general manager after Mike and Marian Ilitch bought the franchise in 1982, the Wings had a good run starting with the 1983 draft, when they chose Steve Yzerman, Bob Probert, Joey Kocur, and Petr Klima. Multiple players from successive drafts advanced to the NHL. The 1987 draft, though, didn't yield much—the first-round pick, Yves Racine, played 508 games, but 10 of the players never reached the NHL and the two others combined for 41 games. But at least Racine did make it. The next year was dreadful—the team wasted a first-round pick on Kory Kocur, a cousin of 1983's Joey Kocur—but Kory never developed into anywhere near the same player and never reached the NHL. Kory Kocur had put up 71 points and 95 penalty minutes in 69 games in the Western Hockey League and was projected by most scouts as a late second-round pick, and he was as shocked as anyone to hear his name called at No. 17. "I'm so happy, my knees are shaking," Kocur said. "I was hoping it would be me, but I didn't know. I thought it might be in the second round."

The Wings had their sights on Reggie Savage, a small but talented scoring machine who had 122 points in 68 games in the Quebec junior league, but he was snatched two picks earlier by the Washington Capitals. (Savage didn't fare much better at the NHL level, appearing in just 34 games.)

"My heart went down when Reggie Savage was picked," chief scout Neil Smith said. "You get a little disappointed. But we're very happy to have Kory Kocur. He was on our priority list of 17 players. He was somebody all of our scouts really felt good about."

The only player the Wings drafted in 1988 to make it to the NHL was their fourth-round pick, Sheldon Kennedy, who appeared in 310 NHL games.

The Wings had the best draft class in NHL history in 1989 (Nicklas Lidström, Sergei Fedorov, Vladimir Konstantinov), but the 1993 edition was a forgettable one. Defenseman Anders Eriksson played 572 games and was used to acquire Chris Chelios, but none of the other picks had an impact. Two years later there was even less to like: Maxim Kuznetsov, a first-round pick, lasted 136 games; the second-round pick, Phillippe Audet, lasted four games, and the third-round pick, Darryl Laplante, 35 games. The Wings were a Stanley Cup contender, so the draft had taken a back seat, but it was still a way to continue to feed the organization's pipeline.

That pipeline got not one drop in 1996. Jesse Wallin was a promising defenseman in juniors, but injuries derailed his development, and he appeared in just 49 NHL games. None of the other eight picks ever made it. The 1997 draft was a bust, too: Yuri Butsayev, the team's first pick at No. 49, played 99 games, which led a very weak crop. Pavel Datsyuk, Henrik Zetterberg, and Niklas Kronwall saved the 1998, 1999, and 2000 drafts, respectively, but there was nobody to stop the bust label being attached to the 2001 draft. Igor Grigorenko, a Russian selected in the second round, was highly touted but a severe car accident delayed his development, and when he did come to Detroit, he balked at being assigned to the minors and sulked his way back overseas. The Wings didn't get anything out of the other six picks, either.

Johan Franzén was the only player from the 2004 draft class who made it to the NHL, with the other seven players lost causes. The 2006 off-season was notable for Steve Yzerman's announcement that he was retiring—it certainly wasn't notable for the Wings' draft class, which didn't give them anyone other than Shawn Matthias, used to acquire Todd Bertuzzi in an attempt to maintain Cup-contender status. Fourth-round pick Gustav Nyquist was the only player from the 2008 draft to make an impact on the Wings. The only other player out of the six they drafted who appeared in the NHL was first-round pick Tom McCollum, a goaltender who played three games. Four of the nine players the Wings drafted in 2011 played at least 100 games in the NHL, but the lingering takeaway from that year is that the Wings had a chance to draft future Stanley Cup champion Nikita Kucherov three times in the second round, and fumbled every time.

The Wings have a richer history of boons than busts at the draft, but they have come away empty-handed some years, even when it led to two old foes finding a neutral talking point over a Swiss goalie.

NOTABLE FIRSTS

The first time the Wings had the first overall pick in a draft was 1964—but that's the extent of Claude Gauthier's claim to a fraction of franchise history. He never made it to the NHL.

As much of a boon as Steve Yzerman turned out to be—the youngest and longest-serving captain in franchise history, winning three Stanley Cups as a player—the first time the Wings had the fourth overall pick was in 1976. Alex Delvecchio, the former franchise All-Star turned general manager, selected a center from Saskatoon, Saskatchewan, named Fred Williams. It was a miserable time for the Wings, who that spring had missed the playoffs for the sixth straight year. Williams looked like a good pick at the time, having recorded 31 goals and 87 assists in 72 games in 1975–76 with the Saskatoon Blades in the WCHL (later renamed the Western Hockey League). Williams was fast and skilled, his talents on display in two playoff runs during which he produced 51 points in 37 games.

Williams scored in his NHL debut on October 7, 1976, but when no points came the next 10 games, he was sent to the minors. Brought back to Detroit at the end of January 1977, Williams only scored one more goal, finishing his first—and what would be his only—NHL season with seven points in 44 games. The Wings waived him a year later. Williams is the highest-drafted, least-productive player in team history.

Willie Huber was the first European player the Wings drafted in the first round, selecting the 6'5" German defenseman at No. 9 in 1978. He lasted 655 games in the NHL, but his lack of physical play earned him the scorn of Wings fans, and Jimmy Devellano got rid of Huber in 1983. The next time the Wings drafted a European with their first pick was in 1993, when they selected Anders Eriksson, a 6'3", 212-pound, chubby-cheeked defenseman out of Sweden. The Wings settled for him after Bryan Murray's attempts to move up in the draft from No. 22 to No. 3, where Murray thought he might be able to land Chris Pronger. But any deal would have been contingent on getting Pronger, and that was rendered moot because Hartford did succeed in moving up by making a deal with San Jose, and the Whalers snatched Pronger at No. 2. (The first overall pick was Alexandre Daigle, whose tepid 327 points in 616 NHL games earned him renown as one of the league's biggest busts.) Eriksson was okay—though the guy chosen in the next spot, Todd Bertuzzi, went on to be one of the league's premier power forwards who late in his career played for the Wings—but he was an easy sacrifice at the 1999 trade deadline in order to acquire Chris Chelios from the Chicago Blackhawks.

In 1994 the Wings chanced their first-round pick, at No. 23, on a Russian, selecting Red Army defenseman Yan Golubovsky, whose promise lay in his exceptional skating and passing skills. He tried to make it in North America, spending three seasons with the Wings' AHL affiliate and another three seasons splitting time between the Detroit and Adirondack Wings, but Golubovsky never developed into a top-tier defenseman and was used in December 2000 in the trade that brought Igor Larionov back to Detroit. Golubovsky only appeared in 56 NHL games, his notability limited to his nationality.

38

THE 10 BEST PICKS IN FRANCHISE HISTORY

IN THE MORE than half a century since the NHL instituted a draft, the men in charge of the Red Wings' selections have made incredible picks. Some have transformed the franchise directly, such as Steve Yzerman and Nicklas Lidström. Others indirectly impacted the franchise—Keith Primeau's value, for example, was realized when he was used to acquire Brendan Shanahan.

From the first draft in 1963, when the Wings chose a future NHL All-Star n Pete Mahovlich, more than 500 players have been selected by the Wings. While the 1970s were heavy on quantity, it is the quality of the picks in the 1980s that leads off the 10 best draft picks in franchise history.

1.   Forward Steve Yzerman

Drafted in the first round at No. 4 in 1983, Yzerman famously was the player the Wings drafted when they couldn't have Pat LaFontaine. But the shy teenager from Canada soon endeared himself to Detroiters with his hard work, and eventually he became known simply as "The Captain." Fans shared his pain as the playoffs kept ending too early—or didn't come at all—and gave him a standing ovation when there were rumors he might be traded. That gap-toothed grin he flashed on June 7, 1997, when he hoisted the Stanley Cup became an iconic image. Yzerman revived the Wings, captaining the team to three Stanley Cups and retiring in 2006 having played 1,514 games. He became the face of the franchise, and his return as general manager in 2019, nine years after he had left the club, was heralded as superman's return. No other player has had a more emotional and lasting impact on the Wings.

2.   Defenseman Nicklas Lidström

Drafted in the third round at No. 53 in 1989, Lidström was the best-kept secret in Sweden. Wings scouts noticed how well he did little things and convinced general manager Jimmy Devellano to take him in the third round. The reward was a defenseman who carried the franchise for two decades. Lidström played 1,564 games for the Wings, topping Yzerman's 1,514 for most in franchise history. Lidström defined consistency, giving the same steadfast, positionally sound performance game after game, season after season. He shut down opposing superstars without seeming to exert himself and commanded the ice with the puck. Lidström made everything look effortless, and he matched his off-ice demeanor to his on-ice implacable steadiness. He hoisted the Stanley Cup four times, the last as captain, and won the James Norris Memorial Trophy, awarded to the top defenseman in the NHL, seven times. When he retired in 2012, the former best-kept secret in Sweden was regarded as one of the best defensemen to have played the game.

3. Forward Sergei Fedorov

Drafted in the fourth round at No. 74 in 1989, Fedorov was a bold pick. No one doubted his skills, but around the NHL, people doubted he'd ever be able to leave Russia. A year later, the Wings had engineered Fedorov's escape, and he embarked on making the pick look like the best gamble of the draft. Fedorov dazzled; he was a phenomenal skater and puck handler. In 1993–94, Fedorov won the Hart Memorial Trophy (awarded to the NHL's most valuable player of the regular season), the Frank J. Selke Trophy (top defensive forward), and the Lester B. Pearson Award (most outstanding player as selected by NHL players). Fedorov won the Stanley Cup in 1997, 1998, and 2002. To the great disappointment of ownership and management, Fedorov left the Wings in 2003, having played 908 games. When he returned to Detroit in other teams' uniforms—the Mighty Ducks of Anaheim, Columbus Blue Jackets, Washington Capitals—Fedorov was soundly booed by fans at Joe Louis Arena. His 2015 induction into the Hockey Hall of Fame helped restore good relations with the franchise. While his tenure in the NHL ended elsewhere,

Fedorov's best years came in a Wings uniform, proving the gamble in 1989 was worth it.

4. Forward Tomas Holmström

Drafted in the 10th round at No. 257 in 1994, Holmström began his NHL career in the press box, where he watched while waiting for Scotty Bowman to put him in the lineup. Impatient, Holmström did what few would have dared do, and complained to owner Mike Ilitch. But that was Holmström at his core: pure determination. He was the rare Swede who was not a good skater, but he didn't need to be to position himself in front of opponents' nets. That drive pushed Holmström to win four Stanley Cups and appear in 1,026 games. He is the best 10th-round pick in franchise history, and his 530 points ranks second all-time in NHL history among 10th round picks.

5. Forward Henrik Zetterberg

Drafted in the seventh round at No. 210 in 1999, Zetterberg had matured as a player in his native Sweden by the time he joined the Wings for the 2002–03 season. He was quiet but effective, and had instantaneous chemistry with Pavel Datsyuk. Zetterberg was a workhorse at both ends of the ice, and his one-on-one battles against Pittsburgh Penguins superstar Sidney Crosby were the talk of the Stanley Cup Finals. Zetterberg was a key part of the Wings' Stanley Cup championship in 2008, and served as captain from 2012 until his retirement in 2018. His 960 career points in 1,082 games ranks second all-time in NHL history among seventh-round picks.

Tomas Holmström tries to block Nashville's goalie Pekka Rinne during Game 4 of the first-round playoff between the Red Wings and Predators on April 17, 2012, at Joe Louis Arena in Detroit. *Photo by Julian H. Gonzalez*

6. Forward Pavel Datsyuk

Drafted in the sixth round at No. 171 in 1998, Datsyuk joined the Wings in the fall of 2001, when he was 23 years old. He made an instant impression with his wizard-like skills with the puck, so much so that veteran Brett Hull was delighted to find himself playing on a line with the rookie center. Datsyuk was a part of that magical 2002 Cup-winning team, and played a big role in the 2008 title. He dazzled with the puck while playing with such sportsmanship he was awarded the Lady Byng Memorial Trophy four straight times. Datsyuk spent his entire career with the Wings, and his 918 points in 953 games ranks fifth all-time in NHL history among sixth-round picks.

7. Forward Bob Probert

Drafted in the third round at No. 46 in 1983, Probert fought and scored, establishing himself as the premier tough guy of the 1980s. His tenure with the Wings was tainted by a long list of off-ice problems centered around his substance-abuse disorder, but on the ice, Probert was a huge part of bringing the franchise out of the "Dead Wings" era. He was as tough as they come—he amassed 3,300 penalty minutes in his career, 2,090 of them in a Wings uniform to hold the franchise record—and was beloved by fans. Whatever trouble he got into, chants of "Probie! Probie!" greeted him at Joe Louis Arena. Probert played for the Wings from 1985 to 1994, appearing in 474 games. When he showed up for Yzerman's retirement ceremony at the Joe, Probert received a standing ovation.

Chris Osgood in the final seconds of Game 6 of the first round of the 1994 playoffs. *Photo by Julian H. Gonzalez*

8. Goaltender Chris Osgood

Drafted in the third round at No. 54 in 1991, Osgood back-stopped the Wings to the Stanley Cup championship in 1998 and 2008. He won his first Cup in 1997 as a spectator. Quiet and shy, Osgood withstood the spotlight of playing goal in Detroit, lashing back when he felt unfairly judged, but mostly keeping his thoughts within the locker room. He didn't want to leave in 2001 when the Wings acquired Dominik Hasek, and was happy to return in 2005. When he retired in 2011, Osgood had played 565 games with Detroit, and 317 of his 401 career victories came with the Wings, a record for a franchise-drafted goaltender.

9. Defenseman Vladimir Konstantinov

Drafted in the 11th round at No. 221 in 1989, Konstantinov was captain of the famed Red Army team before joining the Wings in 1991. Stoic to the core, Konstantinov quickly endeared himself to Wings fans with his quietly effective play. Opposing coaches despaired of what they considered his dirty tactics, but Konstantinov had the last laugh. He was a runner-up for the Norris Trophy in 1996–97, and played a central role in the Wings ending a 42-year championship drought. His career ended the weekend after the Cup celebration when he was in a limousine accident, but in just 446 games over six seasons he made a mark as one of the franchise's best picks.

10. Defenseman Niklas Kronwall

Drafted in the first round at No. 29 in 2000, Kronwall grew into a premier defenseman. He stood 6', 194 pounds, but

Niklas Kronwall smiles during the second period of the Wings' 3–2 preseason win over the Chicago Blackhawks in Detroit on September 24, 2010. *Photo by Julian H. Gonzalez*

played much larger and had impeccable timing for delivering big hits at open ice. The term "Kronwall-ed" was born to describe the impact Kronwall's hits had on foes. Kronwall was deft with the puck, too, and played a central role in the 2008 championship. He played 953 games in a Wings uniform, second among franchise-drafted defensemen.

39

WHAT MIGHT HAVE BEEN

T IS FASCINATING to look back at drafts and consider the impact decisions make on a franchise's fortune. Had the Wings made, for example, a different choice with their first pick in the 1990 draft, it is unlikely Brendan Shanahan would have been needed. The Wings passed on right wing Jaromír Jágr at No. 3, choosing instead center Keith Primeau. Primeau grew disgruntled playing behind Steve Yzerman and Sergei Fedorov, and the Wings grew tired of being pushed around in the playoffs. Their desire to add a power forward who played wing led to a blockbuster deal on the eve of the 1996–97 season, when the Wings used Primeau as part of a trade package to land Shanahan.

It worked out spectacularly well: Shanahan played a key role in ending the Wings' 42-year Stanley Cup drought and was a key part of three championships. He was a fan favorite, his personality as glib as his performances were glorious. But would he have been needed if the Wings had had Jágr? Selected instead by the Pittsburgh Penguins at No. 5, Jágr went on to record 766 goals, 135 game-winning goals, 1,921 points, and won two Stanley Cups. Imagine him and Sergei Fedorov on the same line. They would have been unstoppable.

The Wings had drafted a player from what was then Czechoslovakia, having chosen Petr Klima in 1983 and then masterminding his escape two years later. By 1990 the Iron Curtain was falling and players could leave without the cloak and dagger moves the Wings had used to free Klima. But it was one thing to use a fifth-round pick on a European, another to use a first-round pick. Ultimately the decision fell to Devellano, who opted to pick Primeau, a big Canadian forward. Primeau was a good player—he played 909 games—but Jágr was one of the best ever. The Quebec Nordiques, Vancouver Canucks, and Philadelphia Flyers passed on him, too.

Jágr tops the list of players the Wings should have chosen in hindsight, but the list goes back decades. They passed on Hall of Fame goaltender Ken Dryden in 1964, choosing instead Claude Gauthier with the first pick in the draft and Brian Watts with the first pick in the second round. Gauthier never played in the NHL, and Watts played four games. Dryden, chosen by the Boston Bruins at No. 14 but traded days after the draft to the Montreal Canadiens, won six Stanley Cups with the Canadiens in the 1970s, while in Detroit fans derided the "Dead Wings" for a decade.

Bill Lochead, a forward the Wings chose at No. 9 in 1974, was part of that Dead Wings era. They could have had Bryan Trottier, a forward the New York Islanders selected at No. 22 who went on to lead the franchise to four consecutive Stanley Cup championships and then won back-to-back Cups with the Penguins. The Islanders (whose staff included future Wings general manager Jimmy Devellano from 1972 to 1982) made a better choice in 1977, too, drafting Mike Bossy at No. 15 while the Wings chose Dale McCourt at No. 1. McCourt was an average player, while Bossy scored surpassed the 60-goal mark five times and was a key part of the Islanders reign as Stanley Cup champions from 1980 to 1983.

The Wings didn't have their own first-round pick in the 1981 draft and used their second-round pick, at No. 23, on forward Claude Loiselle. The guy selected at No. 40 by the Canadiens would go on to play a pivotal role for the Wings: Chris Chelios—but not until they traded for him in 1999.

The Canadiens made another savvy pick in 1984 when they selected goaltender Patrick Roy at No. 51, two spots after the Wings selected Milan Chalupa, whose NHL career encompassed 14 games. Roy's history is notably intertwined with the Wings: they were the ones who pounded the puck by him on December 2, 1995, scoring nine times on 26 shots. Incensed that he wasn't pulled earlier, Roy swore that he was done in Montreal. He was traded to the Colorado Avalanche, where he became a central figure in the Wings-Avalanche rivalry.

That rivalry was ignited by Claude Lemieux when he shoved Kris Draper from behind into the boards in the 1996 Western Conference Finals. There was no sports figure more despised in Detroit the rest of the decade, but Lemieux could have been a Wing: the Canadiens drafted Lemieux at No. 26 in 1983, one spot after the Wings took Lane Lambert.

Joe Sakic, who captained the Avalanche, could have been the Wings' in 1987. Instead, before a hometown audience at Joe Louis Arena, the Wings drafted defenseman Yves Racine at No. 11, four spots before the Quebec Nordiques took Sakic. Sakic became a Stanley Cup champion and Hall of Fame inductee. Racine had a respectable career but did not make an impact.

No team left the 1989 draft with a better overall selection of picks than the Wings, who took Nicklas Lidström in the third round, Sergei Fedorov in the fourth, and Vladimir Konstantinov in the 11th. That class was what the Wings needed to once again become Stanley Cup winners. With that came a change in philosophy from the early years under Devellano—a willingness by general manager Ken Holland to trade picks, even first-round ones, for players that fed the team's championship contender status.

It wasn't until the mid-2000s, when most of the principal players responsible for the 1997, 1998, and 2002 Cup titles had dispersed, that the draft took on renewed importance for the Wings.

They used their first-round pick in 2005, at No. 19, on defenseman Jakub Kindl, who never developed into more than a part-time player and ended up on waivers. It was an incredible draft class—Sidney Crosby at No. 1, Bobby Ryan at No. 2, Carey Price at No. 5, and even where the Wings picked, they could have had goaltender Tuukka Rask (No. 21, Toronto Maple Leafs) or forward T.J. Oshie (No. 24, St. Louis Blues).

The Wings didn't pick until the second round in 2006, when their choice at No. 41, Cory Emmerton, had a short career (139 games) as a fourth-line grinder. Brad Marchand, drafted by the Bruins at No. 71, became one of the NHL's premier pests and a Stanley Cup champion.

Goaltender Tom McCollum was the last pick in the first round of the 2008 draft. He played three games in the NHL. The guy picked immediately afterward, goaltender Jacob Markstrom, became an All-Star.

Marchand and Markstrom would have been good additions, but the guy the Wings passed on in 2009 would have been stellar. The Wings' choice at No. 32, forward Landon Ferraro, played sparingly before being put on waivers. The guy who went at No. 33 was forward Ryan O'Reilly, who went on to win a Stanley Cup, was awarded the Conn Smythe Trophy, and also won the Frank J. Selke Trophy. He could have been the Wings' at a time they had Henrik Zetterberg and Pavel Datsyuk in their prime, and still had Nicklas Lidström anchoring the defense.

Evgeny Kuznetsov became a first-line center for the Washington Capitals after being drafted at No. 26 in 2010, as opposed to Riley Sheahan, whom the Wings took at No. 21 and who became a journeyman grinder.

By the second decade of the 2000s, the Wings really needed an infusion of talent in their system. They had three chances at the forward who emerged as the best of the class—but then, nobody, not even the ones who drafted Nikita Kucherov, realized how good he would become. The Tampa Bay Lightning—then under the management of Steve Yzerman—drafted Kucherov in the second round, at No. 58, using the team's first-round pick on Vladislav Namestnikov. Kucherov emerged as a a premier goal-scorer and Stanley Cup champion. The Wings selected forward Tomas Jurco at No. 35, defenseman Xavier Ouellet at No. 48, and defenseman Ryan Sproul at No. 55; none became anything more than bit players, their NHL careers over before their twenties were.

Kucherov and Jágr would have looked spectacular in Wings uniforms, but given how history turned out, it's anathema to picture Claude Lemieux in one. Ultimately the Wings' history at the draft is partly judged by what might have been—but more so by what was in 1983 and 1989, when the selections resurrected the franchise.

40

CONSOLATION TO CORNER SUITE

THE FIRST TIME Steve Yzerman was employed by the Red Wings, they gave him a stall at Joe Louis Arena. The second time, they gave him a corner suite at Little Caesars Arena overlooking Woodward Avenue.

After retiring in 2006 following 22 seasons playing for the Wings, Yzerman segued into a front-office role. He already had been a sort of apprentice for five years, with general manager Ken Holland seeking Yzerman's opinion on free agents and trades. Yzerman was styled a vice president of hockey operations, and set about immersing himself in the daily grind of management, the way in 1983 he had immersed himself in the daily grind of being an NHL player.

"We all have these ideas that this is what this team needs, this is what they should do," Yzerman said six weeks into his new role. "I throw these ideas at Kenny all the time, and he listens and then he explains why some things are done or why they're not done. It's just not as easy as we all want it to be to do things. That's the one thing that I've found very interesting, is just trying to get things done. It's not that simple. I'm observing and trying to stay on top of everything and asking a lot of questions. It's been a great transition for me."

Ultimately, Yzerman wanted to be the boss, not an assistant to the boss. In May 2010, that led him to accept the general manager's job with the Tampa Bay Lightning. Yzerman went to Mike and Marian Ilitch's home to tell them the news. He had never worked for another pro team, he had not known any NHL organization other than the Wings for nearly three decades, and to the Ilitches, Yzerman was another son.

"I mean, talk about family," Ilitch said. "That's legit family. But he's 45 now, and it's time. It's the American way, you know. You don't want to hold anybody back. From the day Steve retired, we talked about his future, and he made it clear that he wanted to become a GM. I told him, 'Well, geez, Kenny doesn't want to be president, he wants to stay as GM.' Steve understood that. He didn't want to put pressure on me. He's not the kind of person to flex his muscle. He was so grateful that he got this training."

The 2010 draft was June 25–26. That didn't give Yzerman much time to prepare for his first draft as a GM.

"I didn't really know the scouting staff that well," Yzerman said in 2021. "I'm just trying to get through it without any major mistakes. There's lots of different ways teams run the draft, but generally you leave it up to your scouting staff. The first one was a little tough because you're working with people you really don't know that well. And in the role I was in with the Red Wings, I wasn't super focused on the draft. It was a good experience, but I left it a little bit hands off. I was aware of the players and who we were taking with the first pick, but once you get later into the rounds, you really don't know the players. You rely on the scouting staff."

Yzerman spent eight years as GM of the Lightning, during which time they drafted Nikita Kucherov, Andrei Vasilevskiy, and Jonathan Drouin. In the fall of 2018, Yzerman announced he would step back and serve out the final year of his contract in an advisory role.

On April 16, 2019, the Lightning were eliminated from the playoffs. Three days later, on Good Friday, the Wings held a news conference at Little Caesars Arena to welcome him home. The Captain was now the general manager.

Yzerman took control of a team that, just as when he arrived as a player, was trying to regain competitiveness. It had only been two years since the Wings missed the playoffs for the first time in 25 seasons—and while that streak led to glory that culminated in four Stanley Cups, it also left the farm system depleted. Holland had traded first-round picks as late as 2012 in an effort to sustain success, and when the Wings had first-round picks, they were in the mid-teens or higher. When the Wings had the ninth pick in 2017, it marked the first time picking in the top 10 since 1991.

Yzerman had experienced as a player how hard it was to build a championship team through the draft, and that was before the lottery, before everyone had eyes everywhere, and before the NHL supersized. When Yzerman entered the NHL in 1983, there were 21 teams. When he won his first Cup, in 1997, there were 26. When he went to Tampa, there were 30. Two years after he returned to Detroit, the NHL had grown to 32 teams. For all the advances since the early 1980s, building a competitor through the draft had become a Herculean labor.

"Back in the '80s, you didn't have video, it was harder to travel, and you didn't have nearly as much information," Yzerman said. "You have a lot of resources now to help you identify a player. Kids play a lot more, and play a lot more in international tournaments. A lot of European players come over and play in North American leagues.

"It's easier to see the players and identify them, but the reality is that now there are 32 teams instead of 21, so the talent pool is spread out even more throughout the league, and it makes it harder and harder, and it makes the process longer and longer for all of us."

When he accepted his second job as GM, Yzerman had two months to prepare for the draft. The Wings held their first pick at No. 6. On the opening night of the 2019 draft, held in Vancouver, British Columbia, Yzerman boldly chose a defenseman who had been projected to go in the mid-teens. Yzerman had scouted Moritz Seider extensively, and presented his case before his scouting staff in draft-preparation meetings.

"Not everyone was on board, but Steve steered everybody in the direction of Seider with good argumentation," chief European scout Håkan Andersson said in 2021. "I was happy with that because I liked him. I had watched him, and he was dominant."

As Yzerman's experience in the GM position grew, so did his comfort level in readying his team for the draft. "At some point you just have to set your list and leave it," Yzerman said in 2021. "If you want to keep reviewing it, you'll find a reason to do so. You just keep rearranging it. At some point leading up to the draft, the week before or so, you get your list together and then you leave it so. It takes a little bit of discipline to stick with it. There might be a case where you draft two left-handed defenseman early. Now later on you're looking at a couple more left-shot defensemen, and you have to make a call—do we really want to take another defenseman, or should we look at another position? A lot of times these kids are rated equally, and you have to decide if you want a defenseman or a center or a winger or a goalie."

Yzerman joined the Wings at 18, three years after the draft age had been lowered from 19. As a general manager, he saw the advantage of the later age. "We all have children, and trying to predict at 17 and 18 what they are going to be at 23 and 24, where they are going to be, what their interests are going to be—it's difficult," Yzerman said. "If you pushed it back a year or two, kids are a little more mature. I think theoretically it would help in the assessment of players. I would support it later. For the odd phenom that plays at 18, there's another 200 that don't."

From its inception in 1963, the NHL Draft grew into the primary source for teams to build its rosters. Yzerman headlined the draft class that revived the Red Wings and played with the class that transformed the team into Stanley Cup champions. The NHL Draft is a gamble—and the Red Wings have left the table with some of the best picks in history.

APPENDIX: DETROIT RED WINGS DRAFT HISTORY

(Games current through the 2021–22 season)

2021

Rd.	No.	Name	Pos.	Country	Games
1	6	Simon Edvinsson	D	Sweden	0
1	15	Sebastian Cossa	G	Canada	0
2	36	Shai Buium	D	U.S.	0
3	70	Carter Mazur	LW	U.S.	0
4	114	Redmond Savage	C	U.S.	0
5	134	Liam Dower Nilsson	C	Sweden	0
5	155	Oscar Plandowski	D	Canada	0
6	166	Pasquale Zito	LW	Canada	0

2020

Rd.	No.	Name	Pos.	Country	Games
1	4	Lucas Raymond	LW	Sweden	82
2	32	William Wallinder	D	Sweden	0

2	51	Theodor Niederbach	RW	Sweden	0
2	55	Cross Hanas	LW	U.S.	0
3	63	Donovan Sebrango	D	Canada	0
3	70	Eemil Viro	D	Finland	0
4	97	Sam Stange	RW	U.S.	0
4	107	Jan Bednar	G	U.S.	0
5	132	Alex Cotton	D	Canada	0
6	156	Kyle Aucoin	D	Canada	0
7	187	Kienan Draper	RW	U.S.	0
7	203	Chase Bradley	LW	U.S.	0

2019

Rd.	No.	Name	Pos.	Country	Games
1	6	Moritz Seider	D	Germany	82
2	35	Antti Tuomisto	D	Finland	0
2	54	Robert Mastrosimone	LW	U.S.	0
2	60	Albert Johansson	D	Sweden	0
3	66	Albin Grewe	LW	Sweden	0
4	97	Ethan Phillips	C	Canada	0
5	128	Cooper Moore	D	U.S.	0
6	159	Elmer Soderblom	LW	Sweden	0
6	177	Gustav Berglund	D	Sweden	0
7	190	Krill Tyutyayev	LW	Russia	0
7	191	Carter Gylander	G	Canada	0

2018

Rd.	No.	Name	Pos.	Country	Games
1	6	Filip Zadina	RW	Czech Republic	160
1	30	Joe Veleno	C	Canada	71
2	33	Jonatan Berggren	C	Sweden	0
2	36	Jared McIsaac	D	Canada	0
3	67	Alec Regula	D	U.S.	18
3	81	Seth Barton	D	Canada	0

3	84	Jesper Eliasson	G	Sweden	0
4	98	Ryan O'Reilly	RW	U.S.	0
6	160	Victor Brattstrom	G	Sweden	0
7	191	Otto Kivenmaki	C	Finland	0

2017

Rd.	No.	Name	Pos.	Country	Games
1	9	Michael Rasmussen	C	Canada	182
2	38	Gustav Lindstrom	D	Sweden	92
3	71	Kasper Kotkansalo	D	Finland	0
3	79	Lane Zablocki	RW	Canada	0
3	83	Zachary Gallant	C	Canada	0
3	88	Keith Petruzzelli	G	U.S.	0
4	100	Malte Setkov	D	Denmark	0
5	131	Cole Fraser	D	Canada	0
6	161	Jack Adams	C	U.S.	0
6	164	Reilly Webb	D	Canada	0
7	193	Brady Gilmour	C	Canada	0

2016

Rd.	No.	Name	Pos.	Country	Games
1	20	Dennis Cholowski	D	Canada	115
2	46	Givani Smith	RW	Canada	83
2	53	Filip Hronek	D	Czech Republic	245
4	107	Alfons Malmstrom	D	Sweden	0
5	137	Jordan Sambrook	D	Canada	0
6	167	Filip Larsson	G	Sweden	0
7	197	Mattias Elfstrom	LW	Sweden	0

2015

Rd.	No.	Name	Pos.	Country	Games
1	19	Evgeny Svechnikov	RW	Russia	113

3	73	Vili Saarijarvi	D	Finland	0
4	110	Joren Van Pottelberghe	G	Switzerland	0
5	140	Chase Pearson	C	Canada	3
6	170	Patrick Holway	D	U.S.	0
7	200	Adam Marsh	LW	U.S.	0

2014

Rd.	No.	Name	Pos.	Country	Games
1	15	Dylan Larkin	C	U.S.	504
3	63	Dominic Turgeon	C	Canada	9
4	106	Christoffer Ehn	C	Sweden	114
5	136	Chase Perry	G	U.S.	0
6	166	Julius Vahatalo	F	Finland	0
7	196	Axel Holmström	F	Sweden	0
7	201	Alexander Kadeykin	F	Russia	0

2013

Rd.	No.	Name	Pos.	Country	Games
1	20	Anthony Mantha	RW	Canada	353
2	48	Zach Nastasiuk	RW	Canada	0
2	58	Tyler Bertuzzi	LW	Canada	276
3	79	Mattias Janmark-Nylen	C	Sweden	420
4	109	David Pope	LW	Canada	0
5	139	Mitch Wheaton	D	Canada	0
6	169	Marc McNulty	D	Canada	0
7	199	Hampus Melen	RW	Sweden	0

2012

Rd.	No.	Name	Pos.	Country	Games
2	49	Martin Frk	RW	Czech Republic	124
3	80	Jake Paterson	G	Canada	0
4	110	Andreas Athanasiou	C	Canada	378

5	140	Mike McKee	D	Canada	0
6	170	James De Haas	D	Canada	0
7	200	Rasmus Bodin	D	Sweden	0

2011

Rd.	No.	Name	Pos.	Country	Games
2	35	Tomas Jurco	LW	Slovakia	221
2	48	Xavier Ouellet	D	France	178
2	55	Ryan Sproul	D	Canada	44
3	85	Alan Quine	C	Canada	106
4	115	Marek Tvrdon	LW	Slovakia	0
5	145	Philippe Hudon	RW	Canada	0
5	146	Mattias Backman	D	Sweden	0
6	175	Richard Nedomlel	D	Czech Republic	0
7	205	Alexey Marchenko	D	Russia	121

2010

Rd.	No.	Name	Pos.	Country	Games
1	21	Riley Sheahan	C	Canada	635
2	51	Calle Jarnkrok	C	Sweden	574
3	81	Louis-Marc Aubry	C	Canada	0
4	111	Teemu Pulkkinen	LW	Finland	83
5	141	Petr Mrazek	G	Czech Republic	295
6	171	Brooks Macek	RW	Canada	0
7	201	Ben Marshall	D	U.S.	0

2009

Rd.	No.	Name	Pos.	Country	Games
2	32	Landon Ferraro	C	Canada	77
2	60	Tomas Tatar	LW	Slovakia	701
3	75	Andrej Nestrasil	RW	Czech Republic	128
3	90	Gleason Fournier	D	Canada	0
5	150	Nick Jensen	D	U.S.	407

| 6 | 180 | Mitch Callahan | RW | U.S. | 5 |
| 7 | 210 | Adam Almquist | D | Sweden | 2 |

2008

Rd.	No.	Name	Pos.	Country	Games
1	30	Tom McCollum	G	U.S.	3
3	91	Max Nicastro	D	U.S.	0
4	121	Gustav Nyquist	C	Sweden	652
5	151	Julien Cayer	C	Canada	0
6	181	Stephen Johnston	C	Canada	0
7	211	Jesper Samuelsson	C	Sweden	0

2007

Rd.	No.	Name	Pos.	Country	Games
1	27	Brendan Smith	D	Canada	571
3	88	Joakim Andersson	C	Sweden	205
5	148	Randy Cameron	C	Canada	0
6	178	Zack Torquato	C	Canada	0
7	208	Bryan Rufenach	D	Canada	

2006

Rd.	No.	Name	Pos.	Country	Games
2	41	Cory Emmerton	LW	Canada	139
2	47	Shawn Matthias	LW	Canada	551
2	62	Dick Axelsson	LW	Sweden	0
3	92	Daniel Larsson	G	Sweden	0
6	182	Jan Mursak	RW	Slovenia	46
7	191	Nick Oslund	RW	U.S.	0
7	212	Logan Pyett	D	Canada	0

2005

Rd.	No.	Name	Pos.	Country	Games
1	19	Jakub Kindl	D	Czech Republic	331

2	42	Justin Abdelkader	LW	U.S.	739
3	80	Christofer Lofberg	C	Sweden	0
4	103	Mattias Ritola	RW	Sweden	43
5	132	Darren Helm	LW	Canada	812
5	137	Johan Ryno	C	Sweden	0
5	151	Jeff May	D	Canada	0
6	175	Juho Mielonen	D	Finland	0
7	214	Bretton Stamler	D	Canada	0

2004

Rd.	No.	Name	Pos.	Country	Games
3	97	Johan Franzén	RW	Sweden	602
4	128	Evan McGrath	C	Canada	0
5	151	Sergei Kolosov	D	Belarus	0
5	162	Tyler Haskins	C	U.S.	0
6	192	Anton Axelsson	RW	Sweden	0
7	226	Steve Covington	RW	Canada	0
8	257	Gennady Stolyarov	RW	Russia	0
9	290	Nils Backstrom	D	Sweden	0

2003

Rd.	No.	Name	Pos.	Country	Games
2	64	Jimmy Howard	G	U.S.	543
4	132	Kyle Quincey	D	Canada	586
5	165	Ryan Oulahen	LW	Canada	0
6	170	Andreas Sundin	LW	Sweden	0
6	194	Stefan Blom	D	Sweden	0
7	226	Tomas Kollar	LW	Sweden	0
8	258	Vladimir Kutny	RW	Slovakia	0
9	289	Mikael Johansson	C	Sweden	0

2002

Rd.	No.	Name	Pos.	Country	Games
2	58	Jiri Hudler	RW	Czech Republic	708

2	63	Tomas Fleischmann	LW	Czech Republic	657
3	95	Valtteri Filppula	C	Finland	1,056
4	131	Johan Berggren	D	Sweden	0
5	166	Logan Koopmans	G	Canada	0
6	197	Jimmy Cuddihy	C	Canada	0
7	229	Derek Meech	D	Canada	144
8	260	Pierre-Olivier Beaulieu	D	Canada	0
9	262	Christian Soderstrom	LW	Sweden	0
9	291	Jonathan Ericsson	D	Sweden	680

2001

Rd.	No.	Name	Pos.	Country	Games
2	62	Igor Grigorenko	LW	Russia	0
4	121	Drew MacIntyre	G	Canada	6
4	129	Miroslav Blatak	D	Czech Republic	0
5	157	Andreas Jamtin	RW	Sweden	0
6	195	Nick Pannoni	G	U.S.	0
8	258	Dimitry Bykov	D	Russia	71
9	288	Francois Senez	D	Canada	0

2000

Rd.	No.	Name	Pos.	Country	Games
1	29	Niklas Kronwall	D	Sweden	953
2	38	Tomas Kopecky	RW	Slovakia	578
4	102	Stefan Liv	G	Poland	0
4	127	Dimitri Semenov	F	Belarus	0
4	128	Alexander Seluyanov	D	Russia	0
4	130	Aaron Van Leusen	RW	Canada	0
6	187	Par Backer	C	Sweden	0
6	196	Paul Ballantyne	D	Canada	0
7	228	Jimmie Svensson	LW	Sweden	0
8	251	Todd Jackson	LW	U.S.	0
8	260	Evgeni Bumagin	F	Russia	0

1999

Rd.	No.	Name	Pos.	Country	Games
4	120	Jari Tolsa	LW	Sweden	0
5	149	Andrei Maximenko	F	Russia	0
6	181	Kent McDonell	RW	Canada	32
7	210	Henrik Zetterberg	C	Sweden	1,082
8	238	Anton Borodkin	LW	Russia	0
9	266	Ken Davis	RW	Canada	0

1998

Rd.	No.	Name	Pos.	Country	Games
1	25	Jiri Fischer	D	Czech Republic	305
2	55	Ryan Barnes	LW	Canada	2
2	56	Tomek Valtonen	LW	Poland	0
3	84	Jake McCracken	G	Canada	0
4	111	Brent Hobday	LW	Canada	0
5	142	Carl Steen	C	Sweden	0
6	151	Adam DeLeeuw	LW	Canada	0
6	171	Pavel Datsyuk	C	Russia	953
7	198	Jeremy Goetzinger	D	Canada	0
8	226	David Petrasek	D	Sweden	0
9	256	Petja Pietilainen	RW	Finland	0

1997

Rd.	No.	Name	Pos.	Country	Games
2	49	Yuri Butsayev	LW	Russia	99
3	76	Petr Sykora	C	Czech Republic	12
4	102	Quintin Laing	LW	Canada	79
5	129	John Wikstrom	D	Sweden	0
6	157	B.J. Young	RW	U.S.	1
7	186	Mike Laceby	C	Canada	0
8	213	Steve Wilejto	C	Canada	0
9	239	Greg Willers	D	Canada	0

1996

Rd.	No.	Name	Pos.	Country	Games
1	26	Jesse Wallin	D	Canada	49
2	52	Aren Miller	G	Canada	0
4	108	Johan Forsander	LW	Sweden	0
5	135	Michal Podolka	G	Czech Republic	0
6	144	Magnus Nilsson	LW	Sweden	0
6	162	Alexandre Jacques	RW	Canada	0
7	189	Colin Beardsmore	C	Canada	0
8	215	Craig Stahl	F	Canada	0
9	241	Evgeny Afanasiev	F	Russia	0

1995

Rd.	No.	Name	Pos.	Country	Games
1	26	Maxim Kuznetsov	D	Russia	136
2	52	Philippe Audet	LW	Canada	4
3	58	Darryl Laplante	C	Canada	35
4	104	Anatoly Ustyugov	F	Russia	0
5	125	Chad Wilchynski	D	Canada	0
5	126	Dave Arsenault	G	Germany	0
6	156	Tyler Perry	C	Canada	0
7	182	Per Eklund	RW	Sweden	0
8	208	Andrei Samokhvalov	F	Russia	0
9	234	David Engblom	C	Sweden	0

1994

Rd.	No.	Name	Pos.	Country	Games
1	23	Yan Golubovsky	D	Russia	56
2	49	Mathieu Dandenault	RW	Canada	868
3	75	Sean Gillam	D	Canada	0
5	114	Frederic Deschenes	G	Canada	0
5	127	Doug Battaglia	D	Canada	0
6	153	Pavel Agarkov	F	Russia	0

8	205	Jason Elliott	G	Canada	0
9	231	Jeff Mikesch	C	U.S.	0
10	257	Tomas Holmström	LW	Sweden	1,026
11	283	Toivo Suursoo	LW	Estonia	0

1993

Rd.	No.	Name	Pos.	Country	Games
1	22	Anders Eriksson	D	Sweden	572
2	48	Jon Coleman	D	U.S.	0
3	74	Kevin Hilton	C	U.S.	0
4	97	John Jakopin	D	Canada	113
4	100	Benoit Larose	D	Canada	0
5	126	Norm Maracle	G	Canada	66
6	152	Tim Spitzig	RW	Canada	0
7	178	Yuri Yeresko	D	Russia	0
8	204	Vitezlav Skuta	D	Czech Republic	0
9	230	Ryan Shanahan	RW	U.S.	0
10	256	Jamie Kosecki	G	U.S.	0
11	282	Gordy Hunt	LW	U.S.	0

1992

Rd.	No.	Name	Pos.	Country	Games
1	22	Curtis Bowen	LW	Canada	0
2	46	Darren McCarty	RW	Canada	758
3	70	Sylvain Cloutier	C	Canada	7
5	118	Mike Sullivan	C	U.S.	0
6	142	Jason MacDonald	F	Canada	4
7	166	Greg Scott	G	Canada	0
8	183	Justin Krall	D	U.S.	0
8	189	C.J. Denomme	G	Canada	0
9	214	Jeff Walker	D	Canada	0
10	238	Dan McGillis	D	Canada	634
11	262	Ryan Bach	G	Canada	3

1991

Rd.	No.	Name	Pos.	Country	Games
1	10	Martin Lapointe	RW	Canada	991
2	32	Jamie Pushor	D	Canada	521
3	54	Chris Osgood	G	Canada	744
4	76	Mike Knuble	RW	Canada	1,068
5	98	Dimitri Motkov	D	Russia	0
7	142	Igor Malykhin	D	Ukraine	0
9	186	Jim Bermingham	C	Canada	0
10	208	Jason Firth	C	Canada	0
11	230	Bart Turner	LW	U.S.	0
12	252	Andrew Miller	C	Canada	0

1990

Rd.	No.	Name	Pos.	Country	Games
1	3	Keith Primeau	C	Canada	909
3	45	Vyacheslav Kozlov	LW	Russia	1,182
4	66	Stewart Malgunas	D	Canada	129
5	87	Tony Burns	D	U.S.	0
6	108	Claude Barthe	D	Canada	0
7	129	Jason York	D	Canada	757
8	150	Wes McCauley	D	Canada	0
9	171	Tony Gruba	F	U.S.	0
10	192	Travis Tucker	D	U.S.	0
11	213	Brett Larson	D	U.S.	0
12	234	John Hendry	LW	Canada	0

1989

Rd.	No.	Name	Pos.	Country	Games
1	11	Mike Sillinger	C	Canada	1,049
2	32	Bob Boughner	D	Canada	630
3	53	Nicklas Lidström	D	Sweden	1,564

4	74	Sergei Fedorov	C	Russia	1,248
5	95	Shawn McCosh	C	Canada	9
6	116	Dallas Drake	RW	Canada	1,009
7	137	Scott Zygulski	D	U.S.	0
8	158	Andy Suhy	D	U.S.	0
9	179	Bob Jones	D	Canada	0
10	200	Greg Bignell	D	Canada	0
10	204	Rick Judson	LW	U.S.	0
11	221	Vladimir Konstantinov	D	Soviet Union	446
12	242	Joe Frederick	RW	U.S.	0
12	246	Jason Glickman	G	U.S.	0

1988

Rd.	No.	Name	Pos.	Country	Games
1	17	Kory Kocur	RW	Canada	0
2	38	Serge Anglehart	D	Canada	0
3	47	Guy Dupuis	D	Canada	0
3	59	Petr Hrbek	RW	Czech Republic	0
4	80	Sheldon Kennedy	RW	Canada	310
7	143	Kelly Hurd	RW	Canada	0
8	164	Brian McCormack	D	U.S.	0
9	185	Jody Praznik	D	Canada	0
10	206	Glen Goodall	C	Canada	0
11	227	Darren Colbourne	RW	Canada	0
12	248	Don Stone	C	U.S.	0

1987

Rd.	No.	Name	Pos.	Country	Games
1	11	Yves Racine	D	Canada	508
2	32	Gord Kruppke	D	Canada	23
2	41	Bob Wilkie	D	Canada	18
3	52	Dennis Holland	C	Canada	0
4	74	Mark Reimer	G	Canada	0

5	95	Radomir Brazda	D	Czech Republic	0
6	116	Sean Clifford	D	Canada	0
7	137	Mike Gober	LW	U.S.	0
8	158	Kevin Scott	LW	Canada	0
9	179	Mikko Haapakoski	D	Finland	0
10	200	Darin Banister	D	Canada	0
11	221	Craig Quinlan	D	U.S.	0
12	242	Tomas Jansson	D	Sweden	0

1986

Rd.	No.	Name	Pos.	Country	Games
1	1	Joe Murphy	RW	Canada	779
2	22	Adam Graves	LW	Canada	1,152
3	43	Derek Mayer	D	Canada	17
4	64	Tim Cheveldae	G	Canada	340
5	85	Johan Garpenlov	LW	Sweden	609
6	106	Jay Stark	D	Canada	0
7	127	Par Djoos	D	Sweden	82
8	148	Dean Morton	D	Canada	1
9	169	Marc Potvin	RW	Canada	121
10	190	Scott King	G	Canada	2
11	211	Tom Bissett	LW	U.S.	5
12	232	Peter Ekroth	D	Sweden	0

1985

Rd.	No.	Name	Pos.	Country	Games
1	8	Brent Fedyk	RW	Canada	470
2	29	Jeff Sharples	D	Canada	105
3	50	Steve Chiasson	D	Canada	751
4	71	Mark Gowans	G	U.S.	0
5	92	Chris Luongo	D	U.S.	218
6	113	Randy McKay	RW	Canada	932
7	134	Thomas Bjuhr	LW	Sweden	0

8	155	Mike Luckraft	D	U.S.	0
9	176	Rob Schena	D	U.S.	0
10	197	Erik Hamalainen	D	Finland	0
11	218	Bo Svanberg	C	Sweden	0
12	239	Mikael Lindman	D	Sweden	0

1984

Rd.	No.	Name	Pos.	Country	Games
1	7	Shawn Burr	LW	Canada	878
2	28	Doug Houda	D	Canada	561
3	49	Milan Chalupa	D	Czech Republic	14
5	91	Mats Lundstrom	F	Sweden	0
6	112	Randy Hansch	G	Canada	0
7	133	Stefan Larsson	D	Sweden	0
8	152	Lars Karlsson	F	Sweden	0
8	154	Urban Nordin	F	Sweden	0
9	175	Bill Shibicky	F	Canada	0
10	195	Jay Rose	D	U.S.	0
11	216	Tim Kaiser	RW	Canada	0
12	236	Tom Nickolau	C	Canada	0

1983

Rd.	No.	Name	Pos.	Country	Games
1	4	Steve Yzerman	C	Canada	1,514
2	25	Lane Lambert	C	Canada	283
3	46	Bob Probert	LW	Canada	935
4	68	Dave Korol	D	Canada	0
5	86	Petr Klima	LW	Czech Republic	786
5	88	Joey Kocur	D	Canada	821
6	106	Chris Pusey	G	Canada	1
7	126	Bob Pierson	LW	Canada	0
8	146	Craig Butz	D	Canada	0
9	166	Dave Sikorski	D	U.S.	0
10	186	Stu Grimson	LW	Canada	729

| 11 | 206 | Jeff Frank | RW | Canada | 0 |
| 12 | 226 | Chuck Chiatto | C | U.S. | 0 |

1982

Rd.	No.	Name	Pos.	Country	Games
1	17	Murray Craven	C	Canada	1,071
2	23	Yves Courteau	RW	Canada	22
3	44	Carmine Vani	C	Canada	0
4	66	Craig Coxe	C	U.S.	235
5	86	Brad Shaw	D	Canada	377
6	107	Claude Vilgrain	RW	Haiti	89
7	128	Greg Hudas	D	U.S.	0
8	149	Pat Lahey	C	Canada	0
9	170	Gary Cullen	C	Canada	0
10	191	Brent Meckling	D	Canada	0
11	212	Mike Stern	LW	Canada	0
12	233	Shaun Reagan	RW	Canada	0

1981

Rd.	No.	Name	Pos.	Country	Games
2	23	Claude Loiselle	C	Canada	616
3	44	Corrado Micalef	G	Canada	113
5	86	Larry Trader	D	Canada	91
6	107	Gerard Gallant	LW	Canada	615
7	128	Greg Stefan	G	Canada	299
8	149	Rick Zombo	D	U.S.	652
9	170	Don Leblanc	LW	Canada	0
10	191	Robert Nordmark	D	Sweden	236

1980

Rd.	No.	Name	Pos.	Country	Games
1	11	Mike Blaisdell	RW	Canada	343
3	46	Mark Osborne	LW	Canada	919

5	88	Mike Corrigan	RW	Canada	0
6	109	Wayne Crawford	C	Canada	0
7	130	Mike Braun	D	Canada	0
8	151	John Beukeboom	D	Canada	0
9	172	Dave Miles	F	Canada	0
10	193	Brian Rorabeck	RW	Canada	0

1979

Rd.	No.	Name	Pos.	Country	Games
1	3	Mike Foligno	F	Canada	1,018
3	45	Jody Gage	RW	Canada	68
3	46	Boris Fistric	D	Canada	0
4	66	John Ogrodnick	RW	Canada	928
5	87	Joe Paterson	LW	Canada	291
6	108	Carmine Cirella	LW	Canada	0

1978

Rd.	No.	Name	Pos.	Country	Games
1	9	Willie Huber	D	Germany	655
1	12	Brent Peterson	RW	Canada	620
2	28	Glenn Hicks	LW	Canada	108
2	31	Al Jensen	G	Canada	179
3	53	Doug Derkson	C	Canada	0
4	62	Bjorn Skaare	C	Norway	1
5	78	Ted Nolan	LW	Canada	78
6	95	Sylvain Locas	C	Canada	0
7	112	Wes George	LW	Canada	0
8	129	John Barrett	D	Canada	488
9	146	Jim Malazdrewicz	RW	Canada	0
10	163	Geoff Shaw	RW	Canada	0
11	178	Carl Van Harrewyn	D	Canada	0
12	194	Ladislav Svozil	F	Czechoslovakia	0
13	208	Tom Bailey	C	Canada	0

14	219	Larry Lozinski	G	Canada	30
15	224	Randy Betty	LW	Canada	0
16	226	Brian Crawley	D	Canada	0
17	228	Doug Feasby	F	Canada	0

1977

Rd.	No.	Name	Pos.	Country	Games
1	1	Dale McCourt	F	Canada	532
3	37	Rick Vasko	D	Canada	31
4	55	John Hilworth	D	Canada	57
5	73	Jim Korn	D	U.S.	596
6	91	Jim Baxter	G	Canada	0
7	109	Randy Wilson	LW	Canada	0
8	125	Ray Roy	C	U.S.	0
9	141	Kip Churchill	C	Canada	0
10	155	Lance Gatoni	D	Canada	0
11	163	Rob Plumb	C	Canada	14
12	170	Alain Belanger	LW	Canada	0
13	175	Dean Willers	LW	England	0
14	178	Roland Cloutier	C	Canada	34
15	181	Ed Hill	RW	U.S.	0
16	184	Val James	LW	U.S.	11
17	185	Grant Morin	RW	Canada	0

1976

Rd.	No.	Name	Pos.	Country	Games
1	4	Fred Williams	C	Canada	44
2	22	Reed Larson	D	U.S.	904
3	40	Fred Berry	C	Canada	3
4	58	Kevin Schamehorn	RW	Canada	10
5	76	Dwight Schofield	D	U.S.	211
6	94	Tony Horvath	D	Canada	0
7	111	Fern LeBlanc	LW	Canada	34
8	120	Claude Legris	G	Canada	4

1975

Rd.	No.	Name	Pos.	Country	Games
1	5	Rick Lapointe	D	Canada	664
2	23	Jerry Rollins	D	Canada	0
3	37	Al Cameron	D	Canada	282
3	45	Blair Davidson	D	Canada	0
3	50	Clark Hamilton	C	Canada	0
4	59	Mike Wirachowsky	D	Canada	0
5	77	Mike Wong	C	U.S.	22
6	95	Mike Harazny	D	Canada	0
7	113	Jean-Luc Phaneuf	C	Canada	0
8	131	Steve Carlson	C	U.S.	52
9	148	Gary Vaughan	RW	Canada	0
10	164	Jean Thibodeau	C	Canada	0
11	176	Dave Hanson	D	U.S.	0
11	178	Robin Larson	D	U.S.	0

1974

Rd.	No.	Name	Pos.	Country	Games
1	9	Bill Lochead	LW	Canada	330
3	44	Dan Mandryk	LW	Canada	0
3	45	Bill Evo	LW	U.S.	0
4	63	Michel Bergeron	RW	Canada	229
5	81	John Taft	D	U.S.	15
6	99	Don Dufek	LW	U.S.	0
7	117	Jack Carlson	LW	U.S.	236
8	134	Greg Steel	D	Canada	0
9	151	Glen McLeod	D	Canada	0

1973

Rd.	No.	Name	Pos.	Country	Games
1	11	Terry Richardson	G	Canada	20

3	39	Nelson Pyatt	C	Canada	296
3	43	Robbie Neale	F	Canada	0
4	59	Mike Korney	D	Canada	77
5	75	Blair Stewart	LW	Canada	229
6	91	Glen Cickello	D	Canada	0
7	107	Brian Middleton	D	Canada	0
8	118	Dennis Polonich	C	Canada	390
8	123	George Lyle	LW	Canada	99
9	135	Dennis O'Brien	D	Canada	0
9	138	Tom Newman	D	Canada	0
9	139	Ray Bibeau	D	Canada	0
10	151	Kevin Neville	G	Canada	0
10	154	Ken Gibb	D	Canada	0
10	155	Mitch Brandt	D	U.S.	0

1972

Rd.	No.	Name	Pos.	Country	Games
2	26	Pierre Guite	LW	Canada	0
3	42	Bob Krieger	RW	U.S.	0
4	58	Danny Gruen	LW	Canada	49
5	74	Dennis Johnson	LW	U.S.	0
6	90	Bill Miller	D	Canada	0
7	106	Glen Seperich	G	Canada	0
8	122	Mike Ford	D	Canada	0
9	138	George Kuzmicz	D	Canada	0
10	150	Dave Arundel	D	U.S.	0

1971

Rd.	No.	Name	Pos.	Country	Games
1	2	Marcel Dionne	C	Canada	1,348
2	16	Henry Boucha	C	U.S.	247
4	44	George Hulme	G	Canada	0
5	58	Earl Anderson	RW	U.S.	109

6	72	Charlie Shaw	D	Canada	0
7	86	Jim Nahrgang	D	Canada	57
8	100	Bob Boyd	D	Canada	0

1970

Rd.	No.	Name	Pos.	Country	Games
1	12	Serge Lajeunesse	D	Canada	103
2	26	Bob Guindon	LW	Canada	6
3	40	Yvon Lambert	LW	Canada	683
4	54	Tom Johnston	RW	Canada	0
5	68	Tom Mellor	D	U.S.	26
6	82	Bernie MacNeil	C	Canada	4
7	95	Ed Hays	C	Canada	0

1969

Rd.	No.	Name	Pos.	Country	Games
1	10	Jim Rutherford	G	Canada	457
2	21	Ron Garwasiuk	LW	Canada	0
3	33	Wayne Hawrysh	C	Canada	0
4	45	Wayne Chernecki	C	Canada	0
5	57	Wally Olds	D	U.S.	0

1968

Rd.	No.	Name	Pos.	Country	Games
1	11	Steve Andrascik	RW	Canada	0
2	17	Herb Boxer	RW	U.S.	0

1967

Rd.	No.	Name	Pos.	Country	Games
1	9	Rob Barkwell	RW	Canada	0
2	17	Al Karlander	C	Canada	212

1966

Rd.	No.	Name	Pos.	Country	Games
1	6	Steve Atkinson	RW	Canada	302
2	12	Jim Whittaker	D	Canada	0
3	18	Lee Carpenter	D	Canada	0
4	24	Grant Cole	G	Canada	0

1965

Rd.	No.	Name	Pos.	Country	Games
1	3	George Forgie	D	Canada	0
2	8	Bob Birdsell	RW	Canada	0

1964

Rd.	No.	Name	Pos.	Country	Games
1	1	Claude Gauthier	RW	Canada	0
2	7	Brian Watts	LW	Canada	4
3	13	Ralph Buchanan	D	Canada	0
4	19	Rene LeClerc	C	Canada	87

1963

Rd.	No.	Name	Pos.	Country	Games
1	2	Pete Mahovlich	F	Canada	884
2	8	Bill Cosburn	F	Canada	0

The author with the Stanley Cup in 2002 in Prague, Czechia.

HELENE ST. JAMES joined the *Detroit Free Press* in 1995 after a globetrotting life: she was born in Denmark, grew up in Colombia, graduated from Michigan, and taught English in Taiwan. She was on the scene when the Wings ended their 42-year Stanley Cup drought in 1997 and again for their Cups in 1998, 2002, and 2008. She followed the Cup to Czechia in 2002, where she rode next to the Cup in the back seat of Red Wings defenseman Jiri Slegr's Mercedes en route to Dominik Hasek's Cup party.

She also has covered Olympics in Russia, China, and Italy.

She was selected Michigan's sportswriter of the year for 2017. Her first book, *The Big 50: The Men and Moments that made the Detroit Red Wings*, was published in 2020.